NAVY SEAL
SHOOTING

CHRIS SAJNOG

Produced in the United States

Graphic design & layout by Wesley Ligon @ MadDogDesigns.com
Images and front cover by Triple Horse Studios

ISBN: 978-1-943787-00-5

First Edition:
10 9 8 7 6 5 4 3 2 1

Contents

Dedication

To my wonderful wife Laura, for giving me the time and support to follow my passions.

Foreword

When our country needed someone to write the instruction manual for the elite US Navy SEAL Team Sniper program, they looked to one man — Chief Petty Officer Chris Sajnog. He wasn't chosen because he had the most confirmed kills or because he won any national shooting titles. He was chosen for the same reason you should chose this book: because he's the best in the world at teaching others not just how to shoot any firearm with deadly accurate precision under stress, but also how to train them most effectively so they learn faster than ever before. Simply put, when it comes to learning how to shoot, Chris is a firearms training guru with the magic touch. There is no one else on earth who even comes close.

I met Chris during a radio interview when we were each promoting our books. I was on to talk about the bestselling *American Sniper* that I was lucky enough to co-write with Chris Kyle, the deadliest sniper in American history. Chris was promoting his new book, *How to Shoot Like a Navy SEAL*, a book that went on to become a bestseller in the firearms market and, two years later, still maintains a five-star rating.

American Sniper was successful because of the amazing true story of an American hero who risked and sacrificed his life to protect and help his SEAL team brothers, members of our Armed Services and this great nation.

How to Shoot Like a Navy SEAL reached its success because it teaches the skills that allowed heroes like Chris Kyle and others to successfully complete their missions by putting effective rounds on target every time. Although it is only 124 pages, the value of its content, with its easy to understand directions and access to videos from a master instructor, did not go unnoticed.

That book was written from the twenty years of knowledge and techniques Chris developed during his highly successful Naval career. His new book, *Navy SEAL Shooting,* was written after Chris learned the trouble others have in being able to train the same way he trained the SEALs. After retiring from the Navy in 2009, he started Center Mass Group and began teaching law enforcement and civilians his elite methods. Chris realized that outside of the Teams, people don't have the same amount of time or money to dedicate to firearms training. So what do Navy SEALs do when they're given a challenge? They figure out a way to be successful despite any obstacles. And that's what Chris did...

Chris spent four years studying how the best athletes and musicians in the world got to where they are today — how they learned, how they trained. He studied mechanics and physics and applied them to every shooting technique he developed, eventually changing or modifying almost every "traditional" way people have been taught to shoot. Finally, he studied the amazing scientific advances in how the brain and body actually acquire new skills and developed his unique firearms training program, *The New Rules of Marksmanship*, based on building perfect neural pathways.

The result is *Navy SEAL Shooting* and I'm honored to be able to introduce Chris and his groundbreaking book to you. But it comes with a warning: if you're looking for flashy techniques that look good when others are watching, this isn't the book for you. Read my *Sniper Elite* series to fill your need for exciting action stories, but if you're looking for a way to improve your shooting and are willing to put in the time to train — you've found the right book.

This book is broken up into four sections: Training, Mindset, Marksmanship and Operations. Chris always says, "How you train is more important that what you train" and he reinforces that by starting the book with a full section on what other books don't even cover — how to actually train! He then discusses how your mind learns and masters new skills and how to use this knowledge to best accomplish your goals. After that, he took the marksmanship lessons from *How to Shoot Like a Navy SEAL*, rewritten and expanded, and included it as its own section. He finishes with a section called *Operations* where he covers movement, malfunctions, manipulations and a section called *Mastery*, where he covers advanced skills such as shooting multiple targets and how to shoot faster without losing accuracy.

Chris and I have become close friends over the past few years, sharing our passion for firearms and defending our nation's freedom. We've spent countless hours talking, traveling and speaking together on our *Teaching Freedom* speaking tour. I can tell you that reading this book is just like having a conversation with him — witty and intelligent. He's a man of few words, but he ensures that each one hits its mark.

You literally can't find the techniques taught in this book anywhere else because Chris developed them! He taught the US Navy SEALs to become masters of shooting under extreme conditions and now he's offering you the same opportunity.

You never know when you'll need to defend yourself, your family or your country.

Are you ready?

Scott McEwen
#1 New York Times Bestselling Co-Author
AMERICAN SNIPER and the national Bestselling
Sniper Elite series of novels.

Introduction

"If you can't explain it simply,
you don't understand it well enough."
—Albert Einstein

As a Navy SEAL I learned that there is no such thing as good enough, and as a SEAL sniper I learned that close enough is enough to get someone killed. Everything we did in training and on missions was done with the goal of perfection—anything less and we went back to the drawing board and figured out a way to go from good to great to ensure that we were better than the enemy. When it comes to firearms training, if you want to be a truly great shooter, you too need to seek perfection in every aspect of your training program. Because unlike leisure endeavors, shooting is literally either hit or miss.

There is no "close enough" when it comes to taking low-percentage shots in high-stress environments. This means not only a strong foundation in the shooting fundamentals, but performing the fundamentals exceedingly well, with virtuosity. So before I get into the how of shooting, I want to explain the importance of virtuosity in firearms training and the theory behind my training model.

There is no "close enough" when it comes to taking low-percentage shots in high-stress environments.

CrossFit coach Gregg Glassman first introduced me to the term *virtuosity* in 2005 in an article about the importance of virtuosity as a CrossFit trainer, where he used the gymnastics definition of "performing the common uncommonly well." As a Navy SEAL sniper instructor, I understood this style of training and had been practicing it for years, but it was not until I read his article that I saw it put into words so well. So my goal here is to explain the importance of virtuosity in firearms training and the theory behind my training model.

Becoming a virtuoso of firearms requires hours upon hours of dedication and perseverance. There are no shortcuts to becoming a master, but many shooters—especially new ones—tend to ignore the fundamentals of marksmanship and want to quickly move on to more advanced or cool-looking techniques, skills, or movements. This pattern of novice training is apparent in all kinds of mechanical skills, such as playing a musical instrument or learning a new sport. This immature yearning is an obstacle to perfection and should be avoided at all costs.

Solid fundamentals are required for mastery, especially in firearms training. The problem comes from shooters having weak fundamentals and a desire for useless originality. Many firearms instructors reinforce this attitude because they're afraid to insist on perfection before moving on, or worse, because they don't understand the importance of these fundamentals. This will only delay true mastery in weapons handling. Especially in firearms training, where mistakes can be fatal, it's important to hammer on the basics.

These include:

1. Shooting platform
2. Grip
3. Sight picture
4. Sight refinement
5. Focused breathing
6. Trigger control
7. Follow-through

You must master these fundamentals before you attempt to move on to more advanced shooting skills. Like the foundation of a building, your fundamentals need to be solid or everything you add on top will come crumbling down. Look at how the masters of any sport train, and you'll see they spend the majority of their time on basic skills. They don't practice for highlight reels—highlight reels happen by performing the basics with uncommon perfection.

I first learned this way of thinking when practicing karate as a child. The key elements of a karate expert are stance, balance, focus, execution of technique, and follow-through. Sounds a lot like shooting, right? Both are martial arts. Both shooters and *karatekas* are warriors striving for perfection. Dedicated shooters practice dry-fire for hours, while *karatekas* do *kata*.

When I talk about perfection and mastery, I'm talking about breaking down each fundamental and practicing it until it's perfect. How you use these skills depends on the situation you're in, or your course of fire. Virtuosity means something different to an International Practical Shooting Confederation (IPSC) shooter than to a Tier-1, door-kicking, beard-wearing operator downrange, or even the average guy who shoots a few weekends a month. Look at what you're training for, and never settle for good enough.

There are a wide variety of firearms instructors out there; some are really good and some . . . not so much. Do they insist on perfection of your fundamentals? Or do they try to teach you cool-looking techniques? If you're training just to shoot cool videos to post on YouTube, that's one thing, but if you want to be a true master of your weapon, take a step back and check your fundamentals. If trained by the best in the business, you will see how simple, basic, and fundamental the training is. The downfall of any training program is a trainer's lack of commitment to the fundamentals and the students' lack of insisting on their instruction.

Instructors range in quality from great shooters I continue to learn from, to others whom I wouldn't feel safe shooting beside on the same range. I'm not saying I'm the best or anyone else is the worst. I just want you to make informed decisions. Anytime you're seeking instruction, consider the candidate's quality as an instructor, not just a shooter. Choose an instructor who insists on perfection of your fundamentals. If you want to be a true master of your weapon, take a step back and check your fundamentals.

As an instructor, naturally I want to show my students fancy movements and advanced shooting techniques—but in the long run, I'm doing them a disservice. There's a natural urge to entertain and impress students with my knowledge and skill. They've paid a lot of money, and I want them to know how good I am. But my goal is to make them good shooters, and I can't do that if I move away from the basics too quickly. Training is about making my students better shooters, not about me. That's why in this book I'll be covering what works, not what you want to read.

When I talk about perfection and mastery, I'm talking about breaking down each fundamental and practicing it until it's perfect.

In firearms training, you need to insist relentlessly on the fundamentals with every shot you take. The sooner you learn that mastery of the fundamentals is the key to effective shooting, the sooner you will become a truly great shooter. Shooters founded in the basics of marksmanship will quickly progress past others who are not lucky enough to have had well-grounded firearms instructors. If you simply commit to the basics, your shooting will improve, you'll advance quickly, and you will earn respect of those around you. Watching someone shoot with virtuosity is awe-inspiring, and it's even better when you reach this level in your own shooting. This book will teach exactly how to do that in the shortest time possible.

My teaching philosophy, explained in this book, is to focus only on what's important to improve your understanding and increase retention. If you're hoping to read a bunch of "There I was . . ." stories, I recommend you go buy yourself a novel. But if you want to learn quickly how to shoot under stress, you've come to the right place. If I can teach you something in three words what takes other instructors five words, I've just compressed that information enough that you're more likely to remember it and use it. Mission accomplished!

All elements must be processed before meaningful learning can continue.

I like using simple techniques (and simple words) whenever possible. If you can draw

and shoot faster by skipping the double backflip, why wouldn't you? So let's just skip those meaningless steps. I will not be teaching you any "advanced" techniques. I believe that advanced shooting is only the basics done smoother and faster.

One "big" term you should understand is *cognitive overload*. Cognitive overload is what happens during complex learning activities when the amount of information and interactions that must be processed simultaneously overloads the finite amount of working memory one possesses.

All elements must be processed before meaningful learning can continue. So if I try to shove too much into your head at once, most of what I've presented will not be retained. I want you to retain as much information as possible, so I'll try to keep my explanations as short as possible. It's also important for you to not take in too much at one time. If you want to learn and actually retain the information, read a chapter or even a single technique, practice it until you understand it, and then move on.

Throughout this book I'll talk about certain habits you need to perfect to become a great shooter. The more time you spend practicing, the better you will become. If you're new to firearms and just want to know the basics of shooting, you can read through the book and you'll be better prepared for an occasional trip to the range. You don't need to set up a training schedule to get where you want to be, and that's fine. Other readers may want to break down each technique and try it out whenever they dry-fire or go to the range. If you like a technique and find it's helping your shooting, add it to your training regime and work on making it a habit whenever you shoot. We all have shooting habits, some good, some bad. Becoming a better shooter involves learning what habits are working and what ones aren't, then replacing the bad ones with good ones and practicing them until you no longer need to think about them. That is, until they are habits.

As a Navy SEAL, I've become very comfortable around firearms. But one thing that makes my fellow frogmen and me so comfortable around weapons is that we are quite vigilant about adhering to the basic rules for firearms safety and handling. Anytime you forget about them, even for a second, bad things can happen—and frequently do.

What would you like to learn from this book? Are you open to change? _____

_____

_____

_____

_____

_____

_____

_____

_____

_____

_____

_____

Safety

*"No one is so good that basic firearms
and range safety rules don't apply."*

One day at a range I was teaching a basic pistol course to some new federal agents. Also coaching the students were other instructors from the unit we were training. The line had been called "cold"—all weapons had been cleared and checked. Another instructor from the unit brought a group together to do a little "private" demonstration on trigger control. He brought his weapon up and slowly pressed back on the trigger . . . as I'm sure you've guessed by now, the next thing that was heard was an ear-splitting BANG! It seems this "instructor" didn't think he needed to follow the same rules as the students. In a word, he got cocky. High-speed, low-drag doesn't mean a thing to me if you don't know the condition of your weapon before you decide it's time to send that firing pin forward. Over the years I've seen it happen to other people on the range, too, and it makes me nervous. So I'd just like to make this clear:

No one is so good that basic firearms and range safety rules don't apply.

The following safety rules apply to any weapon. Every range will also have a list of "range rules" that apply to shooting at that facility, so make sure you follow those too. Never assume that safety doesn't apply to you or that you're "better than that."

To shoot like a Navy SEAL, your shooting needs to be:

1. **Safe:** Firearms skills are worthless if you can't control the business end of a gun.

2. **Effective:** Our actions produce the desired result.

3. **Adaptable:** Every shooting situation is different, and your skills need to be adaptable to address the situation.

4. **Learned:** It's not magic. It takes lots of practice and we also learn from the past.

Keep your weapon on safe until aimed in on target.

Safety is more than just a rule—it's a tactic. It makes it a lot harder to kill the bad guys if you're spending your time patching up a teammate you shot. If it's good enough for the best warriors in the world, it's good enough for you.

Navy SEALs Firearms Safety Rules

1. Treat every gun as if it were loaded, regardless of perceived or actual condition. I think this is the most important safety rule. If you treat all guns as if they are loaded, you really have to want to shoot someone for it to happen. Even if I know my gun is *not* loaded, before I give a demonstration, or dry-fire or clean my weapon, I still check it again to make sure. Make sure you do the same. Treat it like it's loaded until you've checked it by sight and by touch. And never be embarrassed to ask someone else to check your weapon to get confirmation.

2. Keep your finger off the trigger until ready to shoot. Your finger should be extended straight along the receiver until you've made the decision to shoot. It should also be removed from the trigger as soon as you no longer need to shoot, or your weapon is no longer pointed in a safe direction. Speaking of that . . .

3. Always keep a gun pointed in a safe direction, and never point your weapon at anything you do not intend to shoot. Knowing where the muzzle of your gun is pointing at all times is critical to safely handling firearms. When we have problems with students during Close Quarters Combat (CQC) training, we sometimes attach lasers to their guns so they can better see where those guns are pointing and who would be taking rounds in the event of an accidental (AD) or negligent (ND) discharge. Even without a physical laser on your gun, you should imagine a laser coming out of your gun's muzzle, and never let it cross the path of anyone else—unless of course you intend to shoot them.

4. Be sure of your target and know your target's foreground and background. We hear this all the time on the range: "Who shot my target?" Not a big deal there, but what about when it's not training and lives are at stake? You need to be completely sure you know what you're shooting at, as well as what might be in front of it (walls, cars, barricades, trees); what might move in front of it (cars, people, dogs); and what's beyond your target. This could be anything from people in the open to family members in another room during a home invasion.

If your weapon has a safety, you'll need to remember one more: **Keep your weapon on safe until aimed in on target.**

Always make sure a gun is empty before cleaning.

It's not a long list, and there are plenty of variations. Pick whichever verbiage you like and live the rules every day. Could you change the words from "intend to shoot" to "willing to destroy"? Sure, whatever you'll remember. They all mean the same thing and normally if you can remember even one of them, no one is going to die. I recently began teaching my kids how to shoot, starting with a Daisy BB rifle and several Airsoft weapons. Before they could even touch the guns, they needed to be able to not only regurgitate all four rules, but also explain what each one meant. Since the gun has a safety, they also needed to remember to keep the weapon "on safe until aimed on target." These guys were five and seven years old when they started; if they can remember them, I expect everyone else I shoot with to do the same.

Speaking of children and firearms, make sure they know the difference between real guns and "play" guns. My kids love their NERF guns, but they know they are not real. (But they still practice the same rules with them—remember it's "Don't point your weapon at anything you do not intend to shoot." I've been hit by a lot of NERF darts!)

When it comes to the real thing, **avoid horseplay!** Firearms are deadly and must be treated with the respect they deserve. They are not toys and should not be treated as if they were.

If you have children, make sure they know not to touch guns without adult supervision and that they know what to do if they find a gun. This includes when they are at a friend's home. Make sure you talk to your children about what they should do if their friend pulls out a gun, and avoid another tragic story we've all heard on the news.

Always make sure a gun is empty before cleaning. It's impossible to verify if a gun is loaded just by looking at it. Never presume or take another's word that it is empty. As President Reagan said, "Trust, but verify." It only takes a second to check, and that second could save a life.

Before you shoot, make sure the firearm is safe to operate. Guns need regular maintenance to remain operable. If you have any question concerning a gun's ability to function, a professional gunsmith should look at it.

Anytime you go to the range, make sure you know the range rules and wear eye and ear protection. Staying safe on the range is up to you. If you see someone doing something unsafe on the range, make sure you say something. I often see people point out unsafe actions on the range and not say anything. Your not saying anything is as much of a safety violation as the person doing the act. Man-up (women can man-up too!) and tell them they need to stop. Remember, safety is everyone's responsibility.

Happy Shooting!

Write the four weapon safety rules: _____

_____

_____

_____

_____

The Habit of Perfection

"To improve in any area, you first
need to be open to change."

It's happened several times now. I show up at the range to work with a new group of shooters who are supposed to be "past the basics" of shooting, operators whom the government trusts to move around confined spaces with other people, carrying automatic weapons. As we start warming up, I'll go down the line and make corrections on stance, grip, trigger control, and so on. Often they nod their heads in agreement, but when I ask them about the technique, they say they don't know what I'm talking about. I'm talking about the basics of shooting, the fundamentals of marksmanship that everyone with a gun in their hands needs to know to shoot well. As a Navy SEAL, I had these ingrained in my head and repeated on a daily basis to achieve muscle memory.

My goal in writing this book is to cut through all the nonsense we have seen or heard on the range and get to what works. If something I write here doesn't work for you, don't use it. All I ask is that you give it a try. I've found cognitive dissonance to be the biggest limiting factor in helping experienced shooters improve their skills.

> *If you came here looking for confirmation that everything you've been doing is perfect, this might not be the book for you.*

Cognitive dissonance occurs when you've done something for a long time and, even when presented with evidence that there is a better way, you subconsciously fight against it. To improve in any area, you first need to be open to change.

If you came here looking for confirmation that everything you've been doing is perfect, this might not be the book for you. As the saying goes, "There's more than one way to skin a cat." The techniques I present not only work, but they've been tested in combat. Of course there are other ways that work and if you're happy with where you are as a shooter, there is no reason to change. But if you're open to trying something new and possibly going against the way your last instructor taught you was "the right way" to shoot, I'm sure you'll pick up enough nuggets of information to make this read well worth your time.

Keep an open mind and try out the techniques before saying they don't work. And every technique in this book won't work for everyone, but don't throw the baby out with the bathwater as you continue paving the path to perfection.

Shooting is all about habits, and the first habit you need is the habit of perfection. To be a good shooter, you need to be consistent—and to be consistent you need to have good habits. You need to do things the same way every time until they become ingrained and you do them without thinking every time you fire your weapon. When you practice these techniques, never settle for "good enough" and always strive for perfection. Of course you'll never reach this goal, so it will

force you to continue to train. Being a good combat shooter is not magic, and no one is born with the skills. If you want to be good, you need to train. If you want to be great, you need to train more. If you want to be the best, you need to train more than anyone else. Not only do the skills you practice need to become habits, but also training itself must become a habit. It's not something you do only when you have time—you need to make time.

The most important thing is to practice the techniques in this book. I know that sounds simple, but sadly 75 percent of the people who actually finish reading this book will never utilize any of the techniques they've just learned. Some will finish this book, realize they're not magically better from reading it, and start looking for another book or video to make them a better shooter. There is only one way to get better at shooting and that is by practicing.

WARNING: Reading this book will not make you a better shooter. Only training will make you a better shooter!

I _____
                    NAME

am committed to becoming a better shooter. I will read this entire book and practice the techniques described.

_____
                SIGNATURE

____ / ____ / _____
           DATE

SECTION I:
Training

1

What Are You Training For?

"Motion comes from emotion."

I often pose this question to military or law enforcement teams I'm training—it's important to understand the why (drive) to figure out the how (direction). Usually the level of commitment to training seems to wax and wane, and unfortunately I'll sometimes catch a unit on a steep downswing. As an instructor, I can pretty easily tell, not just by how they do during evaluations, but how they act or even talk before training begins.

In a unit dedicated to training, I hear about increasing their tactical advantage or looking for opportunities to hone their skills. In a unit plagued by the disease of mediocrity, talk seems to center around the testing itself or how long we'll be training. Why are people asking me how many negative marks they can get during tactical evaluations? To a true warrior, dedicated to training, the answer is simple: Zero. That's how many times you

can turn your back to a guy with a gun in combat and live to tell the tale.

In this book I'll write a lot about the mental and technical aspects of learning to shoot, but first it's time to ask why you're training and to understand your drive. If your drive is to put holes in paper targets on sunny days, you'll do fine reading the section on marksmanship, and any paper target that comes your way is going down! But if you ever need to defend your loved ones or protect your country, you need to look deeper. A miss on a paper target may give you a lower score or a fail on an evolution, but a miss on a guy who intends harm could mean failing yourself and your family. So you need to know what you are training for.

If you don't immediately know the answer, or it's just to shoot fast, look cool, or pass your next training evaluation, you'll never have the drive to become a true warrior. Even if you're training for competition or hunting, the drive will only come for your love of competition or the hunt. Warriors arise from a strong motivation to survive no matter what obstacles or evils come their way, and that motivation is love. Not to sound like a postcard or motivational speaker, but motion comes from emotion.

There will come a time when you will look back at your training say either "This is why I failed," or "This is why I prevailed."

Love for the people in our lives is the reason true warriors train. We train for battle to make sure we return to the ones we love. As anyone who has brushed death's cold shoulder can tell you, it's those faces we see when our lives flash before our eyes. You don't see the fun times you had or any accomplishments you made, you see the pain and sorrow in their eyes knowing that you're gone and you're not coming back. In combat you're not fighting for a top score or bragging rights, but to spare your wife the pain of crying over your grave as she grows old without you. You're fighting so your parents don't need to bury the son they raised and expected to be burying them. You're fighting so you can raise your

children right and protect them from harm. Because if you die in battle, the permanent pain in their hearts will be worse than any temporary pain you feel in death.

Even if you're training for competition, you need to do it for the love of it. If your only drive is vanity, any success you have will be short-lived.

If you know this, you will train that much harder; you'll wake up early and stay up late making sure you are the best warrior you can be. You'll never be satisfied with your performance and always look for ways to improve your chances of surviving a violent encounter. By knowing that you are training to be with the ones you love and spare them a lifetime of grief, you'll never settle for good enough. Defeating your enemy is the ultimate act of love.

There will come a time when you will look back at your training say either "This is why I failed," or "This is why I prevailed."

So I ask again, what are you training for?

What are you training for? _____

_____

_____

_____

_____

_____

_____

_____

_____

_____

_____

_____

_____

_____

_____

_____

2

Planning Your Training

For shooters, range time is very valuable, in more ways than one. At most ranges it costs money just to shoot. On top of that you have to buy targets, ammo, and cleaning supplies—the list adds up quickly. But the most important thing you have is time. My time is very valuable to me, so I never waste any opportunity to advance my skill set. I know a lot of people who go to the range and just say, "Hey, I'm gonna go shootin'!" They go to the range, set up a target, and start shooting; and they keep shooting until they're out of ammo or time. Even if you're going to practice, what does that really mean? To me it means nothing but wasted range time unless you have a well-laid-out plan.

Before your next trip to the local gunslinging establishment, have an idea of what you want to train before you arrive. This is the direction you need to follow to get where you're going, and without it you're likely to get lost. You might want to work on different stances, grip, trigger control, follow-through, or other skills. To figure this out, of course you need to know accurately where you're at now and where you want to go. A list of drills that works well for your buddy— or even worse, a world-class shooter—will very likely not work for you. What you really need is a plan for you.

We all have weaknesses in our shooting, and you need to spend the majority of your time correcting them.

I believe strongly in weakness-biased training. Weakness-biased training involves taking a serious look at the chinks in your armor and working at correcting them. We all have weaknesses in our shooting, and you need to spend the majority of your time correcting them. Once you've fixed them, there will be something else you need to work on. It's an endless cycle you need to continue as long as your goal is improved performance.

Unfortunately, most people practice with a strength basis, meaning that they practice what they're good at and neglect the areas that need work. Yes, it's easier and it feels good, but we are only as strong as our weakest link, and you can rest assured that when Murphy comes knocking on your door, he'll find that link and expose it.

Years ago Col. Jeff Cooper, the father of modern defensive shooting, laid out what he called the "combat triad." This was a set of three areas that must be honed to up the chances of success in personal combat. His three areas were:

1. Mindset

2. Gun handling

3. Marksmanship

Modern instructors in defensive shooting have grouped gun handling and marksmanship together and added tactics to the mix, thus:

1. Mindset

2. Gun handling and marksmanship

3. Tactics

Over years of training myself and thousands of Navy SEALS and other Special Forces personnel around the world, I've studied the requirements and refined the skills to come up with my own triad for success in personal combat. I call them the Combat-E3:

1. **Education**: All physical and mental skills, gunfighting, tactics, and so on.

2. **Equipment**: Weapons, ammo, kit, communications gear, and physical training (you are a machine!)

3. **Experience**: Real-world, scenario-based training, force-on-force, simulators, and competition.

No matter which one you chose to follow, you need to develop your training plan. There are three elements you need for any firearms training program to be effective. I call them the 3 D's of effective training: definition, direction and drive.

Definition: Aim Small, Miss Small

You need to know exactly where you are in your training and where you want to go. Most training plans out there are cookie-cutter plans that are worthless. Everyone is at a different place in their learning process or skill level and has different goals they want to achieve. How in the world is a training plan for Mike going to work for Michelle? Answer: It's not, and it's the biggest problem with most training methods today. But it's not the methods themselves; it's the plan, and a method developed for someone else is not an effective plan for you.

The first thing you need to do is to get an accurate assessment of your current skill level so you or your instructor knows what you need to work on or what course(s) you should take. Next, you need to get clear about what your goals are and what you want to get good at. It's easy to think that others have the same goals as we do, but ask just a few shooters and you'll find out this is far from the truth. Once you know where you are and where you want to go, you can come up with a plan.

Direction:
The Shortest Route
From Point-A to Point-B

Only when you know where you are and where you want to go will direction be of any use. Your training plan could have the best directions ever invented — super detailed, dyno-awesome-video, surround-sound-audio, with turn-by-turn directions (methods) — but if you're starting at the wrong point, these directions will be meaningless. If your goal is different from the directions, you will NEVER end up

where you want to be. Either way will lead to desultory destruction of your training plan. Normally, the lessons you're getting are not wrong — they're just not what you need.

Figure out what you need to do to get from point-A to point-B or hire a professional instructor if you need help. Write down your plan and include what you need to work on and when you need to do it. Include any courses or classes you need to take, but remember this: A course is not a plan. A course by itself is only one part of your path to perfection.

Drive:
Skinny Pedal on the Right

Drive means that you have a reason for training. You love your family and don't want some worthless P.O.S. to take them away from you or you away from them. You love your country and want to protect it. Hell, you just love to win and want to be on the top of your division! Whatever it is, your drive is the reason you get out of bed early to train. It's what makes you excited and energetic about learning and growing. Without having drive the best you can hope for is to be mediocre; you'll get up early for a week or two, but then your little reserve battery runs out of juice and you find it's easier to sleep in than to get up and train.

In the OLD days we used maps and compasses to get to where we wanted to go. Today we have NEW technology where we have satellites allowing us to use our personal GPS devices to get to where we want to go easier, and faster...the same is true for learning to shoot.

Use a GPS to Plan your Training

Gather information: Find out exactly where you're at and where you want to go.

Plan: Take your time to find the best, fastest way to get there.

Start: You need to get going to get better.

The GPS Firearms Training Model

To get all of these things working together for you (and you do need all three), you want to employ my GPS Firearms Training model. GPS training works just like the one in your car. The first thing you need to do is tell the GPS where you are. If it doesn't know, it can't give you directions. If you don't know where you are, a good instructor can also work like a GPS to define where you're at, but depending on interference (cognitive dissonance) it can take a while to pinpoint your exact location.

Now imagine if at this point the GPS just starting giving you directions. Where are you going? You need to tell the GPS where you want to go or you'll end up wasting your time and gas driving around all day. Even then you may never get to where you want

to go and there's a pretty good chance that you're going in the wrong direction.

So only when the GPS knows exactly where you are and where you want to go can it give you helpful directions. And with well-defined start and end points, the GPS will also be able to tell you as soon as you veer off course and give you new directions to get you to your destination faster.

After you've defined your points, the rest is up to you. Drive! Start moving, do something (this means practice) — if you're heading in the wrong direction your GPS will tell you — "recalculating; make a U-turn as soon as possible." But none of these critical elements will work alone and one or more is missing from most training plans out there (for those that even have a plan).

Again, a method or technique is not a plan, a training course is not a plan, even this book is not a plan — a plan is your personal long-range path to get to where you want to go. Without a plan, you'll never get to where you want to be. Don't let it happen to you!

I want to drive home that you must have a plan and stick to it. It's best to write out your plan in your training notebook, and when you get to the range, just go down the list. Afterward, write down how your training went and what else you need to work on next time, or at your next dry-fire training session. Dry-fire training is the single best thing you can do to improve your shooting. You don't go to the range and just bust caps to get better. You need a plan, and that plan needs to include dry-fire. Live fire just confirms all the dry-firing you've been doing.

What's your Plan? _____

_____

_____

_____

_____

_____

_____

_____

_____

_____

_____

_____

_____

_____

_____

_____

If you want to be able to take precision shots at long range, put in the time and effort to refine your zero until it's perfect.

3

Sighting In Your Carbine

"Sighting in shouldn't take long, but it's also not a race."

Because there are so many types of guns, sights, and optics, I'm not going to cover specifics for any systems but just some general guidelines that will help you sight in faster and more accurately. Sighting in shouldn't take long, but it's also not a race. If do it properly, you should be able to sight in accurately with as few as nine to twelve rounds, and save the rest of the box for other training. You'll get out of sighting in what you put into it. If you just need to hit the broad side of a barn, getting somewhere close to the middle might be good enough, but if you want to be able to take precision shots at long range, put in the time and effort to refine your zero until it's perfect.

Always check your weapon before shooting:

1. Make sure everything on the weapon is tight: upper and lower receiver, carrying handle, front sight, and all else.

2. Check sights (setting, batteries). Check rear elevation and make sure it's not a full rotation off.

3. Set sights to mechanical zero. See manufacturer's instructions.

4. Make sure you are using the small aperture on your iron sights.

5. Make sure your front sight is crisp and black. If you need to, file it flat and hit it with some Birchwood Casey Sight Black.

6. If there is no mark on your front sight post, put one there.

7. Check that your buttstock is in the correct position. Extend as far as possible.

These are general tips to sight in any gun or optic.

1. Always shoot a few rounds to warm up the barrel before sighting in.

2. If you're sighting in your irons, turn your optics off; if you're sighting in your optics, put your iron sights down if you can.

3. Review Data From Previous Engagements (DOPE) book if available, and manufacturer's instructions for your weapon and sights.

4. Make sure you're using the right sight-in target for your optic, gun, and distance.

5. Shoot from the prone position. This is the most stable and takes as much shooter error out of the equation as possible.

6. Get behind your gun. If you don't know how to get into a good prone position, review chapter 2 in the marksmanship section on shooting platform.

7. Use a support if available.

8. Load your weapon before you get set up in your firing position.

9. Place the buttstock in your shoulder.

10. If you're sighting in a red dot, make the dot as dim as possible.

11. Find your natural point of aim (NPA), and take your time. If you're firing three rounds, it should take two minutes to find your NPA and one minute to fire three rounds.

12. Once you come off safe, don't move anything except your trigger finger. Don't move your head, your hands, or your elbow—nothing. You can blink or move your eyes, but that's it.

13. Focus on the mark until you get into the zone.

14. Take at least three shots, calling each one. If one doesn't feel right, take another. You need to adjust off a group, and the more data you have, the better.

15. Remember your exact position before you move—you'll need to fire from the same position to avoid chasing your rounds. This includes your cheek weld; the tilt of your head on both horizontal and vertical planes; your hand, elbow, and leg positions; where the buttstock is in your shoulder; and where your finger is on the face of the trigger. The more you can remember, the more accurate your adjustments will be.

16. Mark shots in a triangle, and number each group. Find the middle and write down your adjustments.

17. Make adjustments on your sights according to the manufacturer's instructions, and do it again until you're happy with your zero. Do not adjust your sights until you are shooting consistent groups. If you're shooting large groups it's impossible to sight in, and it's more important to work on marksmanship than to sight in your gun. If you can, have someone else help you sight in the gun or work with you on diagnosing your shooting problems.

18. If using iron sights and a red dot, you can sight in your irons and then co-witness your red dot to get close. Just make sure you confirm what's happening on paper.

19. I like sighting in at twenty-five yards and then confirming at distance to get better accuracy. (I use a 100-yard zero, as I find that to be the most combat-effective zero for my needs.) See Appendix B to find the best sight in distance for you. This saves a lot of time, and if you can you should do the same.

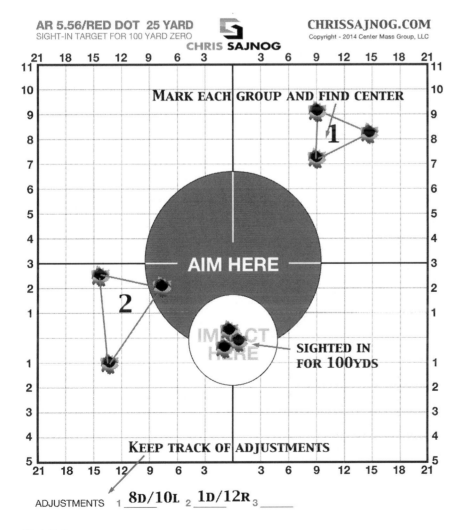

1.3.1 – Example of how to mark your target to sight in your carbine using iron sights. These targets were designed with the help of a sports Ophthalmologist to maximize the eyes' ability to precisely focus and aim while sighting in. Targets may be ordered from chrissajnog.com

4

Training Notebook

"Every shooter, no matter how skilled, will have one skill they need to concentrate on to elevate their game."

Navy SEALS are required to be experts in a variety of disciplines: shooting, demolition, close quarters combat, skydiving, and scuba diving, just to name a few. That's a lot of stuff to keep in our heads, especially when we may not use some of these for months at a time. To accomplish this, we've learned to keep logbooks to document the details needed to employ each skill successfully when the need arises.

This is what makes us good at what we do. We learn from past experiences by recording them in logbooks for each discipline. The same theory applies to shooting.

Many shooters have heard of a DOPE book, meaning Data of Previous Engagements. Snipers use one to record every aspect of each shot they take, so when they need to take a cold-bore (first) shot, they have the information they need to increase their

odds of success. A DOPE book records air temperature, wind direction and speed, specific ammo, distance, and elevation—all critical factors needed to engage targets at distance.

That's it. Keep it simple so you'll be more likely to use it each time you train, and you'll find the information you need much faster.

By contrast, a training notebook is a more general reference log used to document training. I've discussed training notebooks in several articles I've written and cover them in each course I run. What goes in a training notebook is all the vital information about your firearms training: date; weapons used; number of rounds fired (or time for dry-fire training); things you learned that worked for you; things that didn't work for you; and most important, things you need to work on next time.

For SEAL shooting, I use the acronym SEAL:

1. **Safe**: First and foremost, the techniques you use need to be safe.

2. **Effective**: Your rounds must produce the desired effect on target in the time available.

3. **Adaptable**: Your shooting techniques must work in any conditions and translate to any weapons. And finally:

4. **Learned**: Shooting is a learned skill, and you must learn each time you train and continue learning by starting where you left off the last time. This is what makes Navy SEALs the best at what we do.

A training notebook is simply a notebook you keep to document your training. You can use any size, shape, or style notebook you'd like. The key is to actually use it every time you train and review it every time before you train next. I also recommend a main page that lists the current crux in your shooting program. For instance, I had "FRONT SIGHT FOCUS" written in block letters on my main page for years because not concentrating

on the front sight was what made me throw rounds. Later it changed to trigger control. I'd worked on the front sight focus so much that it was no longer a problem, but trigger control was. So I saw "TRIGGER CONTROL" each time before I trained, reminding me to pay special attention to that aspect of shooting.

Your crux could be any fundamental of marksmanship, but every shooter, no matter how skilled, will have one skill they need to concentrate on to elevate their game.

Example training notebook entry:

1/11/2015

Glock 17

200 rounds

Worked on draw from thigh holster, accuracy (50 yards), and multiple target engagements.

Remember to look at the next target and then bring my weapon to my eyes.

Need to practice shooting while moving.

That's it. Keep it simple so you'll be more likely to use it each time you train, and you'll find the information you need much faster. Before you go to the range or dry-fire, review your training notebook's main and last page and take off from where you finished training last time. This way you're not relearning past lessons or mistakes and you'll see your shooting skills improve exponentially. Also remember to come up with a range plan of what you're going to work on so you don't waste your ammo or your time.

Now that you know what a training notebook is, the key is to get one and start using it! All you need is a piece of paper and pencil to get started—I guarantee it will take your shooting to the next level.

What will you use for your training notebook?_____

_____

_____

_____

_____

_____

_____

_____

_____

_____

_____

_____

_____

5

Making Goals a MUST

"The only easy day was yesterday."

Okay, so this is not a motivational course on goal setting, and no workbook accompanies this chapter. My objective is simply to help you understand the importance of having goals, describe effective goals, and give you some tips on how to achieve your goals. To make my goals a must, I use MUST as an acronym for Meaningful, Understandable, Specific, and Timed.

So why are goals important? They are the waypoints along your personalized training plan to ensure you're still on track. Goals should not be end-state goals. For example, don't set a goal to win the IDPA National Championship, but to train fifteen minutes a day. This way you'll know every day if you're on course and be able to adjust as needed, plus you'll be motivated to continue each time you meet your goal—success breeds success. Goals are concrete reminders of

what's important to you. You set goals by stopping and thinking about where you are and where you want to be, and plotting the course for the easiest way to get there. When life throws obstacles in your path, your goals are reminders of the plan you came up with when you could think clearly about your choices.

> *When life throws obstacles in your path, your goals are reminders of the plan you came up with when you could think clearly about your choices.*

When I was going through Basic Underwater Demolition/SEAL (BUD/S) training, my only goal was to make it through each day. That's why we SEALs say, "The only easy day was yesterday." Every day is tough, but if you take it one day at a time, it's more manageable. With attainable goals and a clear and certain vision of where you'll end up, you can accomplish seemingly impossible tasks. I don't call my visions of where I'm going to be goals because to me goals are things you try to do, not something you're sure of, like graduating BUD/S. I pictured myself wearing the Trident and living my life as a SEAL.

I recommend you do the same. Aim high in the vision of where you want to be. Imagine it as if it were true, believe in it. Then set goals that will get you there.

Meaningful

For your goals to work, they need to come from an assessment of what's important to you. Setting a goal to train fifteen minutes a day on dry-fire because you think you should is not going to stick—but setting the same goal because you must be able to protect your newborn baby from intruders will work very well. Think about what's important in your life, and then think about what you need to do to have or keep that in your life. Once you do that, you'll have a goal that will stick and you'll work hard to achieve it.

Understandable

No goal should be overly complex, or you'll use this as an excuse to stop working toward it or explain why you didn't achieve it.

Keep it simple, and your mind will not have an excuse to fight you on it. "Train fifteen minutes a day" is easily understandable—no excuses. But, "Train on the items I have highlighted in the new shooting book I read, working on the items that I scored lowest on the previous week for 25 percent of the time, then working on skills for the upcoming competition for the remainder of the time, unless I need to work on the previous skills more," will never get accomplished.

If a seven-year-old could understand your goal, it's probably good.

Aim high in the vision of where you want to be. Imagine it as if it were true, believe in it.

Specific

For your goals to work, they need to be things you can easily act upon that don't seem too big. "Eat healthy" does not work because it's not specific and you'll fight against it because it seems so big. On the other hand, "switch to 1 percent milk" is very specific, can be acted upon immediately, and seems like a small task. You need to do the same thing with your shooting goals. Make them specific items you can act on. "Work on grip strength in my car on the way to work," is simple, specific, and small.

Timed

Make your goal stick: Set a place and time and immediately do something to move toward your goal as soon as you set it. Many people set a goal to train "someday." "Some" is not a number, and "day" is not a time. But you need both to achieve a goal—"someday" never comes. When you set your goal, make sure you set a time: "Starting Monday, work on grip strength on Monday, Wednesday, and Friday in my car on the way to work."

Timed does not mean training to a clock. Training to a clock is one of the worst guidelines and goals of any training program. Training to a clock means, "You must train for eight hours today." Or like some units I train, they have a mandatory, forty hours of training for a course. This type of objective is always designed by a manager, not a trainer.

So what's the right way? Always train to an objective. Rather than say you're going to train for fifteen minutes, say you're going to complete fifteen perfect repetitions of a specific technique.

The Rider, the Elephant, and the Path

Setting good, effective goals is a great first step, but reaching any goal requires change. To illustrate this, I use the metaphor of the rider, the elephant, and the path, the metaphor Jonathan Haidt first used in his book *The Happiness Hypothesis: Finding Modern Truth in Ancient Wisdom*, and later made famous in *Switch: How to Change Things When Change Is Hard* by Dan Heath and Chip Heath. They used the story to describe why change is hard, and I'll use it to show you the three things you can change to reach your goals.

The rider is your conscious mind, trying to steer a huge elephant down a path. The elephant is your emotions and instinct that walk the path. The path is your environment. To change you can direct the rider, motivate the elephant, or shape the path—and of course it's best to do all three.

Direct the Rider

The rider is your conscious mind, which can come up with all kinds of great ideas, plan ahead, and make short-term sacrifices for long-term gains. The rider's problem is he's very small compared to the elephant and grows tired quickly when he's constantly trying to steer the large beast. The rider's job is getting the right information and planning your training. The better the direction, the easier it will be for you to take the right path.

Motivate the Elephant

The elephant is your emotions, very strong but also very lazy. The elephant is very comfortable on the path and will resist the rider trying to direct him into the dense brush alongside the path. The elephant does not have a big brain, so it will always look for quick rewards, forgetting about the rider's great plan. By coming up with a strong reason for training, you will motivate the elephant and use his strengths to change direction. Just remember that the elephant can get spooked easily, so make the changes small or he will pull against you—and win.

Shape the Path

The path is the final piece of the change puzzle and represents the environment around you. To help make your training easier, shape your path. If the elephant sees an easier path than the one he's on, he's going to take it. Habits are the best way to shape a new path. Every time you train you are breaking brush and either paving an old path or clearing a new one. The rider can shape the path however he likes, and the more consistent he is, the faster it will happen. When the elephant sees it's easier to stay on the new path than the old one, you can take a break and enjoy the ride.

So how does this help make you a better shooter? Direct your rider by setting good goals and coming up with a training plan. Motivate your elephant by knowing what you're training for, and make small changes so you don't spook the beast. Finally, make it easier to train by shaping your path. Keep everything you need to train easily accessible. If you shape your environment so it's easier to train than to watch TV, you'll train more.

What is my motivation? How can I shape my path? _____

_____

_____

_____

_____

_____

_____

_____

My Shooting Goals: _____

_____

_____

_____

_____

_____

_____

_____

_____

_____

_____

_____

_____

_____

_____

_____

_____

One of the biggest hurdles to becoming a good shooter is achieving consistency, which means doing things the same way every time you shoot.

6

Dry Weapons Training

"With consistent, perfect practice you are paving
the path to perfection."

Ever wish you could shoot like a Navy SEAL? I could tell you the "secret" of how we do it—but then I'd have to kill you. Actually there is no secret. It all boils down to practice, and lots of it. Dry-fire is the generic term for practicing weapons manipulation with an unloaded gun. Dry-fire does not mean just pulling the trigger. I can teach a monkey to pull a trigger (though he might slap the hell out of it). Dry-fire training involves everything you do with that weapon, from the fundamentals to shooting on the move. Dry-firing also refers to practicing reloads, drawing your gun, and almost any skill you need to practice. This is why I like to use the term *dry weapons training*.

Got a new piece of kit? You'd be well served to spend some time dry-training and working with that new gear before going to the range to figure out how it works—or

worse yet, waiting until you need to use it in the line of duty or other lethal engagement.

In the SEAL Teams, I had unlimited supplies of ammunition—it was great, but most of us don't have access to endless ammo. Even with all that ammo, I dry-fired all the time—and still do. All great shooters dry-fire a *lot*; it's the "secret" that makes them great! If you want to be great too, try to dry-fire every day for fifteen or twenty minutes, and practice weakness-biased training.

So now you're asking, "Why dry-fire? Why not just go to the range and practice there?" Patience, young Jedi. Think about it; when you dry-fire, you can practice all the skills you normally work on live fire (minus recoil management) without going to the range and paying for targets, ammo, range time, and these days, gas! By taking the time to dry-fire, you'll be able to go to the range and confirm everything you learned dry-firing and become very proficient at shooting.

Shooting like a Navy SEAL is not magic: It's dry-firing!

There are three phases to learning a new motor skill: cognitive, associative, and autonomous. We all start off at the same place, but how quickly we get to the finish line depends on how efficiently we train. Cognitive learning is very slow: You're often using self-talk to work through each step. This requires lots of brainpower to think through each move while you find out what works. This stage is inefficient but necessary to move on.

In associative learning, the basic movement pattern is understood. The learner makes more subtle changes, and movements become more efficient. The last phase is autonomous learning, consisting of fluid, effortless movement. When you get to this phase, your movements are consistent and accurate, with very few mistakes. This is where experts are, and where you want to get as fast as possible. How do you do it? Dry-fire!

Dry-fire improves the neuroplasticity of your brain. Every time you train, you create neural pathways in your brain. Do the

same movement enough, and you'll create perfect muscle memory—your brain knows only one way to do the task, and it can't make a mistake. That's why it's critical not to practice a whole technique from start to finish and then decide it wasn't right.

What most people call "muscle memory" is really the process of myelination.

This is a big mistake I see many instructors commit in letting students make mistakes. Why? To teach them a lesson? Unfortunately it does teach their brains that what they just did was one way to perform that skill—but your learning brain doesn't know right from wrong. Each mistake, no matter how small, teaches your brain one option, even if it's not the option you want to imprint.

What most people call "muscle memory" is really the process of myelination. Think of myelin as insulation around your nerves that your body puts there so it can send messages faster. Practice builds myelin around the nerves responsible for your movements so that the next time you do those movements they will be faster. This happens slowly, but it happens no matter what your movement is— so even if you're training something wrong, you're still building myelin around that pathway, teaching your body the wrong way to do something. To build myelin the fastest, your movements need to be flawless. The speed you move at has no effect on myelin, so the best way to learn and reinforce motor skills is through slow, perfect practice.

With consistent, perfect practice you pave the path to perfection. As in the metaphor with the rider, the elephant, and the path, dry-fire is the best way to clear the new path quickly. If your goal were to get from one side of a dense forest to the other as quickly as possible and you had as much time to train and prepare as you'd like, how would you do it? Would you just keep running different patterns as fast as you could, seeing which route was the fastest? Or would you plot out the best course, remove obstacles along the way, and pave the ground so the path is smooth and fast? Wasting rounds at the range is the first course—dry-fire is the second.

The best way to learn and reinforce motor skills is through slow, perfect practice.

The first time you go down the wooded path it will be slow, and you may even need to backtrack a few times to find the best route. But each time you take the path, the route will be smoother and faster. Stay on the path long enough and you'll be able to

do it with your eyes closed. But take just one step off the path and you're instantly back in deep brush. The key is to recognize what happened. All is not lost, you just need to get back on the path. Slow down and backtrack to where you went off course and you'll be back up to speed.

Professional sports teams don't practice just by playing games—they run drills. In warfare, this is called dry-fire.

When you do your dry-fire training, use your real gun and magazines for drills, working on manipulation of the weapon. If you are practicing skills that are not focused on weapon manipulation, use other tools such as airsoft, Shot Indicating Resetting Trigger (SIRT) pistols, and so on to get more out of the training and make it more interesting. Always figure out exactly what you are practicing and use the best tool for the job.

Tips and Safety Guidelines to Get You Started

Make sure you have been trained by a professional shooting instructor on firearms safety and how to use your firearm. No articles or YouTube videos can replace professional instruction. After you've done this, it's always best to dry-fire with someone watching you when you're first learning. The reason for this is that they can watch your technique to make sure you're doing it right. The only thing worse than not practicing is practicing bad techniques and reinforcing bad habits. Once you've got your technique down, it's fine to practice on your own.

Although you can dry-fire nearly anywhere, pick a place and make it your regular training area. Find a place you can train without distractions, such as a bedroom or garage.

If you're practicing with real firearms, make sure that you're not dry-firing at an interior wall that a bullet could pass through. An interior wall with an outer brick wall on the opposite side or a stone fireplace should work fine. I have a friend who uses a cardboard target with a Kevlar vest behind it—not a bad idea. Never under any circumstances dry-fire at anything you are unwilling to destroy! This includes people, pets, the TV, or anything else you value. Besides being unsafe and irresponsible, you could be charged with a felony in the event of an accident. If there is nothing in your house at which you can safely dry-fire, don't dry-fire at home. Even if the only place you can do it safely is at the range, that's where you should go. I have my students dry-fire every day at the range before we go hot because it's a great way to get warmed up.

You should never dry-fire if you are tired, distracted, or your mind is on anything other than your practice time. Don't burn yourself out. Before you get tired of training or start losing concentration, stop.

Remove all ammunition from the room you are in. Removing it from the weapon is not good enough. You cannot accidentally fire a round if there is no ammunition in the room where you are training. If this is not possible, place all your ammunition in a secured container.

If you are ever interrupted, perform all your safety checks again.

Be very careful when you go from live to dry (or dry back to live fire) with your firearm. This is the time when accidents most frequently happen.

And it should go without saying that *guns, children, drugs, and alcohol* do not mix!

If you have ammunition in your gun, you did not have a negligent discharge while dry-firing—when you are dry-firing, there is no ammunition in the gun.

Here are some simple steps you should take each time before you dry-fire:

1. Come up with a plan for what you're going to practice. You should write this down in your range book as well,

so you can review what you need to work on.

2. If you're at home, go into a room by yourself and shut the door. If others are around or you are at the range, make sure you observe all the normal range safety rules.

3. Turn off the TV, radio, computer, iPod, cell phone, and any other device that could conceivably distract you.

4. Clear the gun, magazines, and any equipment you'll be using of all live ammunition and put it in another room or secure it inside a container.

5. Find a small target in a safe place with a bulletproof backing.

6. Review your training notebook and the fundamentals of marksmanship.

7. Get into position and check your gun again. Be absolutely sure the chamber and magazine well are clear! Check your magazines and any equipment you are wearing or using to ensure they are clear as well.

8. Say to yourself, "I'm beginning dry-fire practice," and mentally prepare yourself.

9. Go through the list of techniques you need to work on. If you make a mistake, go back and correct it

right away to make sure you're not practicing bad habits. If you do it wrong once, you need to do it right seven times to erase that training scar.

10. If you make a mistake while practicing an isolation drill, go back one step and do it right. You don't want to reinforce making and correcting mistakes.

11. To keep it interesting and to advance your skills, you need to vary your practice routines. Start with slow, step-by-step presentations. Make them perfect, then gradually speed up and smooth it out. If you've been taught a four-point presentation, remember those points are not destinations, but waypoints you should move through smoothly. Remember, speed can't be forced: Speed happens. Also, if you have a double-action/single-action (DA/SA) gun, you should practice using both the double-action and single-action trigger. Once you're proficient in the basics, it's time to move on to other skills.

12. Your sessions should last from fifteen to twenty minutes, and you should stop practicing before you get tired or distracted—otherwise you tend to get sloppy in your techniques and build bad habits. I recommend that you practice every day for the first two weeks. For the next two weeks, practice two or three times a week

and after that, practice at least one or two times a week to maintain your skills. If you have the time and want to train more often after that, great! Just don't feel you need to be constantly practicing, as this can seem overwhelming and become an obstacle to training. Goal: Dry-fire four times for every one time of live fire.

13. When you're done, put the gun away in a safe place in your desired carry condition. If you've loaded your gun, make sure you say out loud, "My gun is now loaded" three times so there is no chance you'll forget you're done dry-firing. Make sure you log your progress in your range book and write down the things you need to work on. Then go on with your wonderful and exciting life until your next dry-fire session.

In the end, shooting like a Navy SEAL is easy (as long as your concept of easy

involves years of hard work). We're not born with special powers, and skill can't be programmed into you as in Neo in *The Matrix.* If you've never done it before or don't do it enough, the results from dry-fire training will be dramatic and almost instantaneous. Go ahead and do it for one month—take the thirty-day challenge. I dare you!

Record your dry-fire drills on video to diagnose your own problems. Train in front of a mirror to work on a smooth draw.

Always try to have someone watch you when you train to make sure you're doing everything correctly. Live fire only confirms how much dry training you've conducted, and bullets will magnify your errors.

> Go to **http://chrissajnog.com** for free dry weapons training videos. For those who take their shooting seriously, I also offer several online training courses.

Where and when will I practice dry weapons training? _____

_____

_____

_____

_____

_____

What do I need to buy or do to make sure I can do it safely, effectively and enjoy it? _____

_____

_____

_____

_____

_____

_____

_____

_____

_____

_____

_____

_____

_____

_____

_____

7

Range Equipment

"Like the Boy Scouts... Be prepared."

Although I strongly believe that dry weapons training is a far better method for you to learn with than going to the range, you will actually need to go to a range at some point to check your new ninja-skills. This is a list of recommend items you should carry on every trip. Everyone's bag will be different, depending on how, what, and where they shoot. If you've never been to a range before, this is a good start, and you can add or subtract items as needed.

Range Bag

The first item is the container to keep all your goodies in. The main choices you need to make are size and compartmentalization. Size is determined by what you need. I recommend you compile everything before getting a bag so you have an idea how much space you'll need.

Next, decide if you want an open bag, a bag with lots of compartments, or a combination of the two. There are many range bags on the market, but I actually use a tool bag from a hardware store. Mine has a big open area surrounded by multiple compartments and is the perfect size for my needs. For me, though, the best part is that no one who sees it knows it has anything to do with guns. I see no reason to show that off.

Gun

Depending on your state laws and if you have a concealed carry weapons permit (CCW), you may decide to carry your pistol in your range bag. I do this sometimes for the ease of having just one thing to carry.

Magazines

As with everything else here, check these before you go to make sure they are clean and functioning. I always try to do my first loadout at home before I go to the range.

Ammunition

Always bring more ammunition than you plan to shoot. Of course you have a written training plan, so you know how much you'll use to accomplish your goals. Still, plans are made to be changed! I always like to stop shooting on a high note, so if it's close to the end of my planned drills, I stop and go home with extra ammo. On the other hand, if your plan ends with you not shooting your best, you have extra ammo to shoot a drill you know you'll rock.

Shooting Glasses

I always have two pair in my range bag. Sometimes a pair will break; sometimes a buddy will forget his and I get to feel like the ever-prepared Boy Scout. Make sure your shooting glasses meet or exceed American National Standards Institute (ANSI) Z 87.1 rating. This will be stamped on the glasses. If it's not, find another pair.

Hearing Protection

Don't ruin your hearing! As with shooting glasses, always have more than one set of ear protection in your bag. Also, learn a lesson

I now wish I learned a few million rounds ago: Wear double hearing protection. I recommend wearing disposable foam plugs and a set of electronic ears over those. This will protect your hearing and still allow you to hear what's going on around you. It's a good idea to look up the noise rating (NR) of the firearms you shoot or will be shooting around you, then look up the noise reduction rating (NRR) for your hearing protection to make sure you're adequately protecting your hearing. Always carry extra batteries for all electronics in your bag.

Holster

Depending on your training plan and the size of your bag, you may be able to fit one or more holsters in your bag to practice with. If your holster needs any tools to make adjustments, make sure you keep those in your bag as well. Of course you should have dialed in your holster during all your dry-fire training, but things can and do loosen up when you least expect them to.

Light

If you plan on shooting at night for any reason, make sure you're taking your lights with you to the range to train with them. You don't even need to do most of your low-light training in low light—in fact you shouldn't. But when you have a chance to use your lights, make sure you have them with you, and extra batteries.

Shooting Gloves

If you wear gloves as part of your job as military or LE, or you have a CCW and wear gloves when you carry, bring your gloves and train with them! The amount of gloved training depends on the amount of time you wear gloves. Even if you don't wear gloves for shooting, they are often good to have for working on a gun.

Cleaning Supplies

Bring lube, brushes, patches, and tools— everything to work on or clean your gun. Nothing is more frustrating than having a gun jam and not having the supplies needed to fix it. There have also been plenty of times I was stuck at a range longer than I wanted and I was able to clean my gun because I had the supplies.

Targets

Of course you could probably buy expensive targets at the range, but what if they don't have the ones you need for your training plan? Unless you have a huge bag, you can't keep all your targets in your bag, but I keep about ten small ones rolled up in mine, and they've come in handy on many occasions.

Training Notebook

Last but not least is your trusty training notebook. So important is this piece of gear that it has its own chapter! Make sure you've read that chapter and keep your training notebookwith you.

> Go to **http://chrissajnog.com** for a free list of my recommended training equipment.

What gear do I need before I can go to the range? _____

_____

_____

_____

_____

_____

_____

_____

8

Tools for the Toolbox

"The more you know the more you'll grow as a shooter."

Airsoft

Airsoft cannot completely replace live fire of course, but it's one of the best tools you can use to enhance it. Don't think of it as a substitute for live fire—think of it as a force multiplier. There are plenty of tactics and techniques you can practice with airsoft that you can't (or shouldn't) practice with live fire. Today's airsoft guns are not the toys we grew up with. I remember going to a gun show a few years back and seeing a big sign that read AIRSOFT. I went to investigate and picked up an M4 on the table. As I was checking out the gun, I asked the guy where the airsoft guns were. He said, "You're holding one." Yes, I felt like an idiot—and didn't tell him I was a Navy SEAL—but I was hooked.

There are still lots of salty old shooters who will tell you to stay away because airsofts are

not *exactly* like the real thing. Don't throw the baby out with the bathwater. Properly employed, airsofts have far more positives than negatives as training tools:

- Not the toys we played with as kids.

- Exact replicas of your real gun. Feel the same, work the same.

- Super cheap training.

- Super safe. You couldn't accidentally shoot a real round if you tried!

- Can train and travel (almost) anywhere.

- Will increase the time you actually train.

- Some have recoil. Even if yours doesn't, train that live fire and use airsoft to train everything else!

Blue Guns

These are among the most underutilized tools, especially for instructors. I always use blue guns when I run training because they allow me to quickly demonstrate any aspect of shooting to one person or the whole group without any safety concern about where I'm pointing my gun. If you're practicing tactics, you can often get a lot more training done if you're not worrying about things you don't need, like loaded weapons.

Lasers

Putting a laser on your gun is a great way to dry-fire and practice moving while shooting. Pick a small target like a light switch and walk forward, sideways, and so on, always keeping the beam on the target. Figure out what you need to do and how you need to move to keep the laser's beam steady. If the beam is steady, your sights are steady.

If you're not measuring your training, what you're doing is called playing.

You don't even have to invest in an expensive weapon laser. Just buy a laser pointer for $9.99 and attach it temporarily to your gun.

Video

Film yourself training and then watch it to see what you're doing right and what still needs some work. Don't do too many reps without watching. You don't want to be practicing bad habits. You can use a webcam, your mobile phone, iPad—anything. The footage doesn't need to be studio quality. You watch it and erase it, so don't sweat the small stuff. Just set it down, hit record, do your technique a few times, and then watch it. You'll be amazed at how quickly your skills will progress. To really nitpick what you're doing, you can even play it back at half speed. Sometimes it helps to watch it at a faster speed to check for smoothness. Just try them all out and see what works for you.

Pro Timer or Shot Timer

If you're not measuring your training, what you're doing is called playing. Get a pro timer with a par timer on it and start timing yourself to finish the drill before the buzzer goes off. You can do this with both live fire and dry-fire, and the stress of the buzzer will help you shoot better under pressure.

A great, low-cost alternative to a pro timer is buying a Tabata app for your mobile device. You can use it for live fire by running the headphones under your ear pro, and it's perfect for dry-fire. As an example, you can set up a timer for two seconds of work (this is your timed skill) with ten seconds of rest, when you set back up to repeat the drill. You could practice drawing and firing two shots in two seconds, for example.

Laser Targets, Guns, and Rounds

This is one of the best ways to make your dry-fire training a lot more fun, and if it's fun, you're much more likely to continue doing it. There are dedicated guns like the Shot Indicating Resetting Trigger (SIRT) pistol, and cartridges that can be dropped into your firearm. As with everything else in this chapter, there are both advantages and disadvantages. So make sure you assess your needs and get what fits. I use both for practicing different aspects. And because the SIRT is strikingly similar to my Glock in form and function, I get a lot of use out of it. If you use a different platform, take that into consideration.

Balance Boards and BOSU Balls

Just using these by themselves is a great idea, since improving your balance will improve your shooting. If you've seen the videos of me shooting while on BOSU Balls and balance boards, they were done only after I mastered them without a gun, then with a blue gun, then an airsoft—all conducted safely before I attempted live fire. If you plan to use this tool, I recommend you do the same.

Dummy Rounds

There are many uses for dummy rounds, and having some around is smart. Here are just a few:

1. Teaching kids and new shooters how to load a magazine.

2. Dry-fire training.

3. Practicing handling malfunctions.

4. Testing for anticipation during live fire.

Make sure you buy at least three dummy rounds.

Other Books, Websites, Blogs, and Videos

There are plenty of good resources out there, and the more you know the more you'll grow as a shooter. Just practice the stuff you learn. You'll never get better if you just keep reading books and watching videos. You need to practice to get better.

Instructor-led Training Courses

There is no substitute for learning from a competent firearms instructor. They can assess your skill level and develop a plan for getting you where you want to go. Just do some research before signing up. Find out what instructor experience they have, as this is the most important job you'll be paying them to do. The fact that someone can shoot well in no way translates to their ability to teach their skills to others.

Coach

Even if this person's not a firearms instructor, find a good coach to facilitate your training. If you know what to do, a skilled coach can help you plan your training to be most effective and watch you train and look for the things you tell them to. Sometimes having someone from a completely different discipline can be even better than having someone who knows only shooting. What if they were an expert coach in efficient body mechanics? Could they see things in your draws or reloads that others missed or never thought of? Of course.

Competition

I've heard some people say that competition is bad because it teaches you bad habits that don't translate to "real life." This is an idiotic line of thinking. Competition helps you work on all your shooting skills as well as shooting under stress. Any chance you get to shoot will make you better, period.

Hunting

Again, any chance you get to hone your skills is a good tool to use. Since hunting can put food on the table as well—bonus points.

Join the Military or Police

How about I point out the obvious choice: Support your country or community, get paid, get free ammunition, and free firearms training. This is the route I went, and it's worked out pretty well for me so far.

Paintball

Okay, before you balk, think about it. No, you're not going to practice weapons manipulation, but you can practice other important skills, such as situational awareness, teamwork, tracking moving targets, use of cover and concealment, and more. Remember, these are tools, not your whole program. No one would argue we should not use live fire in training because we can't actually shoot at people.

The fact that someone can shoot well in no way translates to their ability to teach their skills to others.

Apps (not Video Games)

We've all got iPhones or iPads with us all the time, so why not put them to use in our shooting programs? There's an app that has been scientifically tested to improve your eyesight by 33 percent. There are brain games that will help your neurons process information faster, and the faster your brain works, the more likely you'll have a positive outcome during a violent encounter.

.22 Conversion Kits

This is a great way to instill confidence in a new shooter while still using the same platform. Shooting is 99 percent mental, and when you shoot hundreds of rounds dead center with no recoil that will be your reality when shooting your normal load. It's also a great way to save money on ammunition. The only thing cheaper than .22 Long Rifle (LR) ammo is airsoft BBs.

Grip Strengtheners

Grip strengtheners such as green IronMind EGGs, Captains of Crush Grippers, and Dyna-Flex Powerballs are useful tools that can help you improve your shooting skills and overall manual dexterity.

Go to **http://chrissajnog.com** for a free list of my recommended training tools.

List the training tools you will use: _____

_____

_____

_____

_____

_____

_____

_____

_____

_____

SEAL
SLEEP, EAT AND LIFT

Learn to do everything Navy SEALs do
when we're not killing bad guys
(or writing bestselling books)!
NAVY SEAL CHRIS SAJNOG

9

S.E.A.L. – Sleep, Eat and Lift

"You are the weapon and firearms are just tools."

Although the fake book cover to the left is my attempt at humor, the acronym is one we used often to describe "down-time" when we were on deployment.

As a Navy SEAL, I made physical fitness and nutrition the cornerstones of all my training. Because of this, I've had many people tell me I should write a book on exercise and nutrition. I'm not sure I have a book's worth of information yet, but I think they're important enough to include a chapter here.

If you believe, as I do, that you are the weapon and firearms are just tools, it makes sense to take care of your weapon as you do (or should) take care of your firearms. If you want to ensure accuracy, you'll feed your gun high-quality ammunition and practice by working it out as much as possible. You need to give the same care and concern

to your body if you want to be a truly effective weapon.

The idea that physical fitness is important in warfare is not new. The U.S. military discovered after WWI that exercise helped raise combat survival rates, and started implementing physical fitness into daily routines. They didn't require exercise to make the GIs look better with their shirts off, but to improve their combat effectiveness.

You need to be stronger and faster to defeat your enemy.

The first ditty I ever learned about combat in the SEAL teams was, "Shoot, move, and communicate." So how can you move if you're overweight and out of shape? How can you communicate when you're huffing and puffing from being out of breath? And how can shoot accurately when your sights are bouncing up and down from your chest heaving because you never learned the value of exercise? You need to be stronger and faster to defeat your enemy. Whether it's a terrorist or a shot timer, increasing your level of physical health is directly correlated to improved performance with all aspects of firearms training.

Benefits of Exercise and Improved Nutrition

1. Relieves stress, leads to improved performance.

2. Increased self-confidence leads to improved performance.

3. Improved neuroplasticity—good nutrition and exercise literally make you smarter!

4. Improved mental function, improved decision making.

5. Faster reaction times, better scores, and better chance of surviving violent encounters.

6. More endurance, so that hunting, combat, patrol, and competition will be easier.

7. Improved physical strength leads to a better shooting platform and better grip.

8. Better balance and stance.

9. Better looks and increased officer presence and opponent intimidation.

10. Smaller belt size—you can't put as much junk on your belt, so you'll be lighter and faster.

11. Smaller belly—magazines need to travel a shorter distance during reloads.

12. Sick less often, allowing more time to train.

13. Longer life, allowing more time to train.

14. More time to train leads to better mission success.

I hope by now you believe that exercise and nutrition are important parts of becoming a better shooter. I recommend this program for everyone, no matter how old you are, what you weigh, or what color your hair is. Take the first step and get started—the rest is easy!

Functional Fitness

The type of exercise I recommend is called *functional fitness*. What this means is pretty basic: If you work around water, for example, swimming should be part of your training. If you're a running-and-gunning 3-gun competitor, you should be running as part of your exercise routine. Just make sure the exercises you choose are functionally correct. To find out, give it the "bus stop test": Would the exercise you're doing look normal at a bus stop? Squats? Sure, you could be picking up a box. Triceps extensions? Nope. There is no functional reason to extend your triceps like that at a bus stop, so keep that out of your plan.

Now, this is where I'm going to lose some of you, but a few things human beings should not naturally be eating are: soda, chips, candy bars, and bread.

Any successful physical fitness routine will incorporate weights and resistance training, cardio, and some type of CrossFit and/or High-intensity Interval Resistance Training (HIIT) routine, and stretching—after your workouts. Yes, stretch at the end, when your muscles, tendons, and ligaments are warm. It's proven that static stretching prior to lifting weights actually makes you weaker. Stretching prior to exercise fatigues your muscles and leads to injuries.

My Exercise Plan

Monday: Swim in morning, run and foam rolling in evening.

Tuesday: HIIT and core.

Wednesday: Foam roller, balance, and stretch.

Thursday: Mixed martial arts (MMA) training in morning, run in evening.

Friday: Yoga and core.

Saturday: HIIT and balance.

Sunday: Rest.

Nutrition

Key to getting in shape is consuming the right food. It's at the core of physical fitness success and the key to living a better, healthier life. I don't like or use the term *diet*, because people associate the word with something temporary, not what it really means: how you naturally eat.

What's happened since we've been told to follow a low-fat diet? We've gotten fatter.

Now, this is where I'm going to lose some of you, but a few things human beings should not naturally be eating are: soda, chips, candy bars, and bread.

I won't get into the science here. I'll give you a simple prescription that I guarantee—if you follow it—will get you in the best physical *and* mental shape of your life in ninety days.

Simple Plan

1. Stop eating anything white—this means all grains and sugar (milk is okay if you're not lactose-intolerant). Grains include all gluten and sugar, as well as all sweeteners.

2. Take two supplements: fish oil and a probiotic.

> ### *The high-carb diet recommended by the government, not fat, is the reason for the "diabesity" epidemic.*

That's it! Two things—you can do that! And here's some good news to help out. First, stop avoiding healthy fats. What's happened since we've been told to follow a low-fat diet? We've gotten fatter. What is 70 percent of your brain made of? Fat! This includes cholesterol, which your brain needs in large amounts. What's happened to our brains since we were told not to eat red meat and egg yolks?

Alzheimer's, dementia, and attention deficit hyperactivity disorder (ADHD) all increased immediately following the war on fats and cholesterol.

Finally, think of carbohydrates as your new enemy. Carbs turn to sugar as soon as they enter your body and start stressing your insulin pump. The high-carb diet recommended by the government, not fat, is the reason for the "diabesity" epidemic. I watched one of my parents die from being morbidly obese. My dad followed the high-carb, low-fat diet religiously for forty years. The thing was, for him, it wasn't working. He just kept getting fatter. It seemed the better he followed the recommendations, the fatter he got. He even got where he totally eliminated fat from his diet. And remember, 70 percent of your brain is made of fat. In the end I sat with my mom in the ICU as he died. His brain was no longer working, but he followed that diet to the end.

Your Exercise and Nutrition Plan of Attack

1. Just as with your shooting skills, assess where you are now and where you want to be. Come up with a plan. This includes checking with your doctor. I think it's funny when I hear commercials that say, ". . . to make sure you're healthy enough to start exercise." So if you're really not healthy, you shouldn't start? By the way, if you tell doctors

about your new diet, they're going to warn you against it.

2. Decide what you enjoy doing and work that into your plan. The more you enjoy it, the easier it will be to stick to.

3. Find a partner or team to work out with. This will help keep you motivated and on track.

4. Don't spend a ton of money on *anything* when you start out. This means no new exercise equipment, new bike, or lap swimming pool in your backyard. Start doing something, and try different things. When you've found something you like, and if you decide that spending more money on it will make it more enjoyable, then spend the money.

5. Make sure you're doing resistance training.

6. Give yourself rest, one or two days a week.

7. Sleep. You need seven to nine hours of sleep every night, no exceptions. Just because you don't feel tired with only four hours doesn't mean it's not killing you internally.

8. Balance, flexibility, and coordination are just as important as other exercises and even more important as you age. Yoga and sports are great ways to accomplish these.

9. Start now. Anytime you say you're going to start something next week or next month, you're not dedicated to doing it. If you believe that changing the way you eat and exercising could save your life, you'll start *right now*. Put down the doughnut!

10. Variety is the spice of life. Keep your workouts interesting and use different muscles, try new things.

11. Reward yourself. No, not with a jelly doughnut!

My Firearms-Fitness Plan: _____

_____

_____

_____

_____

Notes: _____

_____

_____

_____

_____

_____

_____

_____

_____

_____

_____

_____

_____

_____

_____

_____

_____

_____

_____

SECTION II:
Mindset

One of the most neglected areas I see in any of the combat arts is mental conditioning. Normally when most people think about mental conditioning, they think of a good combat mindset. Having a solid combat mindset is vital and possibly the most important tool for you to have if you plan on defeating your enemies. But there are other mental conditioning skills you can use to increase your odds of hitting your threats under stress and living to tell the tale. Some people say shooting is 80 percent mental and 20 percent physical, but I believe it's 100 percent mental. Even your kinesthetic actions and responses need to be processed mentally. When you train in the manipulation of a firearm, you're really training your brain to give your body a set of neural impulses—without the brain there is no way to even pull a trigger.

When things go to shit, it always happens fast.

When I talk about combat mindset during a course, most people think of kill or be killed, which is important, but there is a lot more to it than that. A good combat mindset is the ultimate weapon, whereas your firearm is just your chosen delivery system. This chapter will help you win battles no matter which tool you employ and will even help during that 99.9 percent of your life you're not fighting for your life.

The truth is, we live in a dangerous world and denial is not a river in Egypt. Like being a faithful follower of the Twelve-Step program, the first step is admitting you have a problem. If you don't think your life is potentially in danger every time you walk out your door, turn on the news for a few minutes. Once you understand the threats that we face every day, it's important to move on to Step Two: Prepare your mind for battle.

I teach the four P's (priorities) of surviving a violent encounter. They are, in order of importance:

> **The 4-P's of surviving a violent encounter**
> - Preparation, mental and physical.
> - Proper use of tactics.
> - Proficiency of skills.
> - Proper selection of equipment.

As you can see, the very first priority is mental, and that's what this section is about. Everything else is completely useless without a strong mental foundation, and mental training is the only thing that will also allow you to simultaneously grow in every other area. When things go to shit, it always happens fast. Your ability to think clearly and quickly, and focus on the solution to the challenge that life has just handed you is what will allow you to survive violent encounters or win the competition.

As you're reading this, some of you may

find yourselves in unfamiliar territory. Some of the concepts and recommendations may be a little too "touchy-feely" for some of the meat eaters out there. Although I'll do my best to describe things in the most manly ways possible, and even start off with a chapter on warriors, I will also cover things like meditation and visualization. So I ask that you hang in there with me and keep an open mind. These techniques work not only for Navy SEALs but for anyone who's at the top of their game. I guarantee if you practice the techniques in this section, you'll be at the top of whatever game you play, too.

One final note I'd like to mention before we get started is regarding what I hear some people call a defensive mindset. Or when people say: "The best offense is a good defense." This is weak-minded crap and will at best lead you to a life of mediocrity, and at worst be the path to certain death if you ever face a true warrior. You need to erase these thoughts from your mind, as they are your mind preparing and planning to lose.

> Go to **http://chrissajnog.com** to get my Mental Marksmanship audio training course.

How am I going to work on each of the 4-P's? _____

_____

_____

_____

_____

_____

_____

_____

_____

Western Lone Wolf Jihadist and Freedom Fighters

SOLDIER OF FORTUNE

MAY 2015

THE JOURNAL OF PROFESSIONAL ADVENTURERS • SOFMAG.COM

WARRIOR CLASS:
NAVY SEALs

Deter, Detect, React

White Death Sniper

Evacuation

False Wall vs. Wall Safe

SHOT SHOW
Inland Manufacturing
Springfield Armory
Rock River Arms, Pro Ears
Black Rain Ordnance, RWC
American Watch, Sellmark

DID THE TROOPS
MISS OUT ON
GOOD GEAR

LONG RANGE FUN WITH RKB
AND THE REMINGTON .338 LAPUA

$5.99

0 71486 02061 5

05>

1

Live Like a Warrior

"The way of the warrior is a never-ending road of self-discovery and self-improvement."

Over the ages, every great society has celebrated and revered a great warrior tradition and passed on the stories of well-known heroes in folklore. We can look back to the Spartans, the Roman Legion, the Vikings, Medieval knights, the samurai, or the Aztecs cuāuhocēlōtl (eagle or jaguar warriors), and each time we will find that a strong warrior class coincided with a strong nation.

A warrior has a certain set of traits that can be used for good or evil, and it's up to each one to choose what path he will follow.

The warrior spirit is alive and well here in the greatest nation in the history of mankind.

Although it lives in the hearts and minds of those who serve in our military and law enforcement as well as other patriots, our society is beginning to shun warriors and move them down the social ladder. At the turn of the 20th Century, warfare began to move away from the martial art of combat and toward a more mechanical, detached system of destruction. This has changed society's view of what it means to be a warrior and paved the way for a society that now teaches our boys to be less masculine and more feminine. Now we're so far off track that it's even okay to choose what gender you'd like to be ("Sorry God, you made a mistake") but not okay to train like a warrior in an effort to defend your family.

Another reason for the cultural shift in thinking is that people have seen an increase in the warriors' dark side. Of course when most of us hear about the Dark Side, we think of Darth Vader in *Star Wars*, and this is a good thing. If you understood how the force worked in the movies, you understand how it works in today's warriors. A warrior has a certain set of traits that can be used for good or evil, and it's up to each one to choose what path he will follow. It's also up to our society to allow boys to be boys and men to be men, and express themselves in manly ways. Sometimes this involves fighting, which, if it's used for the right reason, is a good thing. Too many people think that in times of war we can turn on a magical switch to activate our warriors and protect our way of life, and when the war is over we turn off the switch and our warriors go back to eating tofu and pissing sitting down. I'm guessing that most people reading this would disagree, and understand that being a warrior is a full-time job—a way of life, and something that needs to be trained and tested so we can be ready for our enemies' surprise attacks.

Being a warrior is a full-time job—a way of life.

Going to war is not a prerequisite for the title of warrior. "Warrior" is simply a recognized role that has played a vital part in every great society in history and will continue to do so for time immemorial. The way of the warrior is a never-ending road of self-

discovery and self-improvement. Although it's difficult to travel, and the rewards are few, there is currently plenty of room, since half of our society is still confused about which

Being a warrior means being sure of oneself, having no uncertainty about one's own abilities or successfulness.

bathroom they're supposed to use. So stand up with me, and while we're pissing around the fire eating red meat, let's talk about the traits you'll need to join the warrior class. Warriors are:

Confident

For the people I train, I know this is one of the biggest indicators of success in any combat environment. I can see if they're confident before we even start training. It's why my Navy SEAL brothers and I can spot one another in public, even if we've never met. Being a warrior means being sure of oneself, having no uncertainty about one's own abilities or successfulness. Start with the end in mind—you will win. It's not a question.

Decisive

Displaying little or no hesitation in battle is vital to survival. Warriors are known for their decisive manner.

Assertive

Warriors are leaders. To be a good leader, you need to be confident and direct in claiming your rights or putting forward your views.

Strong

You don't need to bench 500 pounds to join the club, but you do need to make the most of the muscles you have. Even the most skillful swordsman needs the strength to pick up the sword. This applies to mental muscle as well. You need to have a determined will in all that you do. A strong mind can make up for a weak body, but not the other way around.

Skillful

Having the right mindset is vital, but you need a skill set to match that big brain of yours. The skills themselves can vary, but the more mad ninja skills you have, the more balanced you'll become.

Active

You need to be moving, doing, or functioning at all times. Ideas and theories are great, but action is what gets things done. Once you've got a plan, execute.

Aggressive

When most people think about being aggressive, they think about a pit bull with a bad owner. That aspect can and should be used in combat, but I'm talking about being assertive, bold, and energetic.

Disciplined

You've got a plan, you're confident you can do it, and now you need to have the discipline to stick to your plan. Getting up every morning at 0400 so you can hit the gym before work sucks! But being fat and out of shape sucks worse. Not hitting the snooze takes discipline. Warriors are disciplined.

A strong mind can make up for a weak body, but not the other way around.

Adaptable

Navy SEALs have a friend we call Max Flex. It means we need to be able to adjust quickly to different conditions. Being adaptable is what allows species to evolve and survive. The way warriors survive in combat is by adapting to the ever-changing battlefield.

Vigilant

You never know when the balloon will go up, so you have to be ready 24/7. You need to see everything that's happening around you and be prepared to react appropriately. Warriors are always prepared.

Patient

Having patience means bearing pains or trials calmly or without complaint. It means manning up. I'll always remember the whiners in Basic Underwater Demolition/ SEAL (BUD/S) training complaining about how cold or tired they were. Guess what? We were all cold and tired, and complaining didn't make them any warmer (although quitting did).

Clever

A warrior needs to be mentally quick and resourceful. When things go to shit, it always happens fast and you need the mental prowess to quickly invent a new way to do what you were just trying to do. Things rarely go exactly as planned, and you need to be smart enough to adapt.

Being brave means that you are afraid, but you do the offending task in spite of your fears.

Brave

One of the biggest lessons I've taught my kids is what it means to be brave. Like most people (and even some dictionaries) they thought being brave meant that you weren't afraid. This is actually the opposite

of what it means. Being brave means that you are afraid, but you do the offending task in spite of your fears. I'm not afraid to ride rollercoasters, so riding one does not make me brave. When my youngest son was afraid to ride a rollercoaster for the first time, he was afraid, but he was brave enough to go anyway.

Loyal

An arrow without a tip is just a stick. A warrior needs direction, and that comes from being faithful to a cause, ideal, or institution. This could be your family, your country, or a religion. Loyalty will keep you guided along your path; just make sure you keep it in balance with the other traits.

Loving

A warrior has confronted death and understands the value of life. Warriors whose lives are in balance are peaceful, unselfish, and have a compassionate concern for the good of others. The love of his family is what gives the warrior his internal energy to constantly train for battle and strength to survive once he's there.

I know this is a long list, and the kicker is that it's far from complete. My original goal was to come up with a nice-sounding number to write about — like "seven traits of a warrior." But as I started to compile the list, it grew far beyond seven and I simply stopped at a point where I thought would give you a good overview of the complexities inside every warrior. You'll become a true Renaissance man in your quest for warrior status, but just remember to stay away from the dark side.

Like yin and yang, hot and cold, or dark and light, all the above traits have two sides that can manifest. If your life is unbalanced, the dark side will be the stronger force and your actions will demonstrate this fact. There are several ways a warrior can become unbalanced, and it's important to quickly recognize this and take corrective actions.

Not being well-rounded is the quickest way to become unbalanced. We see this with Islamic and other extremists, who concentrate so much on loyalty to their religion that they completely neglect things like patience and love.

Suppression of a warrior's God-given drive will also slowly lead to an imbalance, and manifest itself in negative ways. Telling boys it's wrong to fight is like telling a bird it's wrong to fly. Holding someone back from what they are supposed to do will lead to unwanted consequences down the road.

Sometimes warriors are traumatized, which can effectively short-circuit their systems. It doesn't make them evil; they are the same people displaying the dark side of their traits. We see this with warriors coming home with post-traumatic stress disorder (PTSD) and need to recognize the problem and put them back on the right path.

Finally, being improperly or inadequately trained can lead to imbalances. This is happening all over the Middle East where jihadists are training their children to be warriors. They are loyal to religion, disciplined, confident—they have all the traits, but they are being trained that God wants them to kill infidels while killing themselves in the process. Bad training of good people.

Telling boys it's wrong to fight is like telling a bird it's wrong to fly.

As you train yourself to become a warrior, be on the lookout for these imbalances and correct them as soon as possible. Like a magnet, all warriors have two sides, and you cannot separate them. No matter how thinly you slice a magnet, it will always have a north and south pole. In the same way, no matter how much of the dark side you try to remove, you'll always be left with both sides.

Because of the new society we live in, many men are, let's face it, less manly than they should be. Professionals are telling us that it's okay for boys to play with either Barbie dolls or trucks and that pink is just a color, not an indication of gender. In fact, we're being told that we need to eliminate all gender indicators in a quest for equality. Obviously that whole thought process is out of balance, so here are a few things you can do to avoid that nonsense and join the warrior class.

Don't think for a second that I'm saying woman can't be warriors or that they are in any way not equal. My point is that we are different in the same way that four quarters and a dollar bill are different. By understanding and appreciating these differences, each can be used for their intended purpose. So let's get started...

How to Live Like a Warrior

• **Grow a set of NUTs** (nonnegotiable, unalterable terms) and live by them. These are anything you're not willing to compromise in life, period.

• **Start practicing some form of martial arts:** mixed martial arts (MMA), karate, boxing, jujitsu. Pick one you like, and go get punched in the face a few times. Find a school near you, or start off with a great instructional karate book or video.

• **Meditate**. This may be getting too close to the spiritual realm for some of you, but meditation is one of the most important things you can do for your mind and body. I'll be talking more about this later.

• **Find something you're afraid of and go do it**. If it's a rollercoaster, ride them until you stop crying like a five-year-old girl; if it's public speaking, join Toastmasters. Everyone has fears—warriors overcome them.

• **Work out**. It doesn't matter what you do, just work out hard. Breathe heavy, sweat. If you puke, that's a good indicator that you're getting closer to being a warrior!

• **Embrace competition**. Sign up for a race or fight, or just challenge someone to arm-wrestle. Prove that you're better than someone else at something or work until you are.

• Next time your husband or wife asks you where you want to go to dinner, give an answer and get in the car. **Be more decisive**. The more decisions you make, the easier they become.

• **Start establishing routines and habits in everything you do**. We are what we repeatedly do.

- **Write down your goals and core values**. Review them once a month. If you don't have a map for your life, how can you expect to get where you want to go?
- **Become a master at everything you do**. Everything in life is either worth doing well or it's not worth doing.

- **Stop any addictions**. If you smoke, do drugs, drink to excess, your life is not in balance. **Shoot guns.**

- **Watch warrior movies** to see how you're supposed to be acting. This is my list of inspiring warrior movies:

   The Eagle

   300

   Braveheart

   Red Cliff

   Thor

   Gladiator

   The Lord of the Rings trilogy

   Lone Survivor

   American Sniper

What areas in my life are out of balance? What am I committed to working on? _____

_____

_____

_____

_____

_____

_____

2

The SEAL Loop

"Your mind is always going through some sort of process. You use some method all the time to evaluate every situation, consciously or not."

The SEAL Loop is a concept that I developed to help train operators in how to break down complex situations on the battlefield into manageable pieces. I was inspired by the famous OODA Loop (Observe, Orient, Decide, and Act) originally developed by military strategist and U.S. Air Force Colonel John Boyd. Boyd used this decision cycle at the strategic level for combat operations, and it's still used today in commercial and learning processes.

Although I found the process helpful, I thought it was missing one critical part of the whole "loop" processes, and that was... the loop. You observe something, think about the best options, decide what to do, and then act. That's it—there is no loop in the OODA *Loop*, so it should not be called a loop or a cycle, it should be called a process. The other thing it was

missing was the use of the word SEAL— my favorite acronym!

> *The SEAL Loop is a concept that I developed to help train operators in how to break down complex situations on the battlefield into manageable pieces.*

So that's how I came up with the SEAL Loop (See, Evaluate, Act, Learn). You see, that "L" at the end is not just the critical component to a loop, but is precisely what will make you better every time you train or utilize your skills. I'll break down each of these simple steps, and by the end you'll be well on your way to thinking like a Navy SEAL, not only on the battlefield, but anytime you need to make a decision more complex than what to have for breakfast (although it can be used effectively there, too, if needed).

See

Although I use "see" here, it really means to use all your senses to detect what's going on around you. Let's say you're walking down the street alone at night. Your head is up and you're casually scanning around you and listening to what's going on around you. How tuned you are into your Spidey-sense depends on what your alert level is at that time. Marine Col. Jeff Cooper used four color-coded levels of awareness to denote people's level of awareness at any time. White is the first level, and this means you're oblivious to what's going on around you. Although I believe you should never leave your house in Condition White, this is the mind state of most people as they walk the streets. Head down, headphones in, sending a text, or playing the latest game on their iPhone. The next level is Condition Yellow, which is a state of relaxed alertness. You don't sense any immediate threats, you're in a safe neighborhood, but you're aware of everything around you and ready to react. Once something has caught your attention, you move to Condition Orange, which is where you're in a state of heightened alertness. You know something is or may be dangerous, and you are searching for more

information and preparing physically and mentally for an imminent attack. Finally you reach Condition Red. This is when you're immediately involved in a violent encounter. All of your mental and physical resources are used for dealing with this type of situation.

The closer you are to a situation you've dealt with before, the quicker your mind will be able to give you the correct guidance.

The higher you are on this scale, the less time you will be able to sustain it. That's why it's important to know the lowest level you can operate at safely and also be able to lower the level quickly when the threat subsides. The Marines also use Condition Black, which means that you've moved past Condition Red and have an overload of input, causing an overload of adrenaline. Condition Black is not a safe or sustainable level and should be avoided.

Evaluate

Now you're on your walk and you see someone in the shadows up ahead. Although this neighborhood is not known for gangs, he looks like a gang member and is watching you and reaching in his pocket. This is where you need to analyze everything involved in the situation: where you are, where he is, what weapons do you have on you, where are possible escape routes, who else is in the area, have you been in this situation before, and if so, what did you do and what was the outcome, and how are you feeling? The list goes on. In some situations you might only need to answer a few of these or other questions, while at other times the right answer might come only after playing a game of mental chess and playing out "if/then" scenarios for multiple courses of action. The key to moving through this phase quickly and accurately is scenario-based training. The closer you are to a situation you've dealt with before, the quicker your mind will be able to give you the correct guidance.

Act

This is where you actually do whatever action(s) your mind came up with in the evaluation phase. This phase is missed in people who get that stereotypical deer-in-the-headlights look. There is someone scary coming up, I've never practiced what to do, my mind is searching for a pattern to follow—a neural pathway that I've trained for before. But when it can't find anything close to try, the mind is caught in an endless loop. You, on the other hand, evaluated the situation and decided to cross the street. There were some open stores over there, and a street light. You move across the street and you see the unidentified person pull a cellphone from his pocket. You can also now see that he's not a gang banger, but just a

young boy who was obviously scared of seeing an unknown adult watching him as he was quickly approaching.

When it can't find anything close to try, the mind is caught in an endless loop.

Learn

As I stated earlier, this is the part that completes the loop. Also, it doesn't just need to be the final step—it can and should be the beginning. In our little scenario we just played out, you will likely have learned that at night people can be just as or more afraid than you are. You may have learned to walk on the other side of this street because that's where the lights are. You may have learned what a young boy looks like at night at that distance. The important part is that even though nothing happened, you can still learn just as much from what happened as if he did pull a knife or a gun. Replay the whole scene in your mind and see what you can learn from this. On the other side of the learning spectrum, you could take a course on personal defense and start off at the learning phase of the loop. Then, when you leave your home and walk down that street, you'll have the appropriate level of situational awareness. When you see something, you'll have more tools to use in your evaluation and you can act with an enhanced skill set; then the whole process starts all over again.

One thing to remember is that your mind is always going through some sort of process. Whether it's the SEAL Loop, the OODA Process, or the DITH (deer in the headlights), you use some method all the time to evaluate every situation, consciously or not. The key is to acknowledge this, and hone the skill.

What situations can you simulate so you can practice your reactions? _____

_____

_____

_____

_____

3

Mental Focus

"Meditation increases your ability to focus."

Now that I've got you warmed up to mental training, it's time to expand some of your comfort zones and talk about meditation. For some of you this may seem a little too touchy-feely for learning how to shoot, but my hope is that once you understand its power you will all become converts. I've been meditating now for a little over twenty years, and I'm still amazed by the benefits, not only in shooting but in the rest of my life. Mental and physical preparation are two sides of the same coin—one is useless without the other when it comes to weapons training.

Meditation is proven scientifically to increase your brain's neuroplasticity. This means your brain is growing and changing, something scientists had previously thought was not possible. But the University of Wisconsin studied experienced meditators and found they're able to not get stuck on a stimulus

Mental and physical preparation are two sides of the same coin— one is useless without the other when it comes to weapons training.

and have faster reactions. The study also showed that meditation increases your ability to focus, which is supported by a Wake Forest University School of Medicine study that showed it improves your cognitive processing. Daily meditation offers dozens of other health benefits, but these are some of the ones directly related to shooting and hopefully will help you understand its value.

To be a great shooter you must reach a state where you are not separate from the gun;

SEALSHOOTING

you're no longer just this person back there trying to control it. The gun, the target, your vision, and your whole body become one. To do this you need to clear your mind of all the clutter that it gets filled up with on a daily basis. All the best shooters in the world do this, even if they don't know it. What I mean is that meditation is about being in the zone, it's about clearing your mind and thinking about . . . nothing. It happens to artists in all areas, from music to karate. You do a certain task so much and so often that you're no longer even thinking; you're in the zone. Meditation takes you directly to that zone without the years of practice, and its benefits translate to all areas of your life.

So what is meditation? Meditation is simply clearing the mind of distractions so you can focus. It's actually very simple, but it's not easy at first. This simplicity is what stops a lot of people from continuing to practice. Today, we've got so many things filling up our minds with useless junk twenty-four hours a day that it's hard to get off that fast-moving train. As schoolchildren, we learned that we needed to fill our minds continually, and the fuller the better. Now, I'm not saying that you shouldn't continue to learn, but I am saying that for you to fill up that big brain of yours, there needs to be some space for it to go.

How to Meditate

1.   Find a place where you won't be disturbed during your meditation. Turn off the ringer on your phone and anything else that might interrupt you.

2.   Sit in a comfortable chair, with your back supported, but not your head.

3.   Fold your hands and place them on your lap.

4.   Close your eyes.

5.   Take five deep breaths in through your nose, expanding your belly each time.

6.   Relax all the muscles in your body.

7.   In your head say, "I am"; this is a mantra, and is used to help you clear your mind.

8.   As thoughts come into your head, acknowledge them and go back to your mantra.

9.   Continue this for up to twenty minutes.

10. Before opening your eyes, rest quietly for one to two minutes.

That's actually more information than you really need to get started. All you're trying to do is set the stage so you can clear your mind of all thought. At first you'll think it's impossible, then you will have very short moments when you realize you weren't thinking of anything, but then you realize, that's a thought! Just like everyone has a wobble shooting a pistol, everyone has thoughts coming into their minds. The key to mastering either one is minimizing and accepting. Don't get upset with your thoughts, just let them go away.

Meditation Tips

- Start off with five minutes and work your way up to fifteen to twenty minutes, which studies have found is the optimal length of time to meditate.

- It's better to do five to ten minutes every day than longer times inconsistently.

- Meditate before you eat, or wait two hours after you eat.

- Don't meditate within ninety minutes of bedtime.

- Don't worry about saying your mantra perfectly: "I am." As you repeat it and relax, it will start to slur and have more of a humming sound.

- Try focusing on your breath if your mind wanders.

- Try to meditate twice a day: once before breakfast, and once before your evening meal.

- Try not to skip meditation completely. Do five minutes if you're too busy to do the full time.

- Keep all your muscles relaxed. I've found that your shoulders and jaw tend to tighten up without noticing.

I listen to a brain waves app during my meditation, which helps me clear my mind and drown out any distracting noises. If you find that sounds around you are disturbing you when you meditate, you should try this app or listen to some white noise. I also use this app as a timer; I play it for twenty minutes, then relax for a few minutes before opening my eyes.

If you're interrupted during your meditation, just continue where you left off; do not start over. Give meditation a chance to work. Set a goal of twenty-one to thirty days of daily meditation, and I guarantee you will be a convert.

It may take a week before you notice anything, but the goal is the silence itself. Don't try to "feel it working" because that will only push you away. After a while you will begin to experience visions, feel like you're floating, or maybe you'll see colors. These are normal byproducts of good meditation and should be enjoyed, but do not seek them out in your meditation. They are not the goal—the goal is clearing the mind and saying your mantra. If you seek these feeling or visions, you will be defeating your own practice.

Giving your mind some time to rest will provide you with amazing lifelong benefits and allow you to think faster, clearer, and calmer during any dynamic shooting that you will ever do.

So what should you expect from practicing daily meditation? It's hard to say what your experience will be because everyone is different. For me it took one week of practicing meditation twice a day for twenty minutes before I noticed any changes. It was around the same time I started noticing I was not thinking for a decent amount of time that I felt less stress during the day. I also started to see colors and brief images of random things: a mountain, a forest, the beach. At the time I didn't know you weren't supposed to seek these things, so I started meditating seeking them, and they quickly stopped. After a few days of going back to a goal of clearing my mind and saying my mantra, the colors and images came back. I also notice sometimes that I find myself smiling during meditation without any conscious thought, which I find interesting. Finally, sometimes I feel like I'm floating, and it feels so good, it's hard to not think about enjoying it!

The thing to remember is that these side effects of meditation are not your goal. Giving your mind some time to rest will provide you with amazing lifelong benefits and allow you to think faster, clearer, and calmer during any dynamic shooting that you will ever do.

Where and when will you practice focusing your mind? _____

_____

_____

_____

_____

_____

_____

_____

_____

_____

_____

_____

_____

_____

_____

_____

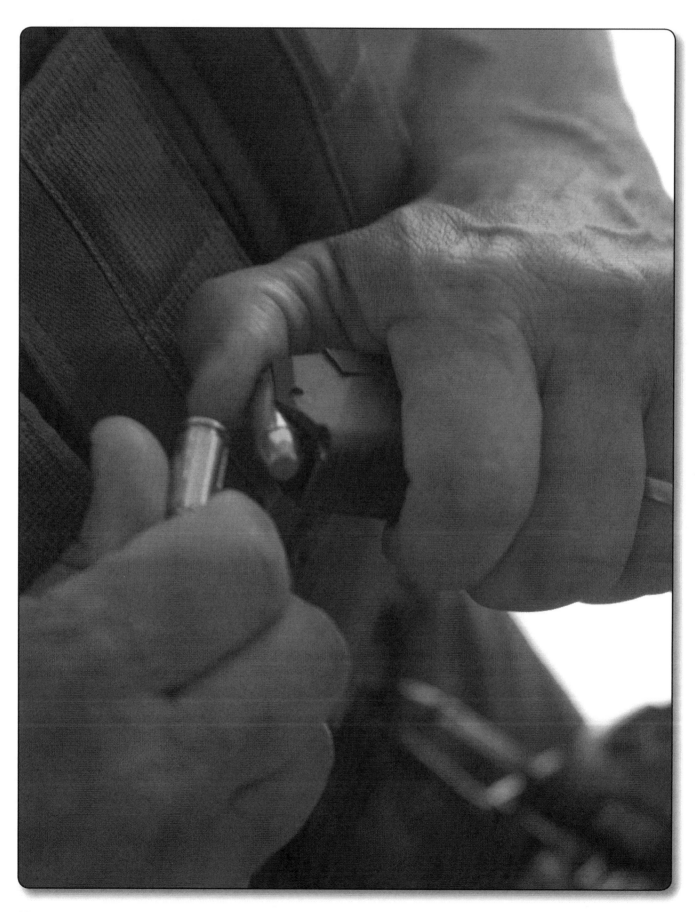

4

Mental Repetitions

"Visualize yourself performing at your absolute best."

The use of mental imagery, visualization, or doing mental repetitions in sports has been around for many years and has a proven track record of success. Visualization primes neural pathways in the same way that physical training does, and your neurons can't tell the difference. You have specialized neurons in your brain made just for this purpose, called *mirror neurons*. These nerves fire the same way when you do something, see something, or even see someone else do the same thing. Top athletes and Special Forces soldiers often credit their success to the use of these tools on a daily basis, and scientific studies back up their claims. So if it works in basketball and golf, will it work in shooting? What about combat?

A recent study by researchers in the Netherlands has shown that simple mental imagery can help law enforcement officers keep their shooting skills from deteriorating in high-threat encounters. They conducted before-and-after firearms performance tests on sixty-six police officers, and the results were quite dramatic. After everyone shot a basic course to get their baseline, they were split into groups where some listened to an audio tape guiding them through mental imagery of a gunfight in which they performed flawlessly, and others listened to meaningless audio.

Simple mental imagery can help law enforcement officers keep their shooting skills from deteriorating in high-threat encounters.

After the audio session, both groups were then presented with a more dynamic scenario where the threat was now shooting back at them with Simunitions (small marking rounds). The group that listened to the guided imagery with a positive outcome consistently outperformed the group that had listened to the unrelated audio.

I became a believer very quickly when I witnessed the power the mind has when you know how to unlock it.

For some of you, this may be a bit too mystical or new-agey at first. It can be hard to go from meat-eating mouth breather to vegetarian belly breather, but you don't need give up your red meat to become more enlightened. In fact, when you do your visualization, you can be as ruthless and barbaric as you want, and if you do it right, you'll be even manlier when you open your eyes! For others, this will just be a simple understanding of the power of your mind and a few tricks on how to focus that power.

I have been practicing martial arts since I was twelve and started using visualization regularly as part of my practice about twenty years ago. I became a believer very quickly when I witnessed the power the mind has when you know how to unlock it. I

would visualize beating my opponent before sparring, and then see every move he threw at me come in slow motion, and his defeat was a foregone conclusion. I continue to use visualization for shooting and other aspects of my life and believe that it contributes to much of my success. Studies have shown that visualization can be even more effective than actually physically practicing the same thing because you can do it perfectly and your neural pathways don't know if you've physically done the movements or if you were just visualizing them. Plus, you can literally train anywhere and ammo is unlimited. What could be better?

If you want to take your shooting to the next level and increase your chances of surviving a violent encounter, just follow these simple guidelines:

How to Visualize

1. Set time aside each day. This is separate from your meditation, but it's great to do it right before or right after your meditation.

2. You can also do it right before an event if you have time.

3. Close your eyes and relax your body.

4. Breathe deeply and relax your mind.

5. Visualize yourself performing at your absolute best.

6. Anchor the act with emotion.

7. End with a positive feeling. That's it!

What you see when you visualize is up to you. You can see things through your own eyes, or like you're watching yourself on TV. Try each one out and see which comes more easily to you. If you've never tried this before, it may take a week or more before you can even start to "see" things with your mind, and the way you see things will likely be different than you do with your eyes open. This is fine and perfectly normal. Just keep trying, and the details will come into focus.

Using all your senses while visualizing is also very important. In the same way that you are seeing things with your eyes closed, you need to learn effectively to feel, smell, and hear things. The more senses you can get into play, the more real this will be in your mind and the more benefit you will get from it. In fact, the most important feeling you need to get is emotional. If you can make an emotional connection with your imagery, the benefit that you get will be the same as if you've physically done whatever you imagined. So if you're visualizing hitting all your targets center mass in the fastest time during a competition, feel that same excitement you would feel knowing that you won the title!

Sometimes your visualization will get away from you and you'll find that the shot missed or that you dropped your gun. Again, this is normal, and this is why you're training. Rewind that video in your mind and keep playing it through until you do it the way you want. If you just let it go, that's teaching

your mind the wrong thing, and you'll be working against yourself. Once you've played it through the right way, make sure you reinforce it with some emotion: Bam!

You can also control the speed, color, and size of your images. Maybe slow down that new technique you're learning so that you can see all the details or make the size of your target huge so you get the feeling that it's easy to hit. Work with all the different options and make the images exciting, to get the emotion that should come with it. Play the images backward or forward at different speeds to see what makes them stick.

It is possible for you to shoot perfectly, and the more clearly you see yourself doing that, the more likely it will happen.

The mind is powerful, but if you push the limits beyond what is possible within the confines of your universe, it's not going to work. If for instance you want to run faster, and you chose to imagine yourself flying, literally flying, your subconscious mind, knowing this is not physically possible, will short-circuit any positive results and you'll just end up spinning your wheels. But that doesn't mean you should limit yourself, either. Say you want to improve your score on a shooting course of fire—you should

NAVY SEAL SHOOTING

CHRIS SAJNOG

picture every round hitting the center of the target. Why? Because it is possible for that to happen. You'll never fly, but it is possible for you to shoot perfectly, and the more clearly you see yourself doing that, the more likely it will happen the next time you're at the range.

Now that you know you don't even need a gun to practice shooting, there are no more excuses! You don't need to find time to go to the range or buy ammo, pick up brass, or clean the gun when you're done. And if you do it right, the benefits you get from ten minutes of visualization could be more than you get from actually going to the range.

Remember, just as with any training you do: Consistent training equals consistent results. Better to do ten minutes every day than seventy minutes once a week. Train hard, and keep eating red meat!

Describe in detail the outcomes you plan to visualize:_____

_____

_____

_____

_____

_____

_____

_____

_____

_____

_____

_____

96

NavySEALshooting.com

Where and when can you practice mental repetitions? _____

_____

_____

_____

_____

_____

_____

_____

_____

_____

_____

_____

_____

_____

_____

_____

_____

5

Confidence and Positive Thought

"Positive thinking is something you do,
while confidence is something you have."

Even I have to admit that confidence sounds cool, but positive thinking sounds like some new-age BS that if we just put on rose-colored glasses, we'll all be seeing roses around nice, tight groups on every target. Well, that isn't the type of positive thinking I want to talk about. What I really want to talk about is the power that your mind, your thoughts, and even your words have, in increasing your confidence and making you a better shooter. And although confidence and positive thinking are very similar, they are not the same thing. Positive thinking is something you do, while confidence is something you have (and can get from having positive thoughts).

So how important are your thoughts to shooting? In its most basic sense, you cannot shoot a gun without thinking of it first. If there is a gun on a table in front of

you, there is no way you're going to shoot that gun or even touch that gun without thinking about it first. So it's clear that our thoughts lead to actions. And if we know that our thoughts lead to actions, wouldn't it make sense that positive thoughts lead to positive results, and negative thoughts lead to negative results?

If you want to shoot better, the first step is being confident in your shooting and thinking positive.

For those who still might not be picking up what I'm putting down, let me ask you this: Do you know anyone who just seems to either have good luck or bad luck with something? For instance, maybe someone who seems to win every drawing they ever enter, or maybe someone who seems to have the worst luck and always gets speeding tickets? If you've said yes, you need to believe one of two things: either there is really a natural "luck" force in nature causing these things, or your thoughts lead to these outcomes, lucky or unlucky. Although they both may seem hard to believe at first, the second option—that the things you think about tend to happen more often—can at least be explained in the realities of the world we live in. In those cases where someone is either lucky or unlucky, they think, and probably say, those things. This is what attracts either good or bad things to them, their thoughts. And if you want to shoot better, the first step is being confident in your shooting and thinking positive.

---

*As a BUD/S instructor, I learned that there are two kinds of students, those who **thought** they would make it through, and those who **knew** they would make it through.*

Not only should our thoughts be positive, but our words should be positive too because the words we hear instantly create mental images, and this can't be avoided.

To prove this, I'm going to ask you to not think about something and then I want you to see if you can do it. Ready? OK . . . don't think about a white bear. You thought about a white bear; you had to. Even if it's something that you're telling yourself not to do, you still have to picture it in your mind as you're telling yourself not to picture it. So even if you're thinking, "Don't miss!" when you're shooting, your mind is going to picture "*miss!*" You have to think and speak positively about your shooting before it will turn around. If you do find yourself thinking a negative thought (and we all do, sometimes), interrupt the thought process any way you can. If you had miss in your mind, say to yourself: "I sure do miss my kids, so I'm going to hit this target dead center, so I can go home and see them!" Does it make sense? No. But it works.

Although we may not talk about it, the reason some people make it through BUD/S and others don't is positive thinking. As a BUD/S instructor, I learned that there are two kinds of students, those who *thought* they would make it through, and those who *knew* they would make it through. Although both think they have the right mindset, only those who were positive they would make it through did so. If you want to be a good shooter, you need to be positive about your shooting. I can't stand it when I hear people on the range shoot, have a bad shot, and then lament over it for the rest of the day. Guess what happens to their shooting? Right down the toilet. If you have a bad shot, or even a bad day (and we all do, sometimes), you just need to let it go and move on.

Both positive and negative thoughts are contagious, and whichever you are using off the range will affect the way you shoot on the range.

One thing you've got to do is think positively in all areas of your life, not just in shooting. Both positive and negative thoughts are contagious, and whichever you are using off the range will affect the way you shoot on the range. It's just not possible to think negatively about everything else in your life, then come to the range and think positive. Your subconscious will call your bluff and give you back what you're putting out. It's a fact that energy cannot be created or destroyed, and this is true for positive and negative energy. Make sure you're putting out positive energy, and it will come back to you on the firing line.

To have positive thoughts, you'll also need to have positive beliefs. What do I mean by this? Well, what if you believed that the gun you were shooting was not very accurate, or you believed that it's impossible to shoot accurately on a windy day? Any of these beliefs is not going to allow you think positively about your shooting. You have to believe in yourself, in your team, your equipment, and the weather. If you don't, you'll sabotage your results and not even know it.

An important point to realize is that as powerful as the mind is, don't expect instant changes to happen, and don't expect them to work by themselves. You can't think positively about your shooting, but never train, because you're still going to suck. Positive thinking is like a light switch: It doesn't hold any power, but it allows it to be released. You'll still need to train to get better, and that takes time, but soon you will see it being released, and your shooting will improve. The next thing you need to do is acknowledge that it's working and let success breed success. As you start shooting better, you will think even more positively, and shoot even better. By allowing this to happen, you will be amazed at how quickly you can reach your full potential.

Positive thinking is like a light switch: It doesn't hold any power, but it allows it to be released.

As Dr. Seuss said, "Bang-ups and hang-ups can happen to you." And they will; expect them, and find a way to turn them into positive thoughts. Did you slap the trigger and let a round fly far off target? Think: That's great! I just learned another way not to pull the trigger so I will shoot even better next time. Or, "Man, I'm glad that happened on the range and not on a crowded street!" Just think about any successful entrepreneur and the way they think. Do they lose money and feel bad about it and decide to stop trying? Hell no, they get excited and consider the lesson a gift. They stay positive!

If you look weak, people will treat you that way.

Once you begin to understand the power of positive thought and you see your shooting improve, it will lead to greater confidence. One thing Navy SEALs are known for is our confidence—even if we're not considered positive thinkers. Some people have even said "overconfident" or "arrogant," but if you can back it up, then I say it's just right!

Just like any other thing you're training, you need to feel it's important in order to commit to doing it and working at it daily. Oftentimes we think about how "lucky" successful people are, how positive things just naturally happen to them. While it is true that things that happen to successful people happen naturally, it is all accomplished through consistent, positive work. If they didn't think the way they thought, they

wouldn't do or have the things they do. It's important to note, too, that most confident people are not born that way. They train and learn and grow into great speakers, leaders, and shooters. If they can learn this skill, so can you.

One last thing to help improve your confidence, and thus your shooting, is your posture, the way your hold yourself and the image you present to others. It's said that emotion comes from motion—the way you move your body—so move in a way that exudes confidence. Pick your head up, put your shoulders back, and look like a warrior. People will treat you differently, and in turn your confidence will grow. Law enforcement officers are taught this in their academies, and it's played out on the streets—if you look weak, people will treat you that way; if you look like you shouldn't be messed with, then they won't. Next time you go to the range, make sure you look confident, and if you're not yet, fake it till you make it.

What limiting thoughts or words do I use and what are positive thoughts or words I can replace them with? _____

_____

_____

_____

_____

_____

_____

_____

_____

_____

_____

_____

_____

_____

Navy SEALs are just
regular people who have
mastered the art
of teamwork.

6

The Teams

"The way a team gets better is by each individual getting better. You're only as strong as your weakest link."

Unless you're a hermit and you're reading this book to keep other life forms off your property, your shooting can benefit from understanding teamwork and what it means to be part of a team. I learned the importance of teamwork twenty years ago when I went through Basic Underwater Demolition/SEAL (BUD/S) training in Coronado, California. In that harsh environment with everything and everyone working against you, you quickly realize you can't make it alone and need to rely on your team (in this case, my classmates) for support. This carried on into my time in SEAL Team Two and throughout my twenty years in the Navy.

As much as I'd like to bask in the glory of being a superhero, with amazing strength or supernatural abilities, Navy SEALs are just regular people who have mastered the art of teamwork. Yes, we are good at a lot of things,

and in fact I often say we are perpetual students of everything. This means that we are constantly learning and perfecting the skills we need to succeed, and we never reach a point where we're satisfied with where we're at in our education. By being part of this awesome group for long enough, you do develop an awesome skill set, and this can often help you outperform others in solo endeavors, but our greatest advancements in learning and dominating our enemies will always stay with "the teams."

I've had the honor to help guide boys into becoming young men as a leader in the Boy Scouts of America, where I've been able to share my experiences and help teach teamwork to these tadpoles. I've also had the opportunity to share the importance of teamwork with youth sports teams on the West Coast. When I first started giving these talks, I thought it was important to package it in a way that the boys would remember, so they could remember and use it. So of course I came up with an acronym. Since I've used SEAL probably one too many times, I decided to go with the next best, or possibly even better: TEAMS, to help them learn and remember the keys to teamwork and to being an effective teammate. Here's what I mean by TEAMS:

Take Responsibility

Don't blame the wind. Don't blame your gun or ammo. Don't blame the guy who shot next to you just as you were about to squeeze the trigger. Anytime you blame anything outside yourself, it gives the power of change to something outside yourself, and it will never make you better. Only you can do that. Let's say someone is punching you in the face. If you decide to blame it on them and use that as your excuse, nothing will change the situation until he gets tired. But once you accept responsibility—"I'm in the way of where this person would like to swing their arm"—you will take action (move/block), and change the situation. What is an excuse? It's something that is often very real. You're not wrong when you use an excuse, it's just that it's what makes the difference between winners and losers.

In BUD/S, most people quit because it's cold—and that's true, it's very cold, and everyone is cold. But some people choose to use that as an excuse to quit—and there's nothing wrong with that—you just won't become a SEAL. Those of us who made it through just didn't use that excuse, even though we were just as cold. So what are you using as an excuse? No time to train? Range too far away? Stupid California gun laws? Those are all excuses you're choosing to use, and that you don't need to. There are plenty of people with busier lives than yours who still get up an hour earlier to train. There are great shooters out there who use dry-fire and mental training as the core of their training plan. There are forty-nine more states for you to move to. The point is that you will find a way to do what you need to do. So how badly do you want to shoot better? Take responsibility and get it done.

Anytime you blame anything outside yourself, it gives the power of change to something outside yourself, and it will never make you better.

Encourage Others

You may not think that Navy SEALs need a pat on the back, but everyone gets down on themselves at times, and a little encouragement can go a long way, especially if it's from someone you care about, like someone on your team. Don't have a team?

6 • THE TEAMS

Start one. Find a shooting buddy, even if it's online, make sure you're training and sharing tips. If you have family, they're part of your team too.

If you go back to chapter 5, you'll see how important this one thing can be, and how the words we use affect how we act. The same is true when we talk about others in a positive way; it's like giving your teammate a shot of confidence when you encourage them. The better your teammates feel about themselves, the better they will perform, which might just one day save your life.

Teamwork calls for everyone to pick up those not having a good day. Go the extra distance, provide positive feedback, keep their energy level up. It is possible to turn that bad day around; it's all in the approach.

Ask for Help or Help Others

You may not think so, but SEALS are not afraid to ask for help. The goal is the performance of the team, so why wouldn't you ask for help? Don't be afraid, or think you're not as good as someone else if you ask them for help. I tell the Scouts it would be like if your arms are too short to reach something, and them feeling dumb asking your legs for a little help getting higher. Your team needs to be like your body—working together for the greater good. And if you find a cancer not playing well with others, cut it out before it destroys everything!

If you find a cancer not playing well with others, cut it out before it destroys everything!

The other thing you need to do is offer to help others, especially if they're not asking for help. In a team environment, these are the people you're going to depend on, and the level of their training may very well save your life. Yes, you'll have to use some tact and not act like a know-it-all, but if you're more experienced in one area, make sure that you pass on as much of that information as possible to the rest of your team. We did this all the times in the SEALs. Even in my first platoon, I was a new corpsman, but I still taught the whole platoon medicine, so they could save my ass if I ever got shot. Of course they schooled me on everything else and weren't as respectful as me, but they made sure I was getting the information. (Yes, you can learn comms while duct-taped to a chair.)

Master Your Job

In every team, everyone has different jobs. The way a team gets better is by each individual getting better. You're only as strong as your weakest link, and you never want to be that link. In the SEAL teams, everyone had to be a great combat shooter, but not everyone was a sniper, medic, or breacher. Those are a few of the specialties I had, so I made sure I was better at those jobs than anyone else. I'm not saying that I ever became the best at anything, but I can tell you that I worked hard to get there every day.

When you see the rest of the team working that hard on their specialties for you, you better work at least that hard on your specialties for them.

The great part about being on a good team is knowing that everyone else is doing the same thing in their jobs. I remember our communicators would be up all night setting up antennas so they could make a "COMMSHOT" halfway around the globe. Not for an operation, and not because they were told to do it. They did it just so they could be the best communicators. They did it so that if they needed to do that in the "real world," they could. They did it for the team. When you see the rest of the team working that hard on their specialties for you, you better work at least that hard on your specialties for them.

Selflessness

I'm sure most of you have seen the movie *Act of Valor* that depicts several real-life selfless acts by some American heroes whom I have the honor to call teammates. Giving your life for your country or your team is of course the ultimate selfless act, but there are many smaller acts that can help the team.

Giving up the time you have to train so you can watch your teammate train and critique him is selfless. Giving up some ammo to your teammate because he needs it more than you is selfless. Getting up early to drive your teammate to the airport is selfless. Anytime you deny yourself something for the betterment of the team, you are being selfless and being a good teammate.

> Go to **http://chrissajnog.com** if you or your organization would be interested in me speaking about teamwork at your next event.

Who is your team and what are you doing to be a good teammate? _____

_____

_____

_____

_____

_____

_____

_____

_____

_____

_____

_____

_____

_____

_____

_____

_____

Notes: _____

_____

_____

_____

_____

_____

_____

_____

_____

_____

_____

_____

_____

_____

_____

_____

_____

_____

SECTION III:

Marksmanship

So far in this book I've covered the bedrock of learning how to fire any weapon system under stress. The fact is, *how* you train is far more important than *what* you train. But if your techniques are not solid, you'll get frustrated with training and give up. So now that you know how to train, let's teach you some proven techniques to practice.

Whether it's in combat, competition, or clearing your home in the middle of the night, the needed skills are the same. You'll learn shooting the way I learned as a Navy SEAL and the way I taught it as the SEAL Teams leading firearms instructor. I'm going to teach you the SEAL fundamentals of marksmanship, lessons learned the hard way on the battlefield that form the foundation for the advanced techniques in the Mastery section.

What's the difference between marksmanship and SEAL marksmanship? Well, quite a bit actually. Although they both require the same components (stance, grip, trigger control, and so on), the best way to accomplish them varies depending whether you're fighting for your life or just for the best score on a course of fire. Learning to shoot under stress requires a mental switch from shooting paper targets on a static range to mitigating the physical and psychological stressors you'll need to deal with to prevail. Many of the traditional marksmanship lessons we were all taught are ineffective when your body gets a rush of adrenaline and your mind is screaming

to fight or flee. They were taught to us by competition shooters with competition guns. They were techniques that work with a heavy gun and a light trigger at a shooting range...not what works when you need to protect yourself, your team or your family.

Don't get me wrong, I think shooting competitions are great and I don't pretend to have the amazing skills the masters of the sport have. But combat is not a sport, and the pressure you feel is a bit more than you get from a Shot Timer. I teach seven Navy SEAL marksmanship fundamentals. Some may like to use three, five, or eight fundamentals. If it's easier for you to take a few of them and combine them in your mind, do so. Just be warned: Leave one out when you're shooting, and the round will miss its mark.

The SEAL Seven

1. Shooting platform

2. Grip

3. Sight picture

4. Sight refinement

5. Focused breathing

6. Trigger control

7. Follow-through

In each chapter, I break down one of these fundamentals so they are not just terms you need to remember. You'll understand what they all mean, how to use them when you're shooting or dry-fire training, and you'll know why they're important in making you a more effective shooter.

> Go to **http://chrissajnog.com** to learn about The New Rules of Marksmanship

What type of shooting do you want to learn? What environments do you need to be effective in?

_____

_____

_____

_____

_____

_____

_____

_____

_____

_____

_____

_____

Even if you have checked before, I'll give you some precision tests that are critical to shooting accurately, but unknown even to some of the best shooters in the world.

1

Finding Your Dominant Eye

"It's the eye your brain says wins the coin toss in the minor differences between the two pictures each eye sends to your brain."

Before we get into shooting, we need to find out which of your eyes is your dominant eye. It's surprising how many people shoot for years without ever knowing which eye is dominant or understanding that this can vary under different conditions. Approximately two-thirds of the population is right-eye-dominant and one-third is left-eye-dominant, but a very small percentage of people have no dominant eye. Sometimes people assume that since they are right-handed they are right-eye-dominant. This is true about 90 percent of the time, but not always. Others learn to shoot from someone who is either right- or left-eye-dominant and just follow what they see. It's important to note that your dominant eye is not the eye with better vision: It's the eye your brain says wins the coin toss in the minor differences between the two pictures each eye sends to your brain.

In shooting it's important to know which eye is dominant because your sights need to move toward the exact spot where your eye intersects the object you're trying to shoot.

The two images your eyes send to your brain come from about 2½ inches apart. These images are close, but not the same. This is called "parallax." So that your brain can provide depth perception, pinpoint exact locations, and track moving objects, it has learned to give a higher priority to one eye or the other—this becomes your dominant eye. In shooting it's important to know which eye is dominant because your sights need to move toward the exact spot where your eye intersects the object you're trying to shoot; this is called "line of sight." If you are shifting the weapon as you're bringing it up to your eyes, it will take longer to acquire a good sight picture and ultimately make an effective shot.

If you've never checked if you are right- or left-eye-dominant, now is the time. If you're new to shooting, this is where you need to start. Even if you have checked before, I'll give you some precision tests that are critical to shooting accurately, but unknown even to some of the best shooters in the world. First the basic tests:

The Miles Test (Static)

1. Fully extend your arms in front of you.

2. Pick out a small object in front of you.

3. Make a triangle with your hands, with the object in the center of the triangle.

4. Keeping your hands in place, alternately close each eye.

5. The eye you can still see the object with (when the other is shut) is your dominant eye.

The Miles Test (Moving)

1. Fully extend your arms in front of you.

2. Pick out a small object in front of you.

3. Make a triangle with your hands, with the object in the center of the triangle.

4. Keeping both eyes open, move your hands toward your eyes.

5. The eye you bring your hands to so you can still see the object is your dominant eye.

3.1.1 – Make a triangle with your hands, with the object in the center of the triangle.

3.1.2 – Fully extend your arms in front of you.

3.1.3 – Keeping both eyes open, move your hands toward your eyes.

3.1.4 – Fully extend your arm in front of you and point directly at the object.

3.1.5 – Keeping your finger in place, alternate close each eye.

3.1.6 – Keeping both eyes open, move your finger toward your eyes, while still pointing at the object.

The Porta Test (Static)

1. Pick out a small object in front of you.

2. Fully extend your arm in front of you and point directly at the object.

3. Keeping your finger in place, alternately close each eye.

4. The eye you are still pointing at the object with (when the other is shut) is your dominant eye.

The Porta Test (Moving)

1. Pick out a small object in front of you.

2. Fully extend your arm in front of you and point directly at the object.

3. Keeping both eyes open, move your finger toward your eyes, while still pointing at the object.

4. The eye you bring your finger to is your dominant eye.

Precision Dominance Testing

After completing these tests, you should have a good idea which eye is dominant. For many people, these basic tests are enough, but for some they are not because your dominant eye can actually change in certain conditions. If you've noticed that you have a harder time focusing on your sights or your accuracy decreases for unexplained reasons, it's very likely that your dominant eye either switches or moves toward the other eye depending on different factors.

How is this possible? Your brain is constantly interpreting the two images it's receiving from each eye to determine distance, position, speed, and so on. If you have something in your hand, your hand is also now sending a signal to your brain saying, "Put this into your formula too." If the lighting changes, your eyes send still more signals to your brain that something has changed and to adjust the formula of determining precisely where that object is in space. Everyone's brain sends this additional information, but our brains process the information differently. If you've never done these additional tests, make sure you do them now to avoid a lot of headaches later.

The precision dominance tests are simple, but critical to ensuring that you can learn or advance your shooting skills as quickly as possible.

Hands-down Test

With your hands at your sides, line up the tip of a thin object (it's usually easiest to have someone hold a pen or pencil) at arm's length with an object at least ten feet away. With both eyes open, line up the two objects and then alternate closing each eye. The eye that is still pointing at the object is your

dominant eye with your hands down. This can be important because this is where your hands will likely be when you first perceive a threat or when a shot timer beeps. Being able to accurately assess where that item is could give you a critical split-second time advantage over your opponent.

One-handed Pistol Test

With one hand at your side and both eyes open, bring your pistol up and line up your sights with a target in the background. Now alternate closing each eye, and see which one is lined up with the object. The eye that's open when your gun is still pointed at the object is your dominant eye. This test can be important because your hands send different signals depending on their positions. Make sure to test with each hand.

Two-handed Pistol Test

Run the same test as when one-handed, but now with both hands on the gun. This is the most likely time to find a shift in the dominant

3.1.7 – One-handed pistol test

3.1.8 – Two-handed pistol test

eye and can cause shooters to struggle. They've done the basic tests and are sure about their dominant eye, but never tested it with both hands sending different signals to the brain. If you notice a shift that you never knew before, your shooting will improve dramatically with this newfound knowledge.

Rifle Test

Perform this just like the tests above, except with a rifle. Because you now have one hand farther out in front, your hands are sending signals from two different locations, which can affect which eye is dominant. This is also fairly common and can explain why some people have a hard time with accuracy or front sight focus when shooting pistol or rifle.

Low-light Test

Before you do any low-light training, take a second to check your eye dominance in low-light conditions. Usually you only need one of the basic tests, but if taking fast, accurate

3.1.9 – Rifle test

shots in low light is important to you, take the time to do all the precision tests, too.

Distance Test

Probably the number two most common shift in eye dominance is distance. This one is easy to do and common enough that everyone must check it. Perform all the tests at ten-yard increments out to the farthest range you will ever shoot. Start with one of the basic tests, and if you notice a shift, make sure you try it with the other tests at that distance.

Stress Test

The final test I recommend is checking your eye dominance while under stress. Do a couple sprints, get your heart rate up, and then do one of the tests.

Possible Outcomes

Normal-eye-dominant: You're right handed and right-eye-dominant, or you're left-handed and left-eye-dominant. You're on easy street!

Cross-eye-dominant: You're right-handed and left-eye-dominant, or you're left-handed and right-eye-dominant. The important thing is that you know . . . you're a mutant! Seriously, with a pistol you may need to simply shift your pistol over to line up with your dominant eye, or you can slightly turn (do not tilt) your head left or right to line up with the sights, depending on which eye is dominant. With a rifle you have a few hard choices. If you're just starting out, learn to shoot off your dominant-eye side. This is easiest if you haven't ingrained a lot of skills. If you have or even if you're older and set in your ways, you can train your other eye to work as your dominant eye, or just close your dominant eye and use the other. Every study on cross-dominant shooters has shown that they have a harder time shooting than normal-dominant shooters. If you have the time and opportunity to fix this, it might be worth it.

Both-eyes-dominant: Don't look up that term because I just made it up. It's not very common, but some people are both-eyes-dominant, or neither eye is dominant. You have a few choices. Some people will be dominant with different eyes at different distances. If this is you, then just be aware and use the correct eye. Some people will have a hard time focusing with either eye and may benefit from covering one of their shooting lenses with clear tape to blur one of their eyes. Finally, if this is a real problem, you can "treat" this and train one of your eyes to become dominant. You'll need to see an optometrist to learn how to do it correctly.

Variable dominance: This is where your dominant eye switches depending on the variables identified in the precision dominance tests. People also have different levels of dominance—some strong, others

weak. The key here is knowing when or how it will shift and to plan accordingly.

> Go to **http://chrissajnog.com** to find out how you can improve your vision.

As you complete each test, write down the test name and results here: _____

_____

_____

_____

_____

_____

_____

_____

_____

_____

_____

_____

_____

_____

Write down the results of your tests: _____

_____

_____

_____

_____

_____

_____

_____

_____

_____

_____

_____

_____

_____

_____

_____

2

Shooting Platform

"The more solid the position, the easier it is to hold the gun and control the trigger without disturbing the sights."

One of the biggest hurdles to becoming a good shooter is achieving consistency, which means doing things the same way every time you shoot. Specifically what I'm talking about is your shooting platform, or what some call body position or stance. Try different positions, see what works and what doesn't, but when you find one you like, stick with it and work on consistency.

Shooting positions should be flexible to allow modifications according to individual body structure.

I use the terms *shooting platform*, *stance*, and *shooting position* somewhat interchangeably, so don't get mixed up. I try to use *platform* when I can—for me the platform is something you work off of and can be moved, whereas when I hear *position* I think of it being static. But few firefights are static. Don't worry so much about the terminology for now since we need to get in a good position before we move anyway! Crawl, walk, run, right?

Regardless what weapon system we're talking about, or what position, a solid shooting platform is essential. The more solid the position, the easier it is to hold the gun and control the trigger without disturbing the sights. Whether you're shooting prone, kneeling, standing, or any unconventional shooting position, you should have as much of your body directly behind the weapon as possible. You must be able to *drive* the gun, and just like when driving your car you need the seat (the platform you operate the car from) adjusted properly. Imagine trying to drive fast if you were sitting to the left or right of the steering wheel. It would be hard to control it, right? Well, it's harder to control a gun if you're not behind it, too.

Shooting positions should be flexible to allow modifications according to individual body structure. Just because I shoot well with my body positioned a certain way doesn't mean it will work the same for you. I'm 6'1", and someone 5'7" might not be able to contort their body the same way I do, so don't push it if it's not working. View my descriptions as a starting point and just make sure you don't violate any of the fundamentals of a good shooting position. This flexibility becomes even more important on the two-way range, as the shooter must assume the steadiest position that also allows for observation of the target area and, if possible, provides cover and concealment. There are innumerable possibilities depending on terrain, vegetation, and the tactical situation. Always stay flexible and adapt to your surroundings. In combat, your feet are going to be where they need to be for mobility, cover, or concealment. Try to keep your weight forward and your center of gravity low—this will help keep your sights on target.

One thing I teach my students is to have as many body parts as possible pointing at the target. This includes your head, eyes, toes, hips, shoulders, fingers, knuckles, and thumbs. In a perfect world, on a flat

range, with no one shooting back at you, this is easy and should be practiced. But ultimately, control of the weapon must come from the upper body. Your lower body has to conform to the current tactical situation while the upper body drives the gun. If you're shooting and moving, think of your lower body like the tracks of a tank and your upper body as the turret. Your lower body is doing everything it can to give your upper body the best possible platform from which to shoot.

Three Elements of Any Good Shooting Platform

Bone Support

A good shooting platform employs bone support, not muscular support. A strong foundation is as necessary to shooting as it is to a well-built house. Think about this: You're using muscles to hold your weapon on target, you bring your focus back to the front sight, and relax. Your body is going to move to its natural point of aim (see below) and you're not going to notice this subtle shift because you're not focusing on the target—you're focusing on the front sight, right?

Muscular Relaxation

Through training and the use of a natural point of aim, you need to develop muscular relaxation in all shooting positions. Undue strain or tension causes trembling, which is transmitted to the gun. When you're shooting in a standing position, try to wiggle your toes. The sciatic nerve—running from the top of the leg to the foot—is the longest nerve in your body, and if you're relaxed enough to wiggle your toes, you're relaxed. In combat, you're going to have enough stress going on; the ability to relax enough to make accurate shots could just save your life.

Natural Point of Aim

Your natural point of aim is the place your sights are aiming when your body is relaxed. You're using bone support and have achieved

muscular relaxation—when you look at your sights, that's your natural point of aim.

To find your natural point of aim in any shooting position:

1. Take any shooting position and mount your weapon.

2. Once a sight picture is established, close your eyes, take a deep breath, and exhale to your natural respiratory pause.

3. Concentrate on relaxing your body

3.2.1 – Natural Point of Aim – Toes out

3.2.2 – Natural Point of Aim – Toes in

completely. This will cause the gun to fall to your natural point of aim.

4. If your gun is clear and safe, use this opportunity to dry-fire once.

5. Open your eyes and adjust your position by shifting your lower body until the gun points to the target at the exact point where you want the bullet to strike. Do not make any adjustments using muscles; you must make even very minor adjustments with the lower body.

Repeat Steps 2 through 5 until, when you open your eyes, your sights are exactly where you want them. This is your natural point of aim.

The upper body (above the waist) is kept in the same position while the lower body (platform) is adjusted to allow firing from different heights or angles.

Obviously in combat or most timed evolutions, you can't go through these steps, but if you practice enough your body will learn what a good shooting platform feels like. You'll naturally end up in a more advantageous position to deal with any threats. Even if you walk up to the firing line

to do some training, take a moment to look at where your hips are pointing when you relax them. If they're pointing two target frames over, you may help yourself out by adjusting them to point at your target. The easiest way to do this is to simply turn your toes toward your target.

In most of the positions described here, the upper body (above the waist) is kept in the same position while the lower body (platform) is adjusted to allow firing from different heights or angles. As mentioned earlier, all these descriptions are just starting points for you to understand the fundamentals of a good stance. Normally, the only place you will ever be in a picture-perfect stance is on the range. In a gunfight, you'll most likely be moving and adjusting your stance to fit your environment and the situation.

As always, use whichever stance works best for you. Whatever stance you choose, it should be athletic—something you can move into and out of quickly.

Pistol Positions

Standing

Although you can use several stances for pistol shooting, I'll describe the stance I use — the modern or modified isosceles. This stance uses the geometric power of a triangle to support the gun, using of bones, not muscles, for support. Think of how you would stand if someone were going to tackle you. You'd be

3.2.3 – Standing Pistol – Front view

3.2.4 – Standing Pistol – Side view

in a fighting position, right? Well, gunfighting is no different. You can see the strength of the position in the picture below. Notice how the arms form a perfect triangle.

There should be no tension in your biceps when your arms are extended. Wherever your arms naturally stop when extended is where you should shoot from. "Locked" does not mean tense.

The standing position is as follows:

1. Stand with feet shoulder width apart (or wider, if it feels better), toes pointed toward the target, knees

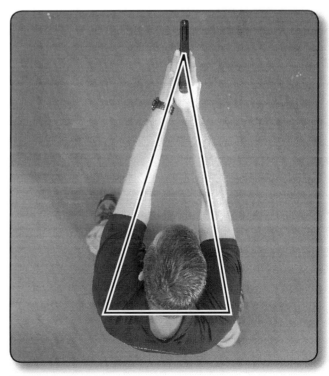

3.2.5 – Standing Pistol – Top view

slightly bent (5 to 10 degrees). Keep in mind that during a gunfight your feet are going to end up where they decide they need to be . . . don't fight it; adapt and make sure your weight is forward—nose over toes.

2. Drop your strong-side leg straight back until the toes are in line with the heel of your other foot. Again, you can slide this foot back farther to get into a more aggressive stance.

3. Both arms are fully extended and locked, but not overextended. If you extend your shoulders out of their sockets, you lose strength from your larger chest and back muscles.

4. The head is upright, leaning forward (nose over toes) at the waist.

5. Bring the sights up to the eyes.

6. Shoulders, arms, hands, and gun will be in a straight line.

7. The barrel of the gun will be in line with the shooter's spine.

Due to the locked joints and chest-forward aspect, in several situations this shooting platform is not the best choice. For instance, if you are shooting out of a vehicle window or need to shoot while moving, a Weaver-style stance with bent arms will likely work better. The key is to train for these situations and find out what works best for you.

Kneeling

As with standing, there are several common kneeling positions from which you can shoot effectively. The differences all have to do with how low you go, for stability, mobility, or use of available cover. You do all these variations with the lower body only while the upper body will be in the same position as standing. The three positions I cover are high, medium, and low kneeling. Some shooters like to shoot from a double kneeling position (both knees down), but I don't find this is a combat-effective position when I need to get up and go.

3.2.6 – High Kneel

With all these positions, learn to go straight down if possible—you may not know what's in front of or behind you, but you know your feet are on solid ground. This may not be possible depending on the situation, terrain, or your body, but it normally is the fastest way to switch positions and keep your sights on target.

High Kneel

Drop straight down on your strong knee from the standing position described above. Bend the toes of your strong-side foot under to allow for quick movement and balance.

Bend the knee of your reaction-side leg. Leaning forward at the waist, you should not be able to see your reaction-side foot. This position is the fastest to get into and out of while lowering the shooter's profile.

Medium Kneel

Drop straight down on your strong knee from the standing position. Bend the toes of your strong-side foot under to allow for quick movement. Bend the knee of the reaction-side leg. Sit back on the heel of the strong-side foot, while leaning forward at the waist. This position lowers your

3.2.7 – Medium Kneel

3.2.8 – Low Kneel

profile from that of a high kneel, and for increased accuracy.

Low Kneel

Drop straight down on your strong knee from the standing position. With the foot of your strong-side leg bent under, sit back on the foot. Extend your reaction-side leg out in front while leaning forward as low as possible. This position is the slowest to get into and out of, has decreased stability, and is used to shoot under very low cover.

Prone

The prone (face down) position is good to know should you find yourself on the ground during a gunfight. Done properly, it's the most accurate position to shoot from and gets you as low as possible. It's also the slowest to get into and out of and limits your field of view, but if practiced enough it can be worth your travel time.

To shoot from the prone position:

1. Lie face down on the ground, with your legs spread apart, heels down.

Your toes can be pointed in or out—just do not have your heels sticking up. Any movement in your heels will translate to the gun and increase your chance of error.

2. The upper body position is the same as standing and kneeling.

3. If possible, keep your forearms and the sides of your hands on the ground for support, and bring your head down to the sights.

4. If unable to get low enough to see the sights, rotate onto the strong-side arm just enough to be able to see them. The arms and gun position do not change. Rotate your entire upper body as a unit

3.2.10 – Prone

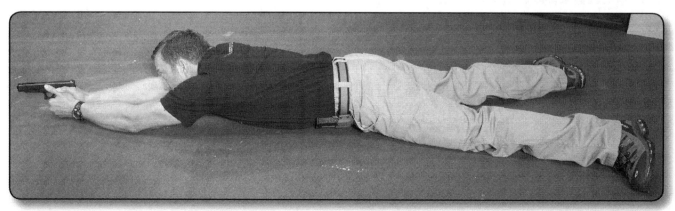

3.2.9 – Prone

until the sights are on target. Make sure the top leg is in front of the bottom leg. It can be bent or kept straight.

Urban Prone

Urban prone is a pretty generic term used to describe most nontraditional prone shooting positions, usually when you're on one side or the other. Generally there are two reasons you might use the urban prone position: to shoot under something low like a car or desk; or to make use of shallow cover like a curb or log.

To shoot from an urban prone position:

1. If possible and practical, go straight down to one side. Lie down on your side parallel with your cover or opening, with your legs spread apart. Put your upper leg back to shoot over low cover, or your upper leg forward to shoot under something. This allows for a better natural point of aim and decreases the amount of your body exposed.

2. The upper body position should be the same as the standing and kneeling positions.

3. Keep as much of your arm as possible on the ground for support.

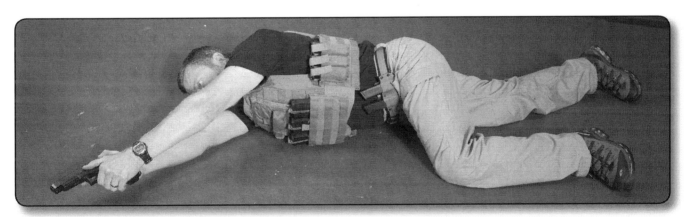

3.2.11 – Urban Prone

3.2.12 – Urban Prone

3.2.13 – Fetal Prone

3.2.14 – Sitting, Split-leg

Fetal Prone

Like urban prone, fetal prone is an unconventional prone position where you're shooting on your side or back, but with your legs tucked in. You'd use fetal prone when getting behind small cover, like the wheel of a car or a ship's cleat and, as the name implies, you're tucked up in a fetal position to avoid incoming fire.

To shoot from a fetal prone position:

1. Remember to go straight down. Lie down on your back with your legs tucked up tight against a small, solid object, as if you're squatting down on the side of the object.

2. Your upper body position should be the same as the standing and kneeling positions.

3. Your pistol will be pointed around the side of the object, as if you're now pointing down if the object and you were rotated 90 degrees.

Sitting, Split-leg

The sitting position is not a common shooting position in stressful conditions, but you never know and it's best to be prepared if that unlikely event happens to you. A good sitting position can greatly increase your stability, but is probably the slowest position to move out of, so make the most if it if you get knocked on your butt. One of the most common situations where you might be sitting and shooting is from a car window. The main change I make is to shoot from a Weaver-type position, as it's nearly impossible to shoot from an isosceles position unless you're shooting through the windshield. There are two variations I teach for sitting pistol, and the first is the split-leg position.

To shoot from a split-leg sitting position:

1. Sit down with your feet about shoulder width apart, straight in front of you with your knees bent about 90 degrees.

2. The upper body position should be the same as the standing and kneeling positions.

3. Your triceps should rest on your knees as support, and your back should be rounded.

4. Make sure that you're not using leg muscles to hold your arms up.

Sitting, Single-leg

The second shooting position for sitting is the single-leg position. Rather than leaning forward and relaxing, this one has you leaning back and using the tension of your arms for stability. I recommend trying them both and using whichever one makes you feel more comfortable.

To shoot from a single-leg sitting position:

1. Sit down with one knee bent about 90 degrees, and the other fully extended.

2. The upper body position should be the same as the standing and kneeling positions.

3. Hook your hands (and gun) in front of one of your knees (I use my reaction side) and lean back to create tension and stability.

4. Make sure you're not using leg muscles to hold your position.

3.2.15 – Sitting, Single-leg

3.2.16 – Squat

Squat

I sometimes use the squat position to teach a good standing position to those who have a hard time getting into an aggressive stance. Getting into it is the same as a good aggressive standing position, but it's still a good idea to practice it because it's by definition lower than your standing position. The squat is a great position to use when standing is too high and kneeling may be too low or too slow.

The squat position works as follows:

1.   Stand with feet shoulder width apart (or wider, if it feels better), toes pointed toward the target, knees bent as much as needed to put your

pistol's muzzle at the desired height. Keep in mind that during a gunfight your feet are going to end up where they decide they need to be. Don't fight it—adapt and make sure your weight is forward, nose over toes.

2.   Both arms are fully extended and locked straight out, but not overextended. If you extend your shoulders out of their sockets, you lose the strength of your larger chest and back muscles. There should be no tension in the biceps when your arms are extended. Shoot from wherever your arms naturally stop when extended. "Locked" does not mean tense.

3.   The head is upright, leaning forward (nose over toes) at the waist. Make sure you keep your back straight by pushing your butt out to help you maintain balance. A good range squat is the same as a good gym squat.

4.   Bring the sights up to the eyes.

5.   Shoulders, arms, hands, and gun will be in a straight line.

6.   The barrel of the gun will be in line with the shooter's spine.

Supine

Supine means on your back and it's a position you'll likely need to shoot from if

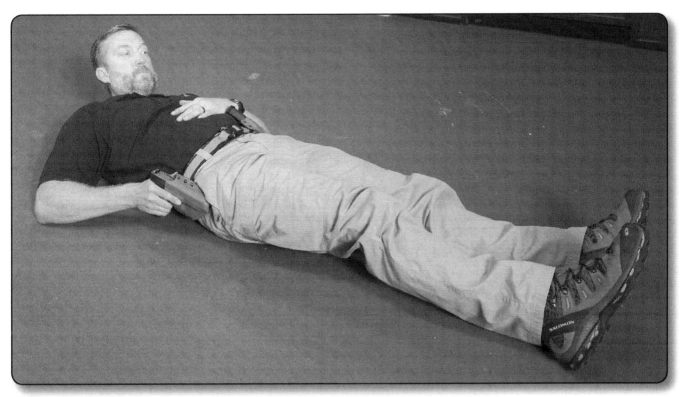

3.2.17 – Supine

3.2.18 – Supine

you ever get knocked down and have an advancing enemy. The position itself is pretty straightforward but you need to be keenly aware of your body position to avoid shooting off your kneecaps. One good drill I teach is defensive shooting, where you shoot from supine, then sitting, then kneeling, then standing.

To shoot from the supine position:

1. Start off lying down on your back with your knees together and bent about 90 degrees. This is so you can safely draw your weapon and move it over your knees. Alternately, you can draw your weapon with your legs straight, move it to between your legs, and then bend your knees.

2. The upper body position should be the same as the other firing positions. The difference is that you will be pointing the weapon "down" between your knees.

3. Your core needs to be contracted and your arms in contact with your abs to create tension and stability.

4. Having your knees bent allows you to use your core to stabilize the position, but with your knees up you need to be constantly aware of where they are or you'll make this position even harder to get up from!

One-handed, Unsupported

One very common shooting position that most people neglect, yet can find themselves in during a gunfight is shooting one-handed, whether that be with your strong or reaction hand, unsupported. Strong-hand unsupported means that you draw your weapon to get into a gunfight, and your reaction hand can't join the party. Maybe you're holding onto a ladder or pulling your teammate behind cover, or maybe your reaction arm or hand is injured. The reason's not important, but perfecting the skill could save your life.

I know many people use the term "weak hand," but the mind is a powerful thing and I don't want to assume that any part of my shooting platform is weak.

Reaction side means only that if you're right-handed, you're able to shoot with your left hand with no help from your right hand, or vice-versa if you're left-handed. I know many people use the term "weak hand," but the mind is a powerful thing and I don't want to assume that any part of my shooting platform is weak. That's why I talk about our support hand (it supports what we're doing) or our reaction hand (it reacts to things so our other hand can remain on fire control). If you do have a "weak hand," keep reading and I'll give you some ideas on how to make your weak hand strong! Also, so as not to focus on right- or left-handed shooters and be biased, I'll use the terms strong and support or reaction hand to keep it simple. But I do remember reading somewhere that left-handed people live on average seven fewer years than right-handed people. Of course I'm kidding, but I am glad I'm a righty!

Many shooters never train in one-handed shooting unless at the range shooting for quarterly or semiannual weapons qualification or someone asks, "What if you're shot in your other hand?" Even then, most military and LE agencies' standard practical pistol courses only have you shoot four to six rounds unsupported at a distance no greater than seven yards. But the FBI has studied over twenty years of actual shooting reports where armed citizens and officers had to defend themselves or others with a pistol, and more than 50 percent of the shooting was done one-handed. So why don't we train one-handed? My guess is because it's hard. Well, stand by for a life lesson: If you want to be hard, push against what's hard. It's how weight lifters build muscle: They push against something hard and grow from it.

Not only will training one-handed prepare you for violent encounters, but doing anything with your nondominant hand actually makes you smarter. And if you wonder how likely it is that you'll get shot in the hand and need to use this skill, consider this: In a deadly situation your mind will focus on the threat, and when that happens your eyes will subconsciously focus directly at the gun.

During training when you're using photo targets (paper targets that look like people) and you're immediately presented with a shoot or no-shoot situation, most people tend to shoot at the weapon. People do this without even knowing it. Despite the fact they're trained at the range to shoot "center mass," it's usually at silhouette targets with no weapons. But during training with live fire or Airsoft, operators doing close quarters combat (CQC) training always use photo targets and very often shoot the weapon. When we do shoot/no-shoot drills with live role players, operators shoot the weapon, too. Every time I'm the "bad guy" I always make sure to wear shooting gloves with carbon fiber or reinforced knuckles, because nothing sucks more than taking round after round to the hand holding the weapon. When a gunfire exchange occurs, many shooters revert to shooting at the threat. So you could easily find yourself taking rounds to one of your hands or arms.

You may find you actually shoot better one-handed, because it forces you to focus more on the fundamentals.

3.2.19 – One-handed

The best way to improve your one-handed shooting is to practice shooting one-handed. Use the same seven shooting fundamentals you use for shooting with all appendages intact, and you may find you actually shoot better one-handed because it forces you to focus more on the fundamentals—probably to the level you should be all the time!

Follow these steps to shoot one-handed:

1. Stand with feet shoulder width apart (feet can be wider if it feels better), toes pointed toward the target, knees slightly bent (5 to 10 degrees). Keep in mind that during a gunfight your feet are going to end up where they decide they need to be. Don't fight it

— adapt and make sure your weight is forward, nose over toes.

2. Drop the strong-side leg straight back until the toes are in line with the heel of the other foot. Again, you can slide this foot back farther to get into a more aggressive stance.

3. Fully extend the arm you're firing with, but don't overextend the shoulder out of its socket. By keeping the shoulder packed in tight, you use your larger chest and back muscles, as opposed to your smaller deltoid muscles. How far you extend is slightly different for everyone, but a good starting place is to shoot from

3.2.20 – Shoulder out

3.2.21 – Shoulder packed in

3.2.22 – One-handed grip

3.2.23 – Thumb up

wherever your arms naturally stop when extended.

4.   The head is upright, leaning forward (nose over toes) at the waist.

5.   Bring the sights up to your eyes.

6.   Keep your shoulder, arm, hand, and gun in a straight horizontal line.

7.   The barrel of the gun will be in line with the shooter's spine.

Helpful tips:

• Make sure you have a high grip on the pistol to help with recoil.

• We have what's called an inner-limb response or reflex. When it comes to grip strength, you can grip something harder with one hand if you also squeeze the other hand. When you shoot one-handed, make sure to make a fist or squeeze something with your opposite hand.

• Rather than having your thumb forward, having your thumb up helps some people control the recoil by giving a little more resistance to the side of the gun from which your other hand is now missing.

One of the most important aspects of fighting with more than one weapons system is utilizing the same position.

Carbine Shooting Positions

In classical marksmanship, there are four main shooting positions: prone, seated, kneeling, and standing—sometimes called off-hand. These positions start with the most stable (prone) and progress to the least stable (standing). In discussing combat marksmanship, we must also note that these move from the least mobile (prone) to the most mobile (standing).

As with pistol platforms, these positions should be modified according to your body type and shooting style. There are several other unconventional positions from which to shoot, including squatting, fetal prone, urban prone, supine, and others I'll describe. For all these positions, it is most important to understand the fundamentals of a good position and make sure you are utilizing them in whatever position you find yourself.

One of the most important aspects of fighting with more than one weapons system is utilizing the same position. You don't want to transition from carbine to pistol and also move your lower body, head, or chest by standing up as you move to your secondary weapons system. If you're in a good fighting position, you should be able to transition with no movement except from the shoulders down to the hands. As you read through these positions, note their intentional similarities not only to each other, but also to the pistol positions.

Standing

This is probably the most common position you will use in any combat situation. It's the quickest to assume and allows for the most mobility to help you avoid getting shot.

To shoot from the standing position:

1. Stand with feet shoulder width apart (feet can be wider if it feels better), toes pointed toward the target, knees slightly bent (5 to 10 degrees).

2. Drop your strong-side leg straight back until your toes are in line with the heel of the other foot. As with pistol shooting, you can slide this foot farther back to assume a more aggressive stance.

3. Mount the weapon so the buttstock is in the shoulder (not hanging over the top) and directly below the strong-side eye. If this is not possible due to body armor, get it as close to the center of your chest as possible. Don't think the buttstock should be placed into the shoulder; think of it needing to be placed in the chest. This more centerline placement helps with recoil management.

4. Keep your head upright, leaning forward (nose over toes) at the waist.

5. Bring the sights up to your eyes.

6. Shoulders, arms, hands, and gun will be in a straight, level line.

7. The strong-side (fire control) hand should grip the rifle the same as you grip a pistol—high up, with the wrist straight behind. Keep this elbow close to the body, and pull the buttstock into your chest.

3.2.24 – Standing – Side view

8. The reaction-side hand should grip the handguard/rail system as far forward and safely as possible. I do not recommend using a vertical foregrip to hold the weapon. (I feel these are possibly the single worst things ever to happen to marksmanship.)

9. Make sure some part of your hand (fingers or thumb) is above the barrel/ on top of the gun to manage recoil.

10. Take away the hinge in your reaction-side elbow by rotating the elbow up and out.

11. Drive the gun with your reaction hand, and leave your strong hand to operate the fire control system.

3.2.25 – Standing – Front view

3.2.26 – Standing – Top view

3.2.27 – Buttstock in shoulder

3.2.28 – Buttstock not in shoulder

3.2.29 – Placement with plate carrier outside strap

3.2.30 – Placement with plate carrier on strap

3.2.31 – Placement with plate carrier inside strap

3.2.32 – Elbow hinge

3.2.33 – Elbow rotated up

Squatting

Getting into a squatting shooting position is the same as a good, aggressive standing position, just lower. If you need to get low quick and move even quicker, the squat may be right for you, and if you practice enough it'll help get you in shape! What could be better than shooting and working out at the same time?

To shoot from the squatting position:

1. Stand with feet shoulder width apart (feet can be wider if it feels better), toes pointed toward the target, and knees bent as much as needed to put your barrel at the desired height. Keep in mind that during a gunfight your feet are going to end up where they decide they need to be . . . don't fight it — adapt, and make sure your weight is forward, nose over toes.

2. If you do have one foot farther back, you will need to rotate that toe outward to maintain a good shooting platform. Keep your back straight, and squat the same as if you were lifting weights.

3. Mount the weapon so the buttstock is in the shoulder (not hanging over the top) and directly below your strong-side eye. If this is not possible due to body armor, get it as close to the center of your chest as possible. Don't think the buttstock should be placed into the shoulder—think of it needing to be placed in the chest.

3.2.34 – Squatting

This centerline placement helps with recoil management.

4. The head is upright, leaning forward (nose over toes) at the waist.

5. Bring the sights up to the eyes.

6. Shoulders, arms, hands, and gun will be in a straight, level line.

7. The strong-side (fire control) hand should grip the carbine pistol grip the same as you grip a pistol—high up, with the wrist straight behind. Keep this elbow close to the body, and pull the buttstock into your chest.

8. The support-side hand should grip the handguard/rail system as far forward and as safely as possible.

9. Make sure some part of your hand (fingers or thumb) is above the barrel/ on top of the gun to manage recoil.

10. Take away the hinge in your support-side elbow by rotating the elbow up and out.

11. Drive the gun with your support hand, and leave your strong hand to operate the fire control system.

SBU

The SBU position is named for my Navy Special Operations friends at the Special Boat Unit (SBU). Though now they're called Special Boat Teams (SBT), we'll stick with the original name. They started using this position from the tactical necessity of getting as low as possible and shooting over the very limited cover of the sides of their boats. It's a simple and effective adaptation of almost any shooting position, where you simply rotate your weapon 90 degrees to bring your sights (and more importantly,

3.2.35 – SBU

3.2.36 – SBU

your head) a few inches lower. If you shoot right-handed you rotate the gun to your left; lefties rotate to the right. Some things to consider when adapting to an SBU position:

- You aren't able to have the buttstock in the same position as in your standard mount. As you rotate the gun, you will need to slide the buttstock out and up to be able to see the sights.

- Use other contact points to strengthen the position.

- Remember to keep your strong-side elbow down. It's not your head, but I'm

sure getting shot in the elbow would not be fun.

Kneeling

I'll cover two kneeling positions: unsupported and supported. Kneeling positions are used to utilize cover or lower your profile and keep you somewhat mobile. Many shooters need to slide their support-side hands back closer to the magazine to find a comfortable position to get into the supported position.

Unsupported

Drop straight down on your strong knee

3.2.37 – Kneeling – Unsupported

3.2.38 – Kneeling – Supported

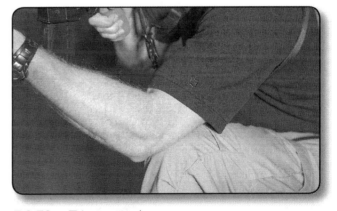

3.2.39 – Triceps to kneecap

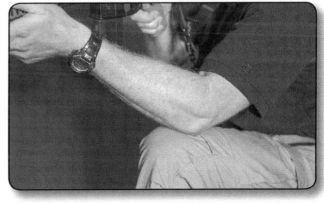

3.2.40 – Elbow to thigh

from the standing position described above. Bend the toes of your strong-side foot under to allow for quick movement and balance. Your support-side leg is bent. Leaning forward at the waist, you should not be able to see your support-side foot. This position is the fastest to get into and out of while lowering the shooter's profile.

Supported

Drop straight down onto the strong knee from the standing position. Bend the toes of your strong foot under to allow for quick movement. Bend your support-side leg. Sit back on the heel of your strong-side foot while leaning forward at the waist. Rest the triceps of your support-side arm on the knee of your support-side leg. If this does not work for you,

you may put your elbow on top of your thigh. Either way, make sure you have hard on soft (elbow bone to thigh muscle) or soft on hard (triceps to kneecap). This position lowers your profile from that of an unsupported kneel and for increased accuracy.

Sitting

There are three combat-effective sitting positions I like to use in the rare event I end up on my ass in the middle of a gunfight. The most common uses of the sitting position are in competitions and shooting from vehicles. Try these out in dry-fire and see which one works best for you and your body type, then take it to the range and practice putting some lead downrange.

Cross-ankle

The cross-ankle sitting position is the most

well known, used in shooting competitions for many years. Getting into the position takes some time, and if you've ever shot a competition where you had to wait with your legs crossed before the whistle blasted and you were able to sit, you know if can be hard on your ankles!

To shoot from a cross-ankle sitting position:

1. Face 45 degrees off toward your strong side.

2. Sit down with your knees bent and legs crossed, with each foot tucked under the other leg.

3. Your upper body's shooting position should remain the same as in the other positions. You may need to slide your support-side hand back to get your sights high enough to see your target,

3.2.41 – Sitting Cross-ankle

3.2.42 – Shift feet/legs to find what works for you

and you may need to collapse your buttstock to get into a good position.

4.   Everybody is different, so you will need to play around with which leg is on the bottom and how far the foot is tucked under your leg. Try different configurations to see what works for you, but make sure you stick to the basics of a good shooting position and use bone support with relaxed muscles in your final position.

5.   If you have the time, it's very important to find your natural point of aim in this position since most people use muscle to support the gun.

Split-leg

The split-leg sitting position is a lot easier to get into and out of and still provides an increased level of stability. For those who have a hard time getting into a good cross-ankle sitting position, this might be a better option.

To shoot from a split-leg sitting position:

1.   Sit down with your feet about shoulder width apart, straight in front of you with your knees bent about 90 degrees.

2.   Your upper body position should be the same as in other positions, but you will need to have your strong-side elbow out as a support on the knee.

3.2.43 – Sitting Split-leg

3.   Your arms should rest on top of your knees and hook around them slightly for support.

4.   Make sure you're not using leg muscles to hold your arms and gun up. To do this, keep the distance between your knees and feet the same—don't let your legs flare out.

One-leg

The one-leg sitting position is one of the few times I recommend holding your magazine while shooting. Normally I cringe every time I see a firearms advertisement with someone holding the magazine with their "support" hand. What are they supporting? Not the end of the gun that's going to be moving! Okay, I'm better now. The key to this position is hooking your hand on the

3.2.44 – Sitting One-leg

front of the magazine well and pinning that to your knee. The three interlocking support points make this one of the most stable sitting positions. I recommend trying them all out and using whichever one makes you feel most comfortable.

Normally I cringe every time I see a firearms advertisement with someone holding the magazine with their "support" hand.

To shoot from a single-leg sitting position:

1. Sit down with your support-side knee bent about 90 degrees, and extend your strong-side leg out in front of you. Some shooters prefer hooking their ankles together, and you should give this a try.

2. As usual, keep the upper body position as close to normal as possible, with the exception of your support-hand grip.

3. Hook your support hand under the upper receiver right where it meets the front of the magazine well, and pin it

to the inside of your knee. Your thumb should be on one side and all other fingers on the other, all pointing back at you.

4. Arch your back and lean back to create tension and stability.

5. Make sure that you're not using leg muscles to hold your position.

Prone

This position is the most stable of all positions and allows for the lowest possible profile and/or the greatest amount of stability. The flipside of this is that it's the least mobile of the fighting positions and reduces your fields of fire both vertically and horizontally.

To shoot from the prone position:

1. Lie face down on the ground, with your legs spread wide apart, heels down (get big). Your toes can be pointed in or out, just do not stick your heels up. Any movement in your heels will translate to the gun and increase your chance of error.

2. The upper body position is essentially the same as standing or kneeling.

3. Both elbows will be on the ground and used as outriggers for support.

4. Your body needs to be directly behind your gun, not off to the side. The barrel should be in line with your strong-side butt cheek.

5. Your support hand should be pulling the gun into your shoulder, and you should be able to let go with your strong hand without the weapon moving.

3.2.45 – Prone – Take your time to get a good natural point of aim

3.2.46 – Prone – Adjust grip to change elevation

3.2.47 – Prone – Using magazine as support

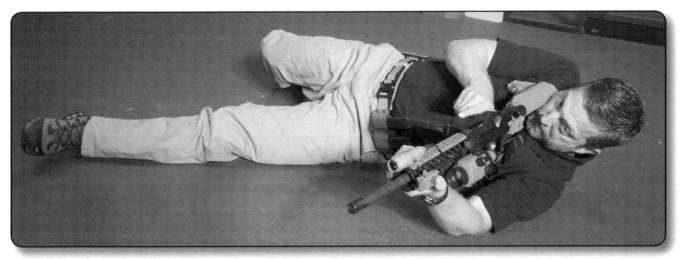

3.2.48 – Urban Prone

6. The magazine should be used as a support if possible. Before relying on this in combat, make sure your gun will not jam if the magazine is used as a monopod. During training, test each type of magazine you have with your gun. If it passes the test, this is a very stable position.

Urban Prone

Urban prone is sometimes called rollover prone, and there are other names for similar shooting positions with the upper or lower body in slightly different positions. My guess is someone wanted to invent a new high-speed move, so they came up with their

3.2.49 – Urban Prone

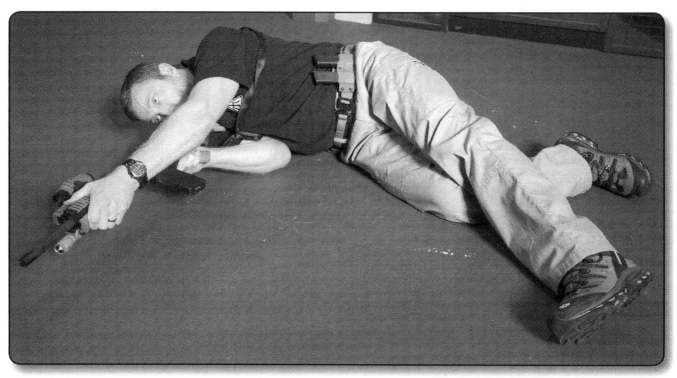

3.2.50 – Urban Prone

own name, but regardless the reasons to use urban prone remain the same: to shoot under something low like a car, or to make use of shallow cover. One thing to keep in mind when shooting a carbine with the ejection port within a few inches of a solid surface (like the ground) is that the ejected brass can bounce back into the port it just left and cause you headaches. You can help avoid this by increasing the distance from the surface or canting the weapon slightly.

3.2.51 – Urban Prone

To shoot from an urban prone position:

1. Lie down on your side with your legs spread apart and your top leg back. This allows for a better natural point of aim and lowers the amount of your body exposed.

2. The upper body position should be the same as standing.

3. If possible, keep as much of your upper arm as possible on the ground for support. If you go down to the left, use your left hand to lower yourself, then use it as your support hand. If you go down to the right, use your right hand. This way you should have good support from your elbow up to the front of the gun.

4. If you are trying to shoot under low cover, use your lower shoulder. If you are shooting over low cover, use your upper shoulder. Either way, use whichever eye lines up with your sights.

Fetal Prone

You'd be amazed what small things you can fit your body behind when someone is shooting at you, and the fetal prone position is the poster child for getting small and

3.2.52 – Fetal Prone

staying in the fight. If all you have is a small piece of cover, get down behind it and tuck your legs up against the wall. You can add to your stability by pressing your feet into the wall like you're standing on it.

You'd be amazed what small things you can fit your body behind when someone is shooting at you.

To shoot from a fetal prone position:

1. Lie down on your back with your legs tucked up tight against a small,

solid object. It should look like you're squatting down on the side of the object.

2. Your upper body position should be the same as standing.

3. Now rotate onto one side with your muzzle pointed around the side of the object. It will look as if you're now pointing down if the object and you were rotated 90 degrees.

Supine

As with a pistol, the supine position with the carbine is not very common, but you must train for every scenario since you could find yourself on your back in competition or a

3.2.53 – Supine

gunfight, and just a little know-how and training could make you the victor.

To shoot from the supine position:

1. Start off lying down on your back with your knees straight and your toes pointed out as far as possible.

2. Unless you're shooting straight up, this is one position where your upper body is going to be different than normal, but who knows, maybe you're being attacked from the sky. If you're not defending an aerial assault, you'll either need to drive the gun out and use your sling as support, or pull it in and use the insides of your arms against your chest as support. Either way, I find it easiest to shoot with a slight inward cant to get on the sights.

3. Your core needs to be contracted and your arms in contact with your abs to create tension and stability.

4. Having your knees bent will allow you to use your knees and core to stabilize

the position, but if you decide to go knees up, make sure you keep the muzzle past your knees!

Obviously there are other positions, and even these are going to be drastically modified depending on the terrain where your firefight takes place. The point is to use these examples as what to strive for and good starting points to train. It's also important to note that everyone's body is different. We all have different levels of flexibility—our body parts are all different lengths, and hinge at different points. Use these as starting points, and modify to what fits your body; just remember the elements that make up a good shooting platform and try not to break any of the basic rules.

If you remember the basic elements of a good shooting platform and put them into practice on the range and in your dry weapons training, you'll be able to apply them no matter what position your body ends up in when it's time to deliver effective customer service to someone who asks for it.

How can I improve my shooting platform? _____

_____

_____

_____

Although many shooters focus on the trigger finger as the key to accurate shooting, I feel the grip holds the title as king of consistency.

3

Grip

"The best connection between yourself and the weapon."

No matter what weapon system you're shooting, a solid grip is vital to placing accurate rounds on target. As sure as having a loose scope mounted on a rifle will make it impossible to hold a group, a loose grip will cause rounds to fly aimlessly off their mark and leave you searching for impacts, as well as answers. So in the same way you need to check your weapon before you shoot to ensure everything is tight, you need to check your grip to make sure you've got the best connection between yourself and the weapon.

Although many shooters focus on the trigger finger as the key to accurate shooting, I feel the grip holds the title as king of consistency. Think of it this way — if your grip is like a gun vise and there is no way the weapon will move, you can do whatever you want to the trigger! Now let's say that you've practiced pulling the trigger straight back until it's literally impossible for you to pull off to one side or the other even a fraction of a millimeter, but...your grip sucks and the weapon moves inconsistently every time you squeeze the trigger (perfectly). Your shots will be all over the place! Maybe once in a while you'll get lucky and the recoil will be straight back (even broken clocks are right twice a day), but people calling you "Shotgun" will be the only constant on your range.

Don't let the tail (your finger) wag the dog (your gun). Your contact with 99 percent of the gun is much more important than where you contact the remaining 1 percent of the gun. The reason most people focus on the wrong thing is that they start off with a poor grip and rather than fix that, think of ways to work around it. Let's start you off on the right path with a good grip.

3.3.1 – Arm behind gun

3.3.2 – Skin tented up

3.3.3 – Fill the natural space

Pistol

Guns are built to a variety of specifications and so are your hands, so it's a good idea to start off with something that fits your hand rather than try to adjust your grip to fit a gun. I recognize if you're in the military or law enforcement you probably don't get to pick the guns you use, so the techniques in this chapter will be particularly important to you. If you do get to pick your gun, make sure you head out to your favorite Gun Mart before you purchase online to see how it feels in your hand. Some guns these days have different grips or back-straps you can change out for a better fit, so check to see if these are available. The gun should fit comfortably in your hand with the forearm of your firing hand in a direct line behind the pistol and your trigger finger should be able to reach the trigger without dragging along the side of the gun. We've all heard the saying, "If the glove doesn't fit, you must acquit." When it comes to guns, "If the gun doesn't fit, you're not going to hit."

Now that you've selected the right piece of equipment, let's talk about how to control that explosion going off in your hands. When you grip the gun, make sure that the forearm of your strong hand is in line with the barrel of the pistol. Just like I talked about in the first chapter, it's important to have as much of your body behind the gun as possible to control recoil, and it starts here with a pistol. Your hand needs to be as high up the gun as possible. In a perfect world you would have your hand directly behind the barrel, but guns have moving parts up there making this impossible. Keeping this goal in mind, your hand should be high enough on the grip so the webbing of your hand is compressed on the beaver-tail. If your grip is too low it will not only affect your shots, but can also cause your weapon to jam from not having a solid recoil abutment.

Wrap your hand around the gun and make sure your trigger finger is not riding along the side of the grip as this can pull the gun off target as you press back on the trigger. Don't get caught up on placing your trigger finger in a certain spot on the trigger. Everyone's hands are built differently and what works well for a paper shooter on a one-way range may not work for you when you hear the snap of rounds whizzing past your pineapple. Just make sure you're able to press the trigger straight back while keeping your sights on target.

If you're using a two-handed technique (and I suggest you do whenever possible), the reaction hand should be placed with the palm of the hand filling the space on the grip left by the strong hand. To do this, your reaction hand should be angled down at about a 45-degree angle. Make sure there is no space between the palms of your hands. Pressure should be equal in both hands as they torque toward each other like a vice. Some people teach a 60/40 grip for how hard you should be gripping the gun, but

3.3.4 – Reaction hand down at 45 degrees

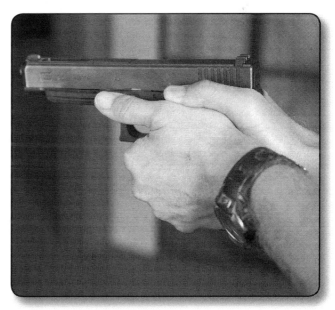

3.3.5 – Thumbs forward

I prefer a 100/100 grip since that's what you're going to do in combat and it's best to think about how you're going to drop the threat rather than how hard you're squeezing the gun with each hand. Both of your thumbs should be pointing forward, toward your target. I've found that the more things you have pointed at your target, the better chance you have at hitting it.

A lot of people have questions about how strong they should grip a pistol and I've found that consistency of grip equals consistency of shots. To be consistent without a pressure gauge there are only 2 options. One is to hold it with no power, just enough so it doesn't drop out of your hand. The other is with 100% power. Which one do you think will produce more consistent shots? How do you think you will be holding your weapon when you're being shot at? Also, the 100% grip cures "milking" the trigger. Try this: relax your hand and pretend to rapidly pull the trigger of a pistol with a heavy trigger pull. See your other fingers moving? This is "milking" the trigger. Now do it with your hand tightly clenched... it's impossible to milk the trigger.

Now that you've got the perfect grip, put the gun back in the holster and take the time to note the position of your hand. You need to establish the proper grip in the holster and you need to practice getting the right grip every time. Did I hear someone say dry fire? Practice drawing the gun from its holster and bringing it up on target making sure you have the right grip. Once you've got the gun in your hand and pointed at your target, the grip you've got is the one you're going to shoot with...get it right.

Here are a few ways you can check for a proper grip:

- Let go with the bottoms of both hands and the gun should hang straight down. (Figure 3.3.7)

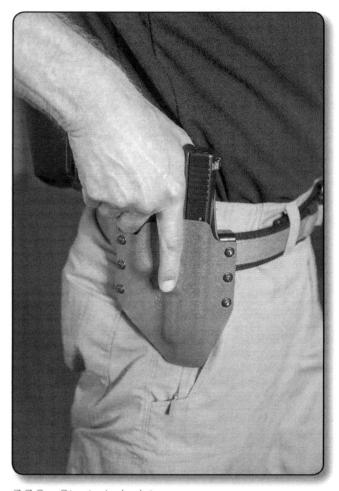

3.3.6 – Starts in holster

- Point the gun straight up in front of your face. The trigger finger should be straight across from the reaction hand thumb. (Figure 3.3.8)

- You should be able to support a pistol only with your reaction hand. (Figure 3.3.9)

- You don't need to adjust your grip between shots.

- Your sights come back the same way after recoil.

- You're shooting consistent groups.

3.3.7 – Let go with bottom

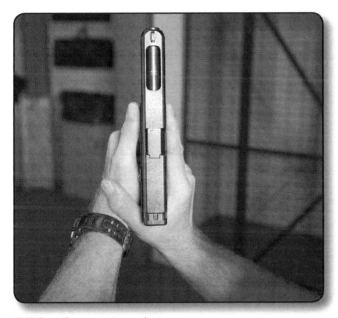

3.3.8 – Gun pointed up

3.3.9 – Reaction hand support

Carbine

The grip for the firing hand of a carbine is basically the same as on a pistol. Grip the rifle with your firing hand as high as possible with your middle finger touching the bottom of the trigger guard. This will help when doing magazine changes and clearing malfunctions. The gun is controlled with the support hand, leaving the strong hand to concentrate on fire-control and pulling the buttstock into your shoulder. Before I talk about the forward grip of the carbine, I need to talk about accessories such as lights or lasers. Before you start tricking out your bang-stick with cool-guy gear, make sure you can shoot it accurately. Take it out to the range and establish a solid shooting platform and note where your forward hand grips the gun. Now look at the open space you have available...this is where you need to mount any accessories. I see a lot of guys on the range saying they can't grip the gun properly because something is in the way. Don't let the tail wag the dog! You need to be able to shoot effectively first or that cool new light is only going to help your teammates find your corpse.

So now that we've cleared the playing field, grip your gun as far out on the handguard/rail as possible. I always ask my students, "If you were going to nail a 2x4 to a wall and only had two nails, where would you put the nails to give you the most support?" The answer is always the same, as far apart as

3.3.10 – Fire control system

3.3.11 – High grip

3.3.12 – Ready to shoot

You need to be able to shoot effectively first or that cool new light is only going to help your teammates find your corpse.

possible. If you want to support your gun, you need to do the same thing.

There are a number of different ways to grip the handguard, but it's important that some part of your hand is above the level of the barrel. The recoil of the gun is going to kick the gun up. If you're trying to hold the gun from underneath it's going to bounce up and pull out of your hand every time. For the same reason it's important that you take that hinge-point (elbow) out of the equation. Most people I see on the range shoot with the support elbow directly beneath the gun giving the weapon a perfect hinge to move around. This may be fine slow-fire on a static range hitting bull's-eyes, but is not going to cut it in combat. By simply rotating the arm out to the side, you eliminate the hinge and are better able to drive the gun with the reaction hand and send accurate rounds down range as fast as needed. As with the pistol I like to point anything I can at the target. In this case, depending on your grip, you can either point your thumb or your index finger.

3.3.13 – Grip far forward

3.3.14 – Grip on top

3.3.15 – Let go with strong hand

Here are a few ways you can check for a proper grip:

- Let go with the strong hand.
  The gun should stay in your shoulder.
  (Figure 3.3.15)

- Let go with the reaction hand.
  The gun should stay in your shoulder.
  (Figure 3.3.16)

- When shooting, your sights come back the same way after they recoil.

- You're shooting consistent groups.

3.3.16 – Let go with reaction hand

Here's a final piece of advice for a good grip, especially with the pistol. This one trick is guaranteed to cure 95.3 percent (made-up statistic) of all grip issues and I'm amazed by how few people do it...Practice grip strength! If you're one of those guys with a "weak-hand," you need to do strength-building exercises with your forearms, hands, and fingers. If you're limp-wristed or yellow-backed, there is nothing I can do for you... seriously though, this training is for anyone who wants to improve their shooting. There are several exercises you can do with weights to develop these muscle groups including the use of rubber bands and stress style squeeze balls or Dynaflex Powerball. This device uses gyro force (gyroscopic training) that is powered by the motion of your own hand/wrist. This motion produces torque that increases the faster you go. It develops forearm, hand, and finger strength all at the same time. It's a very popular training device among the rock climbing community and widely used by many NFL wide receivers and running backs to take their game to the next level. One day in the team room I was sitting there working my Powerball while talking on the phone. I showed one of the guys how to use it and he said he could instantly tell it worked the stabilizer muscles key in shooting. He went online right then and there and bought one. Within a week his pistol shooting improved so dramatically that all the guys had various ones on their desk within a month. It's something that I use for just ten to fifteen minutes a few times a week. If you get one, I recommend also buying the docking station/starter. It's a battery-operated starter that gets the inner ball rotating. Otherwise if you just buy the ball you'll have to get it rotating with the included string. Not a deal breaker, but the

3.3.17 – Captains of Crush

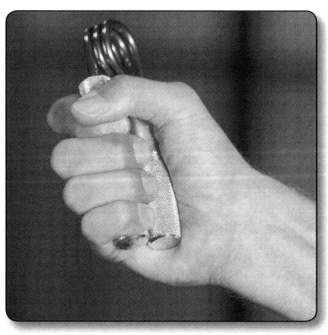

3.3.18 – Captains of Crush

docking station is worth the extra cost. They sell them with just the ball or in a combo set that includes the ball and docking station. I also use Captains of Crush grippers, which are expensive compared to others, but they get results and don't lose their tension. I use these in my car three times per week (Monday, Wednesday and Friday) for about ten to fifteen minutes, normally on my way to or from the range. Find a routine that works for you, just remember if you've got a weak grip, your shooting is likely to be the same.

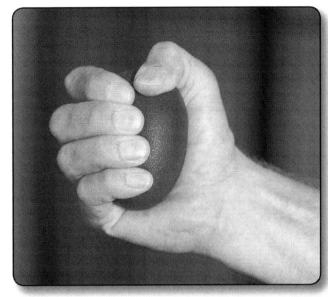

3.3.19 – Green Egg

How can I improve my grip? When will I work on grip strength?_____

_____

_____

_____

_____

_____

_____

_____

_____

_____

_____

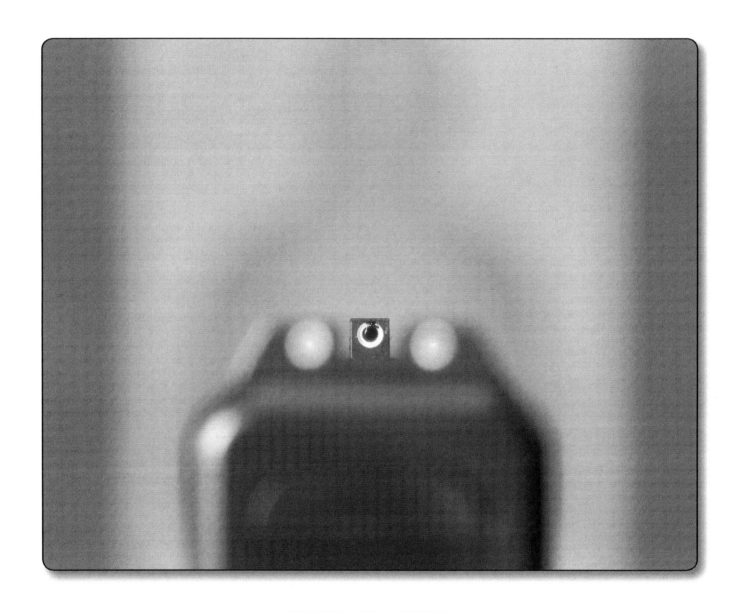

Even if your target is not moving, when the first round hits, your target could fall and you'll need to adjust your point of aim to fire for effect.

4

Sight Picture

"Aim Small; Miss Small."

Sight picture is what most people think about when they visualize aiming because that's exactly what it is—pointing your gun at your target. But rather than thinking about a still picture, I want you to think of it as a video (moving pictures). What's the difference? In home defense, combat, competitions, and hunting, your targets move! The picture you "took" for your first round may not be effective for your second. Even if your target is not moving, when the first round hits, your target could fall and you'll need to adjust your point of aim to fire for effect. The other reason to think video is that even if your target is not moving, you may be, or should be, so your image will be changing. So if sight video works for you, use it. If not, understand the importance of "taking multiple pictures and combining them together in a way that conveys movement."

First, let's talk about some old-school advice that many shooters, myself included, were taught that needs to be corrected. I'm talking about a center mass hold versus a 6 o'clock (aka lollipop or pumpkin-on-a-post) hold. I teach to always aim center mass (hence the name of my training company) and I thought the 6 o'clock went away with the mullet, but I still find students on the range practicing this ancient technique. If you're using a 6 o'clock hold, I'll give you three scientific reasons why you need to change your evil ways to become a better shooter.

The first is speed of accurate shot placement. If you are bringing your weapon up on target, you'll need extra time to figure out where to hold so your rounds land in the center of the intended target area. Why not skip this extra step and just aim center mass from the beginning? Rapid target acquisition is your

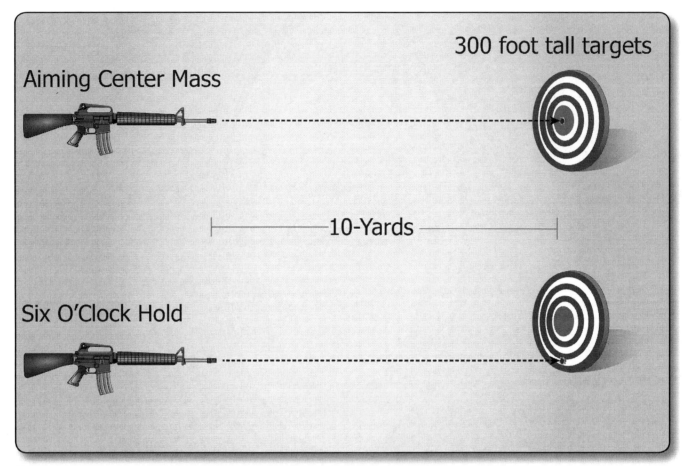

Aiming Center Mass

300 foot tall targets

10-Yards

Six O'Clock Hold

3.4.1 – Comparison of impacts of 6 o'clock hold and center hold

friend when shooting, whether in competition, on the battlefield, or late at night when an intruder enters your home. Of course you need to learn and practice mechanical hold-offs. But don't make that your starting point.

The second reason is that your rounds will hit different places depending on the size of your target and your distance from that target. I'm not sure why someone would practice different holds for different-shaped targets. I was taught that the 6 o'clock hold is used to sight in on bull's-eye targets at 200 yards. Fair enough, if you're only shooting bull's-eye targets, but this book is not about shooting round objects at known

distances. So the problem becomes how big the diameter of the circle is and at what distance you're shooting.

Rapid target acquisition is your friend when shooting, whether in competition, on the battlefield, or late at night when an intruder enters your home.

I sometimes exaggerate things to try to figure out if something will work or how it works. For example (Figure 3.4.1), let's assume you shoot with a 6 o'clock hold. You go to the range after work, but the only target in the back of your car is one that's a 300-foot-diameter bull's-eye. And let's say you're going to shoot from ten yards. (Hey, I said, exaggerate!) After you load up and get that target set up (with the help of a nearby crane), you step up to the firing line and try to decide which hold is better. For the first magazine you decide to use the center hold. The crane is still available, so it hoists you up to the center of the target. You call the line hot, then unload the entire magazine in 3.4 seconds, concentrating on sight alignment while merely pointing in the

Hold center mass and leave the pumpkins on a post for Halloween.

general vicinity of the center of the target. Not the best shooting you've ever done, but all shots are within twelve inches of the center of the target. After you get back down, you reload and try the 6 o'clock hold, which you were taught in boot camp in 1922. You take your time because you're on solid ground now and fire the whole magazine, really concentrating on the fundamentals of marksmanship. (You've got to shoot well to

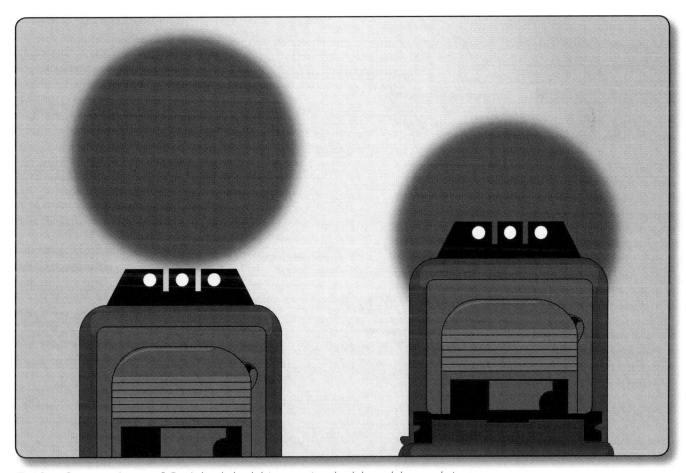

3.4.2 – Comparison of 6 o'clock hold to center hold on blurry dot

prove this is the best way!) Although you've got a tighter group (because you aren't on a crane), the shots are a little low compared to the other group. You break out your tape measure and discover that there is a 149-foot, ten-inch difference in the two groups. To decide which is closer to the center, you hop on your ATV and ride back about half a mile. From this vantage point you can see that the groups shot using the center hold are much closer to the center than the 6 o'clock hold group. If you were wondering if the distances you shot from would have similar effects, they will. Hold center mass and leave the pumpkins on a post for Halloween.

The final reason I put away my 6 o'clock hold with my Walkman has to do with how your eye works. Earlier I wrote about the importance of front sight focus. I assume you read that and you're a good student and already practicing this important point. When you use the 6 o'clock hold and focus on the front sight, the target becomes blurry and this is where the problem lies (Figure 3.4.2). The 6 o'clock hold might have a leg to stand on if the target were not blurry, but it is. Therefore your eye can't find the exact bottom of that pumpkin, so each time you shoot your shots move around as your eye tries to figure it out. The eye is amazing, and one of its attributes is the ability to find the

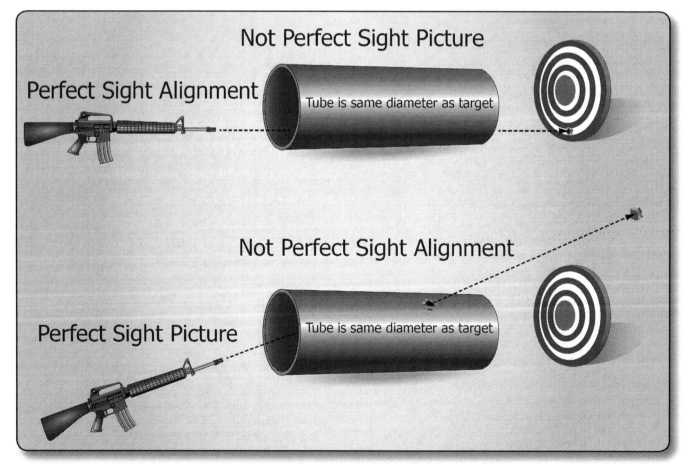

3.4.3 – Comparison of sight alignment and sight picture through tube

center of anything. This is why the center hold wins again. Although the target is blurry, it's still round and your eye can still find its center. This is true no matter what shape the target is, and your eye can do it before you even think about pressing the trigger.

The eye is amazing, and one of its attributes is the ability to find the center of anything.

Proper sight picture happens when you take your sights and place them on (overlay) a target and they are in the center of that target. This is what's meant by "center mass." To shoot quickly and effectively, you want to find the center of the largest part of your target and aim at it. If all you see is the side of your enemy's head, find the center of it and take care of business. The thing to remember is that sight picture only has to be on the target (anywhere on the target) to score a hit. Sight refinement, which I'll discuss in the next chapter, needs to be perfect or you risk missing completely.

To give you a quick idea, imagine shooting at an eight-inch circle with the circle at the end of an eight-inch-diameter tube. This shouldn't be too hard to imagine. If it is, please see Figure 3.4.3. If your sight refinement is perfect, you can fire anywhere into that tube—as long as you're pointing somewhere

at the target—and you will hit the target. But if your sight refinement is off, even just a little, you're likely to miss completely, even if your front sight is pointed directly at the center of the target.

Accept your wobble! Many shooters don't understand this aspect of marksmanship and spend all their efforts worrying about a little wobble, rather than ensuring that their sights are properly aligned. That little wobble will move you around the target, but how big is your wobble area? If you're shooting an eight-inch target, you've got eight inches to wobble. NOTE: If your wobble is eight inches or more, please clear and safe your weapon and go see your doctor. Unless you're trying to shoot gnats at twenty-five yards, don't worry about your wobble and concentrate on what's important: perfectly aligned sights.

To shoot quickly and effectively, you want to find the center of the largest part of your target and aim at it.

If you do shake when you shoot and are presented with a threat, put your sights center mass on your target and pull the trigger. If your sights are aligned, you'll be surprised to see that your rounds hit where you were aiming and your target will not be able to make fun of you for shaking, as it will be dead.

Unless you're trying to shoot gnats at twenty-five yards, don't worry about your wobble.

If you do need to hit a small target or make a low-percentage shot, remember to aim small, miss small. When I say "aim center mass" I don't mean the whole target. When you aim at a target, pick the smallest thing you can see to aim at. If it's bare, divide the target into four and aim at the center. This is especially important when transitioning between targets. If you're aiming at a one-inch target and miss by 10 percent you'll hit 1.1 inches from center. If you're aiming at person and are 10 percent off, you could easily miss completely. Aim small, miss small!

The importance of your sights and their relation to your target cannot be overstated. Everything we do in marksmanship comes down to having proper sight alignment and sight picture when the round goes off. These are really the only things that matter in marksmanship:

Body Position is only important because it allows you to hold proper sight alignment and maintain or adjust your sight picture.

Grip: You need to grip the gun correctly so you can maintain sight alignment.

Breathing: You breathe to relax with a handgun so you can focus on the sights, and you shoot during your natural respiratory pause with a rifle so your sight picture is the same with each shot. You continue to breathe in combat shooting so your eyes can continue to focus on your sight alignment.

Trigger control: The only reason you need to control the trigger is so you don't disturb the sights. If the gun were in a vise, you could slap that trigger and it wouldn't change where the round went.

Follow-through: Once again, this is just to preserve the sight alignment. And the fundamentals of combat marksmanship are just the beginning. The only reason we need to have the same cheek-weld, eye relief, head tilt, or anything else we do is in the quest to establish and maintain sight picture and sight alignment long enough to fire a shot without disrupting either one and quickly follow up with more shots if needed.

Training notes: _____

_____

_____

_____

_____

_____

_____

_____

_____

_____

_____

_____

_____

_____

_____

_____

*To provide exceptional customer service,
you must aim the gun and give the round a definite
direction of travel to the target.*

5

Sight Refinement

"To shoot accurately, it is crucial to maintain front sight focus throughout the entire shot."

I'm always surprised at how many decent (not great) shooters out there have never learned the fundamentals of marksmanship. Sure, they've heard about them or even talked about them, but if you ask them what they mean, they have no idea. Others have learned the fundamentals and have been slinging lead for years but have neglected to practice the skills needed to put effective firepower downrange using those little pieces of metal protruding from the tops of their guns. So here we discuss how to properly align (and refine) your sights in the event your scope, red-dot, or laser ends up quitting the fight before the enemy does.

Just after the invention of rifling, I put sight alignment as the second most important contribution to being able to fire an accurate shot. Sight alignment and sight picture are two terms that are often used interchangeably. It's fine to put them together once you understand both, but it's vital to know they are two different, and very distinct components. Sight alignment has nothing to do with the target (well, besides hitting it) while sight picture has little to do with your sights besides where you put them.

To provide exceptional customer service, you must aim the gun and give the round a definite direction of travel to the target. Accurate aiming with open sights is achieved by placing the front sight exactly in the middle of the rear sight with the top of the front and rear sight posts flush and equal amounts of light on either side of the front sight post. (Figure 3.5.1) With an aperture or peep sight, this is accomplished by putting the tip of the front sight post centered vertically, as well as horizontally, in the rear

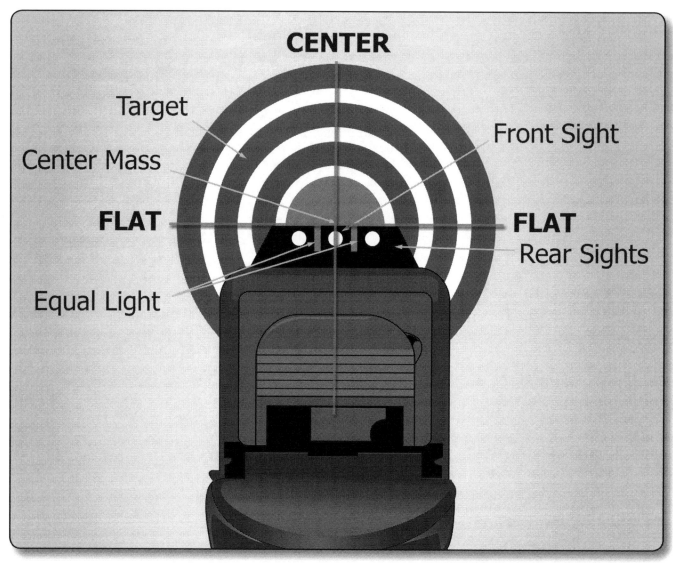

3.5.1 – Properly aligned pistol sights

sight aperture. It then becomes imperative to maintain this relationship between the sights while depressing the trigger and discharging the weapon—this is called sight refinement.

Sight alignment must be worked out with each type of gun you shoot, but the basics remain the same. There are a lot of different sights out there, and it's important to know how the manufacturer intended yours to be used. Some owner's manuals even include pictures or descriptions showing how they

Error is proportional to distance, so the greater the range, the more a small error in sight alignment will throw your impact off target.

should be aligned. If you're like me, you don't read directions, but maybe you could

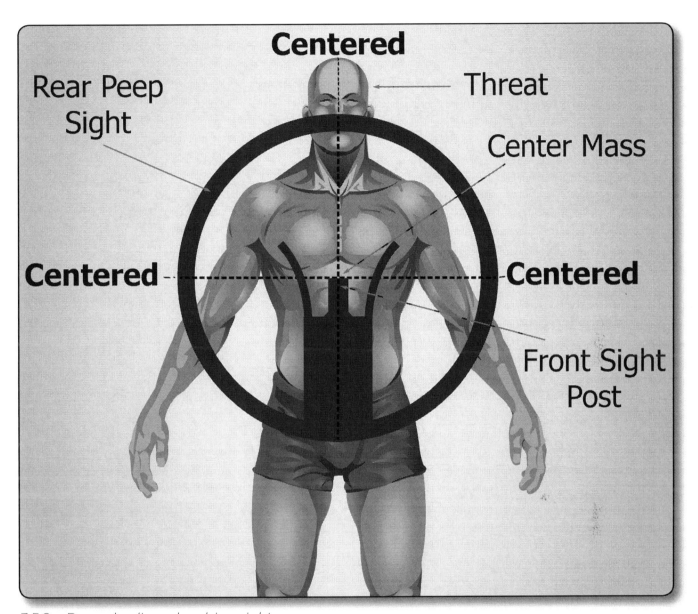

3.5.2 – Properly aligned carbine sights

take a peek when no one is looking—it could save you a lot of headaches on the range.

As you first learn to align your sights, a few things can go awry, but armed with the right knowledge, you'll be better prepared to make self-corrections. The first is known as an *angular shift error*. (Figure 3.5.3) This occurs if you fail to align the sights correctly as described above. As the amount of the

error or distance from your target increases, the hope of hitting the target decreases exponentially. If you're not aligning the sights with the same military precision required of a Marine Corps recruit folding his underwear, each time you shoot, the front sight post will be in a slightly different relationship with the rear sight and it will look more like you're shooting buckshot than a finely tuned instrument. Error is proportional

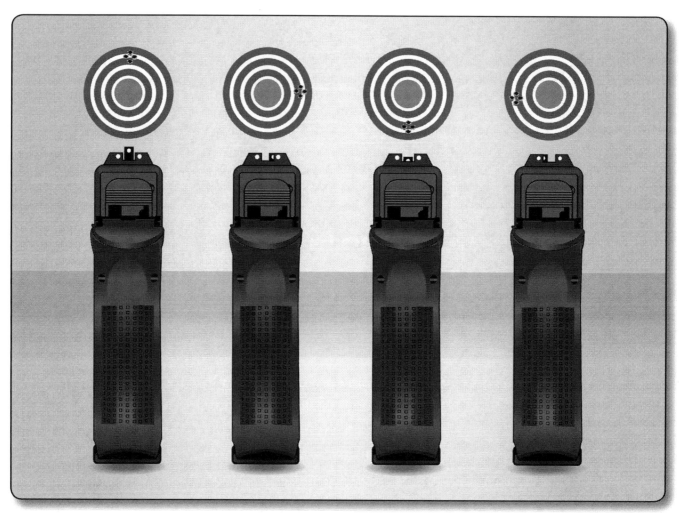

3.5.3 – Four sight angular shift errors

to distance, so the greater the range, the more a small error in sight alignment will throw your impact off target. If your sight alignment is off by just 1/16 inch at twenty feet, the result will be a 4.5-inch separation between point of impact and your intended target—assuming everything else is correct! Luckily there's an easy fix we'll get to soon.

The other problem, which has more to do with sight picture than sight alignment, is called a *parallel shift error*. This happens when the sights are aligned perfectly, but the gun is not aligned perfectly with the target. This means that if you're shooting at an eight-inch target, you can move your gun around in an eight-inch circle, no matter how far away you are, and you'll still hit the target in the same place your gun was in your imaginary circle back on the firing line. (Figure 3.5.4) If you're focused on the target instead of the front sight, small movements (the notorious wobble) appear magnified. This movement, though still there, will appear significantly reduced by focusing on your front sight. The takeaway for all this gunfighting geometry is that a bad sight alignment (angular shift error) is far more

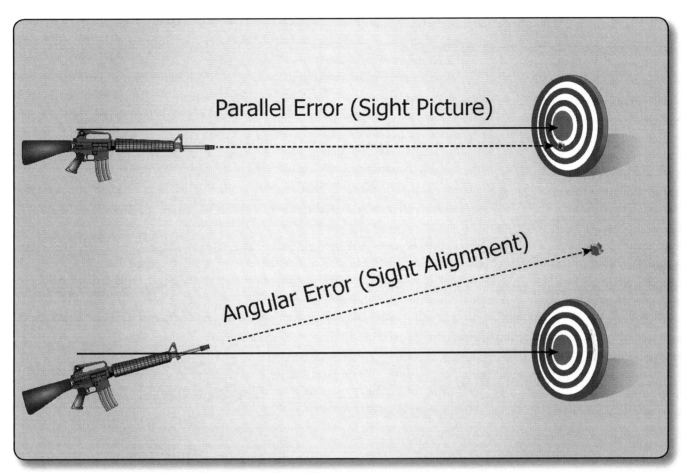

Parallel Error (Sight Picture)

Angular Error (Sight Alignment)

3.5.4 – Comparison of angular to parallel shift errors

detrimental than sight picture (parallel shift error) to hitting your target. Most of your effort should therefore go toward keeping the sights in correct alignment. So don't worry about your wobble. Holding the gun perfectly still is neither required nor possible without support.

Now comes the really tough part: *front sight focus!* If you've been around guns for any length of time, you've heard it, but what does it mean, and can you do it? What it means is that the front sight should be crystal clear, with the rear sights and target appearing blurry. I get it; this goes against everything your mind is screaming at you:

Focus on the target! But you need to fight that internal battle and focus only on the front sight. You also need to keep your eye on the front sight throughout each shot and not look at the target between shots. You know you might be doing this if: 1) your shots are going low; or 2) you can see the impacts of your rounds as you're shooting. Also, shooters focusing on the front sight will sometimes break that focus at the last millisecond before the round goes off and focus on the target. This is just as bad as not focusing on the front sight at all, and it's hard for the shooter to figure out why he's missing—he thinks he's looking at the front sight the whole time.

Every shooter has at least one thing that is the crux of shooting effectively. Mine was front sight focus for years, but then for some reason it changed to trigger manipulation. But if you've never had that "Aha!" moment with your front sight, there is a good chance you're not really focusing on it intently enough. In every course I run, even with experienced shooters, there is always at least one who is not focusing on their front sight. I'll have them bring the gun up, focus on the sight, and then describe in minute detail exactly what the sight looks like as they are pressing the trigger. When the gun goes off, they see that by some "miracle" the bullet fairy delivered the round to its intended target. Aha! If you haven't had that moment, next time you're at the range, just point your gun at a target, focus on the front sight and say, "Okay, I know it is not going to work, but I'm going to keep focusing on the front sight until the gun goes off. I follow

through, and my gun is back on target." I think you'll be pleasantly surprised.

One of the best tricks I learned and later taught in sniper school to help dramatically with front sight focus is to put a mark on the top middle of the front sight post (Figure 3.5.5). With this one step, I've seen people who have struggled for years to shoot tight

---

> ## If you've never had that "Aha!" moment with your front sight, there is a good chance you're not really focusing on it.

---

groups instantly start keyholing rounds. If you're not shooting groups as tight as your weapon will allow, try adding a mark and watch your group size shrink. In the same way that "aim small, miss small" works on your target, the smaller your point of focus, the smaller your groups. Learn to focus on the mark so intently that you get into the zone where you tune out everything around you and all you see is that mark.

To shoot accurately and effectively, you need to be able to shift your focus from very wide (battlefield, target) to narrow (front sight post, mark on front sight post). Getting and maintaining your sight picture is your wide image—now you need to narrow it down as small as possible. You need to focus so

3.5.5 – Front sight post with mark

narrowly, so closely that your whole world becomes a small mark on the middle of your front sight post. Focus on it so intently that you can describe the front sight and every defect on it. Then, stop thinking and get into the zone. You'll know when you're in the zone because you've been there before when you played sports, music, or anything you've focused on so much that your performance was effortless and perfect—that is the zone, and if you let yourself go there when you shoot, your shooting will perfect and effortless, too.

To mark your front sight post, I recommend using black or white metal paint or even nail polish and the tip of a toothpick. If you have a flat black post, put a white dot in the top center of it. If you have a white dot, put a small black dot on the top center of the dot. The goal is to make your focal point as small as you can see and focus on to get you into the zone. One word of caution: Do not paint over tritium sights. You can usually put a mark just above the tritium sights, which works just fine. If you find it doesn't work for you or you don't like it (unlikely) the paint will come right off.

Something truly amazing happens when you detach from emotion, relax, and focus on your front sight. Everything around you slows down and you can actually see more of what's really happening around you. See the images on the next spread. The first (Figure 3.5.6) is a group of dots, then Figure 3.5.7 shows the same image with an image of a

front sight post with a mark on it. Stare at the mark for about thirty seconds and see what happens.

Something truly amazing happens when you detach from emotion, relax, and focus on your front sight.

So what happened when you focused intently on the mark? If you're like most people, when you focus on the front sight the dots fade. When you focus on the mark, they disappear! That's what you want to happen to the world around you when you shoot in the zone. If you didn't see that change, try it again and really concentrate on the mark—bring it into focus until it's crystal clear and don't look away even for a split second. Initially, even blinking or quick shifts in gaze will make the dots reappear. It's important that if you need corrective lenses to bring the mark into focus that you wear them when training. I've seen the addition of glasses instantly fix years of poor shooting.

If that one didn't work for you or you need more proof that focusing on your front sight post is critical to shooting accurately, check out the images below. Figure 3.5.8 is a different type of optical illusion that again demonstrates that your eyes have a hard time focusing on one point when there is an overload of visual input. These lines

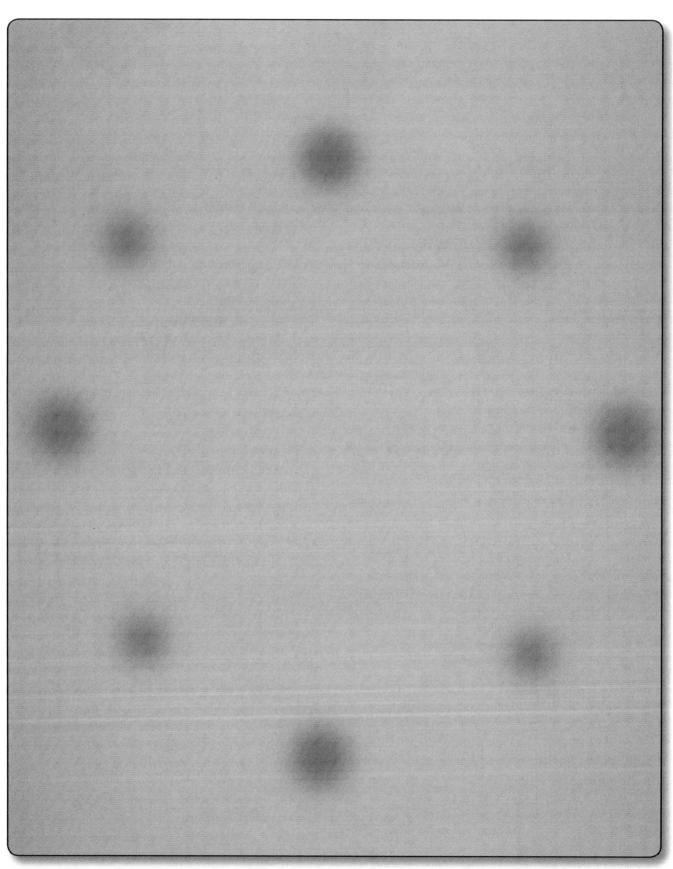

3.5.6 – Look at the circle of dots

3.5.7 – Now focus your eyes on the small mark on the front sight post

3.5.8 – The lines look like they're moving

3.5.9 – If you focus on the mark, the movement will stop

should look like they're moving, but when you concentrate on the mark (Figure 3.5.9) everything slows down.

If you focus on the mark, the image no longer appears to move. Why is that? The apparent movement is actually caused by your eye movements, not by the image. Your eye is trying to focus on too many things at once, and this back-and-forth eye movement is interpreted as movement in the image. The important thing to know is how to stop it. Focus on one point and don't let your eyes move off it until all movement around it stops. This is called front sight focus, and it will dramatically change the way you shoot if you've never seen it this clearly before.

Most of the time when told to "focus on the front sight," shooters let their eyes essentially use autofocus, and this is not enough. Your eye works by using accommodation to bend the lens of your eye to focus on objects at different distances. This is normally done reflexively on autofocus, but to obtain the crystal-clear focus needed for accurate shooting, you need to control the muscles in your eyes consciously. If you can't see or focus on the mark, focus on the space between the front and rear sights. The key is having two things that contrast each other so you can stay fixated on it until you get into the zone.

Rather than merely glimpsing to check for proper sight alignment, force yourself to stare at it for approximately thirty seconds.

Especially when you're first learning, this will help imbed the image of proper sight alignment into your mind so that it's more recognizable when you're on the range or, more important, in a personal-defense situation. One thing that will help is to take a picture of your front sight post and look at it repeatedly every day until it's ingrained in your mind. Anytime you need to shoot quickly, your mind will be instantly drawn to the familiar image and your eyes will instantly focus on the mark and be able to align the sights quickly.

Too many shooters try to force a shot that's not there and waste a round, or worse.

To shoot accurately, it is crucial to maintain front sight focus throughout the entire shot. It's also important to maintain that focus from when the round goes off until you get your next sight picture. The way to do this is to work on all the mechanical parts of shooting to the point where they become natural movements (muscle memory) and you can then spend all your mental power processing the continuous visual input you're receiving. Just as when you are learning to drive a stick shift, all your movements are very mechanical—clutch in, move stick, blinker on, clutch out—but once you learn to manipulate the controls you do all those movements subconsciously by following the directions from your eyes—you're driving with your eyes.

You must shoot the same way. Practice your trigger press until it's smooth and consistent, then you can relax and focus on the mark. Let your eyes focus on the front sight as your mind relaxes and takes in and processes all the data needed to deliver a well-placed shot. With an open mind and the picture of what your eye needs to see in your mind, let your eyes pull the trigger, and practice visual patience. If the shot is not there, you need to be patient and wait until it is. Too many shooters try to force a shot that's not there and waste a round, or worse. I've heard it for many years and it's true: You can't miss fast enough!

You may have heard this before, but I don't believe in the "front sight, front sight, front sight" mantra I was taught (I was taught you're supposed to just say this in your head as you shoot).

As a Master Training Specialist (MTS), I learned that people learn and perform much better from visual input than from auditory (this is why visualization works, while people who talk to themselves are crazy). So rather than saying the words "front sight," I recommend putting a picture of what the front sight should look like in your mind and not continue pressing the trigger unless that is what you see with your eyes. Again,

a great way to ingrain this image quickly is to take a picture of your front sight post and look at it often.

Inattention to correct sight alignment can often be traced back to the failure to fully understand its importance—now you don't have that excuse. Without this knowledge, you may very well start off on the right track, getting everything lined up just right, but then something catches your eye you and lose that perfect sight alignment as you continue to press the trigger. Or if you start to notice a wobble, you'll lose focus on the front sight to make sure you're still on target and will then lose sight alignment (angular), which as we learned earlier is much more important than sight picture (parallel). No more excuses!

Now that you understand the importance of always focusing on your front sight, I can tell you that there are definitely times when you will not want to (or need to) focus so keenly on your sights. Proximity negates skill, so depending on the threat, distance, time available, and possible collateral damage, you will need to decide where you should

---

To obtain the crystal-clear focus needed for accurate shooting, you need to control the muscles in your eyes consciously.

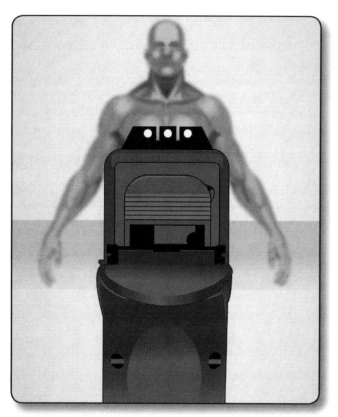

3.5.10 – Sight Priority Focus

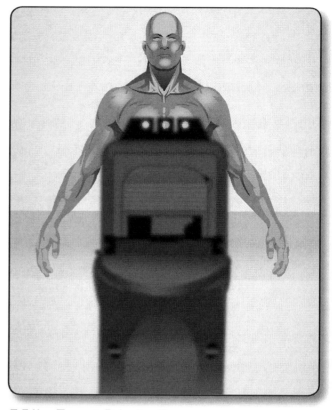

3.5.11 – Target Priority Focus

direct your focus during any engagement. If you're close to your target and speed is more important than pinpoint accuracy, you will use a target priority focus (TPF). On the other hand, if you're farther away from your target, have more time, or need to make a precision shot on a low-percentage target, you'll need to use a sight priority focus (SPF).

This is called front sight focus, and it will dramatically change the way you shoot if you've never seen it this clearly before.

When making this decision on where to focus, it's important to note that it's not an all-or-none decision. You're not focusing only on the sights or only on the target. As with exposure on a camera, it's a sliding scale of where your priority is, and that scale will be constantly changing throughout the gun battle or competition. You could have someone pop up close to you with his gun drawn. You're only three yards away and he's facing you, standing up against a brick wall. This means target priority focus, engage. You then look up and see another threat twenty-five yards away. He is looking at your team, waiting for a chance to take another shot at them. You can just see the side of his head and the angle you're at is not optimal since if you were to miss, your round could sail past and hit a bystander. This means sight priority focus, engage. Check you out, hero!

So now that you understand there are different places to focus and reasons for each, it's important to practice them. Even if you are far enough away that you want to focus on the sights rather than the target, you may not be physically able to, due to your body alarm response (BAR). Your body alarm response is your body's way of trying to help you out, but it usually doesn't feel that way. This will affect your shooting through changes like increased respiratory rate (hyperventilation), auditory exclusion, and changes in your ability to focus on close objects such as your front sight post. You can reduce the effects through constant proper practice, but you can never eliminate them completely. It's important to practice shooting while focusing on the target so you'll be better prepared when the time comes.

Another way we miss shots is what I mentioned earlier: lack of visual patience. You're waiting for the shot to break and it's taking longer than expected, so you just start slapping the trigger like it owes you money. In the process, you lose sight alignment and the round. Don't get anxious for the round to go off. Relax and let your mind process what's going on. If you've been told to just keep steady pressure on the trigger until the gun goes off, make sure you also keep your foot on the gas as your car spins out

of control. Don't feel bad—I was taught the same thing. Treat your trigger like a gas pedal, and if you're losing control, let off the gas! Once you're back in control, let your eyes control the trigger as you keep the sights aligned until the shot breaks. Remember, you can only shoot as fast as you can see. You need to wait as long as it takes to see what you need to see before you shoot. The only other option is missing the shot. You'll then need to make up the shot (if possible) and hope you didn't hit something you were not willing to destroy. As the saying goes, speed is fine, but accuracy is final.

Don't get anxious for the round to go off. Relax and let your mind process what's going on.

This is why I like to refer to sight refinement, rather than sight alignment. For me, to align something is a one-time deal: Line up the sights and then go to the next step and pull the trigger. But refinement is something that continues—you line up the sights and keep them aligned as you go to the next step. Think in terms of sight refinement instead of sight alignment. It's not a one-time thing (align and shoot), it's a constant process that needs to be adjusted and managed all the way through the follow-through. Missing one-hundredth of a second of visual input is enough to make you have no idea where your shot went. If this slight change of words helps you remember to keep adjusting (refining) your sight alignment as you press the trigger, then use it. If you've used the term sight alignment for more than twenty years and you know you need to keep aligning them, then use that. I don't care what you use as long as it helps you put effective rounds downrange.

Treat your trigger like a gas pedal, and if you're losing control, let off the gas!

Sights: Iron, Backup/ BUS, and Reflex (Red Dot)

The only things I call "backup sights" are the ones in my gun bag that I can install in the event something traumatic happens to the sights on my gun. Iron sights need to be thought of as tools in your toolbox, not something used only in case of emergency. If you run a red dot on your carbine and need to take a long-range precision shot, the right tool for that job may not be your red dot—it could very well be those things you've been calling backups. It's the same reason you shouldn't call your nonshooting hand your "weak" hand. It's just doing something else, but it's still important. It's important to learn how to shoot with your iron sights first before using optics anyway; this will make you a better marksman.

Reflex or red-dot optics do not obviate the need for marksmanship, and I think the "point-and-shoot" ability these offer has made many forget about the other six rules of marksmanship. Before they became popular, taking a shot out past 200 yards with a carbine was commonplace among those claiming the moniker of "marksman." Nowadays I run classes for young military guys who have only used a red dot and are worried when I take them past twenty-five yards!

If you continue to apply solid shooting fundamentals with a red dot, you can still use it to your advantage for long-range engagements. For accurate shots with a red dot, make sure the sight is parallax free, and consider turning down the brightness to force your eye to focus on the dot, just as on the mark on a front sight post.

Sight picture with optics is more important than sight alignment because you get your sight alignment done when you sight in your gun. After you sight in, the only thing you need to worry about is your sight picture, and this is made easier by the way optics are designed. What an optic does is to put the reticle (dot) on the same focal plane as the target, so you just need to put it where you want to hit and hold it there until the shot breaks. Red-dot optics should be mounted at arm's length on your rifle, as they work best at that distance from your eyes. Doing this also helps you to have a wider field of view when acquiring targets and shooting.

If it's too close to your eye, it will be like trying to assess the battlefield while looking through a toilet paper tube.

Red-dot optics should be mounted at arm's length on your rifle, as they work best at that distance from your eyes.

I also recommend you practice shooting a dead optic, which is almost like instinctive fire, except you have the inside ring of your optic and possibly a front sight post to use as sighting instruments. How far can you shoot accurately if your optic dies and you don't have time to flip up your sights? Should you transition? It's best to have all these questions answered ahead of time so you don't need to make a time-sensitive decision when time is short. So why not just run with your iron sights up all the time? Because under stress, your eye will try to help you out by aligning anything it sees in the center of your focal area. This means your rear sight, red dot, and front sight. It will slow down your ability to sight in and reduce your accuracy. Keep your iron sights down and practice flipping them up when needed.

Training notes: _____

_____

_____

_____

_____

_____

_____

_____

Though shooting during your natural respiratory pause helps in long-range shooting, it is extremely detrimental on a fast-paced battlefield or competition course.

6

Focused Breathing

"For effective combat shooting, you should do your best to breathe normally."

Okay, this one has always puzzled me. When I hear the term "breathing," I assume it has something to do with oxygen being exchanged in the lungs via the pie hole. But whenever I hear people talking about it as it relates to marksmanship, it always seems to be some form of holding your breath, or not breathing! So once again I'm here to right a wrong that's been perpetuated throughout our community for many years and get you on the road to recovery. Sit back, take a deep breath, and relax as I discuss proper breathing for combat marksmanship.

I remember being taught what many of you were also taught in regard to breathing as a marksmanship fundamental: to hold your breath. At the time it made sense. I was told this by an instructor who was a better shooter than I and who was running the course of instruction I was attending. I was in the military at the time and being taught by some of the best shooters in the world. Specifically I was told: "Shoot during the natural respiratory pause." I did this for many years as a SEAL sniper and never found any reason to question what I had learned.

Now, before my long-range brethren attack me, there are times when this technique should be used, namely when taking long-range shots. What is long-range? That's a topic for a later discussion, but for now let's define it as any range nearing the

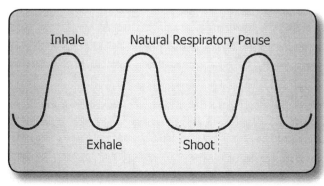

3.6.1 – Natural respiratory pause

maximum effective range of you or your weapon system. For these distances, it is still important to use every fundamental to your advantage to ensure your round finds its target. But though shooting during your natural respiratory pause helps in long-range shooting, it is extremely detrimental on a fast-paced battlefield or competition course.

From a scientific standpoint, your body needs energy to do work. Your body gets the energy it needs by combining food molecules with oxygen in a process called cellular respiration. Your body combines glucose with oxygen to release energy your body can use. The chemical reaction looks something like this:

$$C_6H_{12}O_6 + 6\ O_2 \longrightarrow 6\ CO_2 + 6\ H_2O =$$
energy your body can use

Like your body, fire also needs fuel and oxygen to sustain itself. Your muscles and other parts of your body, like your eyes, need a constant supply of glucose and oxygen to provide energy for your muscles and to support other functions. All parts of your body depend on breathing and circulation working together to deliver the oxygen needed by your body's cells and to remove the carbon dioxide produced by all cells in the body.

The Effects of Lack of Oxygen

The part of your body that is most sensitive to lack of oxygen is your brain. Lacking oxygen, your brain is immediately affected, and if this continues parts of the brain can be permanently damaged. The next body part affected by lack of oxygen is your eyes, and both are critical to combat shooters.

The following is a list of effects on the body from a lack of oxygen. This list is from The National Institute of Neurological Disorders and Stroke:

Motor Skills

The cerebellum is responsible for much of our coordinated movement and balance. Cell death can lead to jerkiness and other motor problems. An onset of poor coordination can be a sign of oxygen deficiency in the brain. With oxygen levels low, brainpower becomes focused on preserving core life functions over fine motor skills.

Visual Acuity

After the brain, the next body part affected by lack of oxygen is the eye. Although the first effects may be minor and hard to notice, your eyes' ability to focus is immediately diminished as the level of oxygen supplied to the eyes decreases. If oxygen is withheld longer, the eye can develop a nystagmus, which is an involuntary movement.

Heart Rate

When the brain is not receiving enough oxygen, the heart rate will increase in an attempt to deliver more oxygen.

Concentration

With mild oxygen deficiency to the brain, you will notice difficulty with concentration and attentiveness. This difficulty with mental tasks can extend to poor judgment.

We all know that breathing is essential to life, but it is also an essential part of shooting. The loss of the attributes listed above is certainly not what you want in the middle of a firefight! Because of many shooters' misunderstanding of this marksmanship fundamental, most shooters I work with are holding their breath as they try in vain to hit their targets. As they hold their breath, their vision quickly deteriorates and their hands begin to tremble. As their shot groups widen, they revert to what they were previously taught and try to hold their breath even more, making the situation worse. Effective shooting is all about relaxing, and you can't relax while holding your breath. Your eyes' ability to focus on the front sight is also hampered while holding your breath, so it's important to give your body the oxygen it needs.

So we know we don't want to hold our breath when we shoot, but we do need to control our breath. If you have been exerting yourself and are huffing and puffing like a three-pack-a-day smoker on a 5K run, you need to slow down your breathing to control your sights. The best way to accomplish this is through a technique called *autogenic breathing*. This is simply taking a deep breath for a count of four, holding for a count of four, and then exhaling for a count of four. Repeat this three times, and it should help to slow down your breathing enough to control your sights. You can do this as you're getting ready to shoot or even while you're shooting. The most important part I've found is to really exhale completely before taking the next breath. It really has a calming effect that will allow you to shoot more accurately. For effective combat shooting, you should do your best to breathe normally. Relax and breathe throughout your trigger pull, and you'll find it much easier to acquire and maintain a good sight picture.

Effective shooting is all about relaxing, and you can't relax while holding your breath.

Try breathing the next time you're dry-firing or are at the range. Not only is it good for your body, but it's good for your shooting as well! If you're taking that long-range shot, go ahead and shoot during your natural respiratory pause, but if not give your brain and your eyes the oxygen they need to do their jobs.

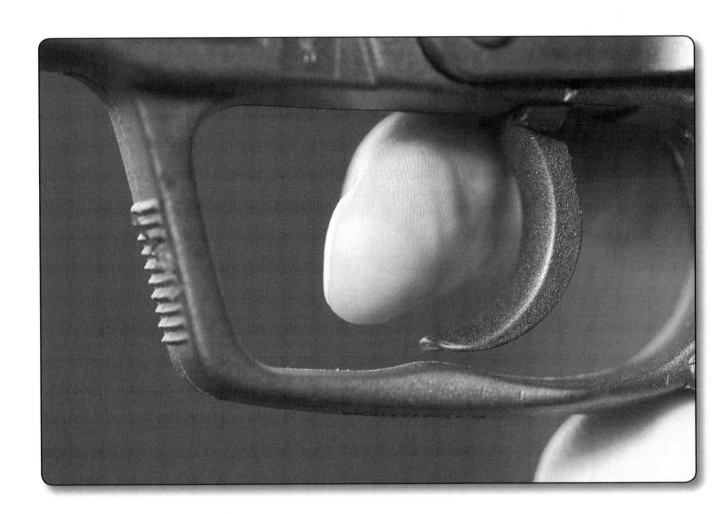

The two main reasons pistols are harder to shoot than rifles are the shorter sight radius and the trigger-to-weapon weight ratio.

7

Trigger Control

"Don't let the tail wag the dog!"

Trigger control is all about touch, and what I'm about to tell you is, to many, a touchy subject. So before I get started I want to talk about cognitive dissonance in training. Cognitive dissonance is the feeling of anxiety when you're presented with conflicting ideas. In firearms training, this would be when you've learned and practiced something one way for years and someone shows you a new way of doing it. This has always been one of the hardest things for me to overcome as an instructor. I experienced this firsthand when I wrote an online article on trigger finger placement. I contended the long-held belief that you must contact the trigger on the middle of the pad at the tip of your trigger finger. Although I gave compelling evidence that there is a better way, I received negative comments from people who didn't even try the new technique. They fought for their beliefs due to strong cognitive dissonance. So before you read any more, you need to ask yourself which is more important: being a better shooter or sticking to traditions.

> ## *Cognitive dissonance is the feeling of anxiety when you're presented with conflicting ideas.*

Trigger control needs to be maintained throughout the firing sequence, and this is especially difficult with a pistol. The two main reasons pistols are harder to shoot than rifles are the shorter sight radius and the trigger-to-weapon weight ratio. Anytime your trigger weight is more than the weight of the weapon, you've got your work cut out for you. This is why "race guns" (used in competitions) are heavy with light triggers, and the guns we shoot in combat, law enforcement and personal defense are the opposite. So what works for someone with a competition gun shooting paper targets will not work downrange with your government-issued sidearm.

The first thing you need to do for good trigger control is establish a good grip. Once that's done, wherever your finger hits that trigger is the best place for you to put your finger.

Unfortunately, a lot of what is being taught comes from these great range shooters and what works for them. I'm not saying that what they teach is wrong, and I'm sure it works with their specially made guns—it just might not be the best technique for combat operations or any off-range shooting when you've got to control a tiny trigger with two gallons of adrenaline pumping though your system.

What if you were learning how to drive a race car and your instructor told you all car seats had to be set to the same distance from the steering wheel? It didn't matter how tall you were, your body shape, or if your arms looked like you came from *Planet of the Apes*—you will keep that seat in the

same position. Of course you're going to listen—he's a great driver!

Does this sound right to you? Of course not; so why should it make sense when a firearms instructor tells you the "law" about where you need to put your finger? Think about all the different sizes, shapes, and strengths of our hands. Look at the finger joints alone of any group of shooters, and you'll see they are all in different places. How then can it make sense that they all put their fingers on a trigger in the same place and be expected to shoot well? Now think about all the different sizes and shapes of handguns out there, and we're all still going to put our finger in the same place?

I know this is going to upset some people. For almost twenty years I was told exactly where to put my finger on the trigger, and when I first started instructing, I was regurgitating the same company line I'd been told. I would tell students where to put their fingers, and if it didn't work for them (normally some whining about their hands being "different")

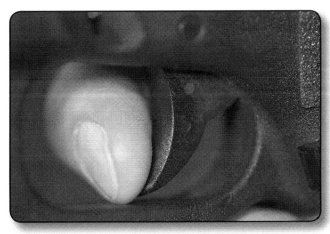

3.7.1 – Tip of the finger on trigger

I would have them change (weaken) their grips so they could put their fingers where they were told. It never worked well, and I usually deemed them "bad shooters."

If you do need to take more than one shot, re-prepping the trigger during recoil will not only help you shoot faster, but you will also be much more accurate.

It took a while, but I finally took off my blinders and realized you shouldn't adjust 99 percent of where your hand comfortably contacts your gun (grip) so that 1 percent (tip of the finger) goes where someone with different hands than yours told you it works best. If you have an instructor who is telling you where to put your finger, give him the finger! Actually, he'll need to give you *his* finger if he's telling you where you need to

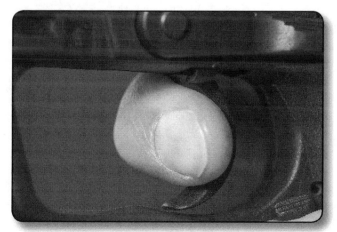

3.7.2 – Trigger placement with good grip

put it. Your hands are not the same as his (go ahead, look), so you may need to put your trigger finger somewhere else.

The first thing you need to do for good trigger control is establish a good grip. Once that's done, wherever your finger hits that trigger is the best place for you to put your finger. Different person = different place. Different gun = different place. With the gun comfortably in your hand, you'll have much better recoil management and trigger control.

The most important thing is being able to pull the trigger while maintaining correct sight alignment. In the end it doesn't matter how you do it, as long as you get it done and can do it quickly and consistently. Anyone who tells you differently is likely more concerned with doing it their way than putting effective fire downrange.

One technique that will help you master the trigger without disturbing the sights is your trigger prep. Prepping the trigger means taking out any slack in your trigger before the hammer even moves. Trigger prep is important, because you can only focus for a limited time. Learning to quickly eliminate this excess movement will help reduce the time you have your gun up and the possibility of disturbing your sights. Just as important is stopping as soon as the trigger breaks and the round goes off. This is called mashing the trigger, which will mess up your follow-through and slow down any follow-on shots that are needed.

If you do need to take more than one shot, re-prepping the trigger during recoil will not only help you shoot faster, but you will also be much more accurate. When you move your finger quickly, you are very likely going to disturb the sights, so doing that during the time when your sights are moving anyway is like using the movement as camouflage. By the time your sights settle on the next target, your trigger is already prepped and you're ready to shoot again.

I was taught years ago that you need to apply consistent pressure to the trigger until the shot breaks. This seemed to work most of the time, but there were times when someone would move in my path, or my tango would move and my shot would break outside of center mass. I realized the problem was the rule I was following: that I had to keep pulling the trigger until the shot broke. I've learned to form a direct link from my eyes to my trigger finger so that when something in my visual field changes, the movement of my finger is ready to respond. A critical aspect of learning this is learning to sense the pressure on your finger. You need to really feel it and connect that feeling to what your eyes are seeing.

As your finger is moving, make sure you press the trigger straight to the rear so you don't pull your shots. If what you're doing now works, don't change it. But if it doesn't, give this a try. (Remember, use what works, not what anyone else tells you.) Keep the second joint of your trigger finger

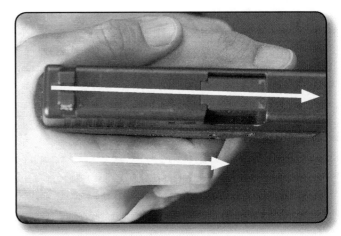

3.7.3 – Second Knuckle Straight

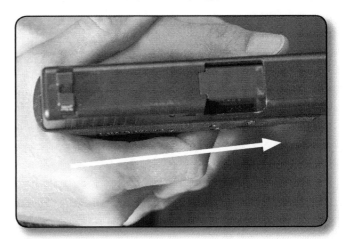

3.7.4 – Second Knuckle "Pushing" Left

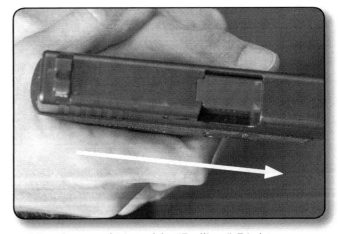

3.7.5 – Second Knuckle "Pulling" Right

pointed straight at your target as you press the trigger. This way, it's nearly impossible to push or pull the shot with your trigger finger. The tip of the finger may work well with a light trigger on a heavy gun, but with a heavy trigger you're much more likely to pull shots when trying to balance the tip of your finger on the trigger. I've used this technique to improve the shooting of many SEAL sniper students over the years, and if you're contorting your hand in the name of finger placement, it will help you too. Give it a try next time you dry-fire (you do dry-fire, don't you?) and then try it out on the range.

Keep the second joint of your trigger finger pointed straight at your target as you press the trigger.

Another aspect to consider is where your finger is vertically along the face of the trigger. The trigger is a lever just like any other, and you need to adjust your finger up or down on the lever to achieve the best mechanical advantage. Lowering your finger just a little may give you just enough

leverage to achieve a smooth pull without disturbing the sights.

As you press back, the pressure on the trigger needs to come only from the trigger finger. To do this, you need to have a good grip and not let any part of your trigger finger drag along the frame of the gun. Some shooters tend to squeeze the trigger with their whole hand, and this will cause the sights to move off target. To train your body to pull the trigger correctly, I recommend dry-fire training. Start with a weapon that has been cleared and safe. Now establish a proper grip on the gun and sit with the gun in your lap. Practice pulling the trigger like this until you really feel how the trigger moves. You can make major improvements in your trigger pull by doing this because there is nothing else to think about. Once you're comfortable with this, stand up, mount your gun, and do the same thing with your eyes closed. Again, all you need to do is manipulate the trigger without worrying about your sights. After that, do the same thing pointing at a blank wall. It's much

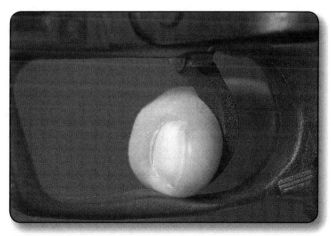

3.7.6 – Finger high on face of trigger　　　*3.7.7 – Finger low on face of trigger*

easier to see if you're maintaining proper sight alignment on a blank wall than it is looking at a target. Of course, the final step is to add a target.

For an effective shot, the pressure on the trigger needs to be smooth and even. This does not mean slow! You can pull the trigger as fast as you want, as long as it's smooth. Smooth is fast, but slow is just slow. Speed in shooting comes from getting the gun out of the holster, mounted, and your sights aligned on target quickly. If you work on doing these things fast, you can use the extra time for sight refinement and smooth trigger manipulation. I see a lot of guys on the range who take their time getting their gun on target and then start mashing the trigger in an attempt to "shoot fast." Remember to make up time anywhere else than your trigger squeeze!

Your trigger finger should never leave the face of the trigger during the shooting sequence. I put my finger on the trigger as soon as I can safely do so after I've identified

3.7.8 – Finger coming off trigger

my target and made the decision to shoot. Normally this is right after my gun is out of the holster and rotated to point at my target. If I need to shoot from the hip I'm ready; if not I'll continue up to fully mount the weapon. My finger will begin moving as soon as my eyes see what they need to see to take the shot. As I stated earlier, I don't pull the trigger with my finger: I pull it with my eyes. As soon as the shot breaks, I pause with the trigger to the rear, normally as the muzzle is coming up. I then let the trigger out, only until I feel the sear reset. By this time my muzzle has settled and I have pressure back on the trigger, ready to shoot again if needed. This is my follow-through, which I cover in chapter 19. It is only after I have decided I no longer need to deliver exceptional customer service that I take my finger off the trigger.

As stated earlier, rather than saying, "front sight, front sight, front sight," I have a picture in my mind of what I need to see for my finger to move, and I pull the trigger with my eyes. If the picture is not there, my finger does not move; but as long as I see that picture my finger will continue to move until the picture changes or the shot breaks. To do this, you need to remember to practice visual patience. Wait for the gun to shoot. Do what you need to do. Your gun is accurate—your job is to not mess it up!

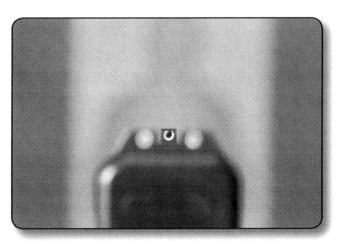

3.7.9 – Keep a picture of a perfect front sight in your head

Let's review:

1. Start off with a good grip. Don't let the tail wag the dog!

2. Let your finger land naturally on the trigger.

3. Consider moving your finger lower on the face of the trigger.

4. Keep the middle knuckle of your trigger finger pointed at your target.

5. Prep the trigger.

6. Pull the trigger with your eyes.

7. Make sure it's smooth and that you feel the pressure on your finger.

8. Keep finger in contact with the trigger.

9. Re-prep the trigger during the recoil.

10. Dry-fire.

Of course, unless you're in the process of engaging a target, you need to keep your finger off the trigger. One of the main reasons to keep your finger off the trigger is the body's startle response. When we are startled our bodies naturally contract muscles, which often leads to unintended discharges if the finger is on the trigger. This could be a bad day if you're pointing your gun at something you aren't willing to destroy.

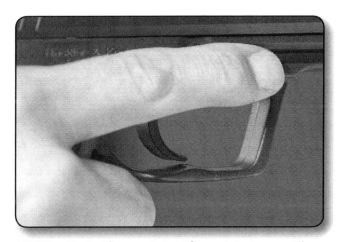

3.7.10 – Keep finger away from trigger until ready to shoot

Training notes: _____

_____

_____

_____

_____

_____

_____

Neglecting follow-through can negate all the steps you previously took to deliver an accurate shot.

8

Follow-Through

"Following through means seeing what you've started through to the end."

A lot of people have a problem with the last fundamental, and not just when it comes to effective shooting. Following through means seeing what you've started through to the end. For instance, what if I wrote the first five or six chapters of this book but never finished it? Lack of follow-through is the reason we can't stand politicians. They tell us they're going to do something, but it never happens. When it comes to shooting, you need to finish what you've started too. You need to see each shot through to completion, and I aim to show you how.

Colonel Jeff Cooper once said: "The best defense against a vicious attack is a more vicious, explosive and overwhelming, offensive counterattack, followed through to the very end with the attacker being down, disabled, and out of the fight." So following through with each shot means maintaining our shooting fundamentals for a fraction of a second after the shot breaks. But it also means we have to follow through with the fight until our enemy is no longer a threat. I will cover this last point later, but let's start with the marksmanship part of follow-through.

Follow-through is a term most of us have heard from the first time anyone taught us about marksmanship. But it is also one of the most neglected. Maybe because it's last on every list that shooters assume it's the least important, but neglecting follow-through can negate all the steps you previously took to deliver an accurate shot. Follow-through simply means that you continue to apply all fundamentals of marksmanship after the weapon fires. A proper follow-through allows the weapon to deliver the round precisely on target and recoil in a natural and consistent manner.

3.8.1 – Trigger Prepped

3.8.2 – Stay relaxed when shot breaks

3.8.3 – Stop moving finger when round goes off

3.8.4– Reset trigger during recoil

3.8.5 – Prepare for next shot

Here's what you need to do to follow through in shooting:

1. Call the shot (more on this later).

2. Stop pressing the trigger.

3. Stay relaxed and do not react to the sound or movement of the weapon.

4. Maintain your shooting platform, including head position.

5. Maintain proper grip.

6. As the gun is recoiling, let out the trigger only until it resets.

7. Re-prep the trigger for follow-on shots.

8. Reacquire sight picture and sight alignment after your muzzle settles.

You know you are actually following though if you can see the muzzle flash in daylight or see the front sight come up out of the rear notch.

Looking at this list, you can see that follow-through is just continuing to employ all the other fundamentals after the gun goes bang and preparing for the next shot if needed. Do not think of the shot breaking as the final step in taking a shot. I see too many people on the line firing a shot and coming straight back to their retention, or low ready, position. If this sounds like you, you're not following through and you'll never master the art of shooting. You know you are actually following though if you can see the muzzle flash in daylight or see the front sight come up out of the rear notch. To shoot faster and more accurately, remember these tips for your follow-though:

1. Don't mash the trigger. Stop pressing as soon as the shot breaks.

2. Keep focusing on the mark on your front sight.

3. Your trigger reset and prep should happen as the gun is recoiling.

4. Keep your finger on the trigger throughout.

5. Stop letting the trigger out as soon as you feel or hear the sear reset.

As you learn to follow through, do so to the same spot on a static target, but as you get better, practice lining up your sights to a new place each time. In combat, your target will be moving—if not, it's dead and you don't need to waste your ammo.

The first step to a successful follow-through is a proper and consistent grip. The reason the grip is important to follow-through is that it will determine how your gun recoils after the shot. If your grip is not even or consistent, your recoil will vary and your shot placement will not be consistent. Even pressure with your grip means both your hands on the gun. If you're trying to grip the gun with different pressures with each hand (i.e., 60/40), the gun will recoil to the side of less resistance and affect your follow-through.

A well-executed follow-through needs to happen after every round you shoot. The math should be pretty simple. However many shots you take, always remember to stay on the target, acquire another sight picture, and be ready to take one additional shot. So for example, if you're firing a two-shot string, you need to be ready to take the third shot. I've found this is the best way to ensure a good follow-through. Rather than trying to think about all the steps needed, simply prepare yourself and your gun to fire another shot.

Speed doesn't come just from doing things faster. It comes from doing things smoothly and consistently.

We've all heard the common shooting expression: "Slow is smooth and smooth is fast." I understand what it's trying to point out, but if you're going slowly, how can that ever be fast? Sure, you need to start off learning things slowly, and you can't push your speed past what your current skill level allows, but if you continue to go slowly, that's never going to equal fast. To be able to shoot fast and accurately, you need to be ready to finish your trigger squeeze—not start it—as soon as your sights settle back down on your intended target. To do this, you need to have a good follow-through by practicing the steps listed above and maintaining contact with the trigger at all times.

Speed doesn't come just from doing things faster. It comes from doing things smoothly and consistently. If your sights are not settling in the same place after each round,

you're going to have to take the time to see where your sights are and make adjustments before taking the next shot. I like to tell my students that "Speed happens." If you're trying to increase your speed without the proper techniques to support it, you're going to fumble and make mistakes. But once you have the proper foundation to support faster shooting, let speed happen.

Regardless of your shooting speed, follow-through is an important fundamental for accurate shooting. Sight alignment and trigger control are the two most important steps in marksmanship, and both need to be maintained during your follow-through. Sight alignment in shooting is more accurately defined as sight refinement, and pulling your trigger is better defined as trigger management. You can't just line up the sights once and slap the trigger once if you're expecting a good result. Your sight alignment needs to be continually refined, and your trigger needs to be actively managed until all threats are neutralized; this means follow-through.

Your trigger needs to be actively managed until all threats are neutralized.

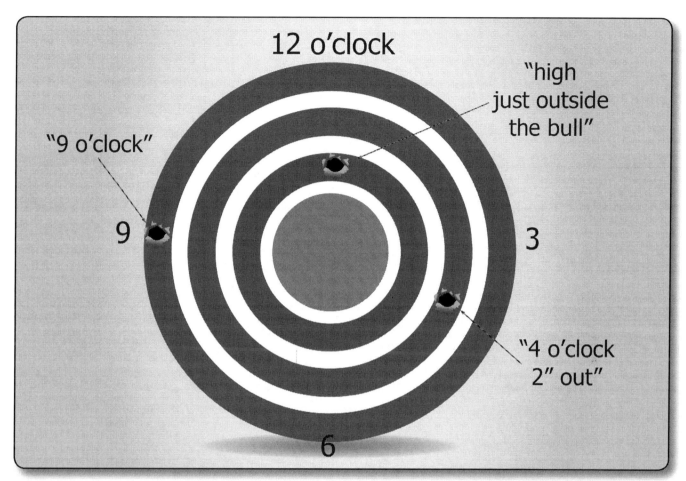

3.8.6 – Calling your shots

Calling Your Shots

For some reason, many shooters think that calling their shots is reserved only for world-class shooters or snipers. I've found that it's like working out—if you just start doing it, you'll see it's fairly easy and quickly becomes second nature. Calling the shot is also extremely simple, as there's just one step: When the shot breaks, remember what the sight picture looked like. By doing this, you should be able to "call" where the impact will be on the target. I tell students to imagine they're taking a picture with a camera, and the trigger is the shutter release button.

When the flash goes off (bang), you've got your picture. Also, don't be afraid to call what you see. Many times when I start working with people on this technique, they just continue to call "center," shot after shot. They're not hitting center, but are just not nitpicking what they saw. Start practicing calling your shots, and you'll be surprised at how quickly your shooting improves.

Practicing these combat fundamentals with every shot you take is the only way to master the art of shooting. And just like anything in life, if you don't follow through your previous work is wasted.

Training notes: _____

_____

_____

_____

_____

_____

_____

_____

_____

_____

_____

_____

_____

_____

_____

_____

_____

SECTION IV:

Operations

Now that you understand how to train and the fundamentals of marksmanship, let's talk about everything else that goes into shooting. Whether you're in combat, competition, or training for self-defense, you need to master more M's than marksmanship alone to put effective rounds downrange. Here I'll cover mounting your weapon, magazine changes, movement, malfunctions, and other manipulations to make you the master of your weapon. Anyone can pull a trigger with the gun up and running, but it's all this other stuff that makes a good shooter.

Control your weapon or it will control you!

Before we get started, let's debunk the "gross motor skill" fallacy when it comes to weapons manipulations. Some trainers claim that when the shit hits the fan in a gunfight, you lose all fine motor skill, and are able to use only gross motor (large muscle) movements to fight back. So if I'm doing a magazine reload while being shot at, I will not be able to press the mag release with my thumb and should swat my whole hand at it. I say hogwash! This is why we train. Do fighter pilots lose fine motor skills when they are flying at Mach 2 and locking onto multiple threats? I've never flown one, but I've seen pictures of the cockpit, and *every* dial, button, and switch looks smaller than my mag release. How do they do it? They

train! If you put in the same time needed to become proficient with your gun, you will not shoot like a caveman but like a finely tuned instrument.

In all manipulations I teach, I try to lower the degree of bimanual interference during movement. Bimanual interference occurs when the movements of the two hands or arms are asymmetrical, or their movements are timed differently. (Think of tapping your head and rubbing your belly.) By moving in a certain way or timing your movements a little differently, you can avoid the inner-limb confusion that frustrates many shooters, and by practicing each technique with deliberate, perfect movements, you will overcome your body's natural resistance.

Finally, we'll cover your ability (or inability) to *shoot*, *move*, and *communicate*. As you begin learning or refining these skills, realize that you cannot effectively multitask. As much as you think you can, you can't. Yes, you can walk and chew gum at the same time, but that's because these are low-sensory-input tasks. But your mind is hardwired to pay attention to the item with the most sensory input at the moment—say, someone shooting at you. This is the time you swallow you gum, and don't know why. To avoid this, you need to give your full attention to *one* thing at a time. So, if you need to draw your weapon and then shoot, put your thought and energy into drawing, and then make the switch to shooting. It sounds simple, but you can't let any other thoughts break your focus. Your partner just got shot, a dog is biting your leg, you're hungry—none of that matters as you press back on the trigger. So remember: Focus on one major task at a time, while the lower-priority items are on autopilot.

Control your weapon or it will control you!

Training notes: _____

_____

_____

_____

_____

_____

_____

_____

_____

_____

_____

_____

_____

Drawing your weapon from a holster is like any other skill—it's perishable. If you don't incorporate drawing your weapon into your training regimen, you're giving the tactical advantage to your adversary.

1

Pistol Mounts

The first things to discuss before drawing your pistol are what type of holster you have and where it's placed. There are lots of choices in pistol holsters, and without getting into the plethora of options, I do want to discuss maximizing whichever one you choose.

First up is the drop-leg holster. It's what I usually used in the SEAL Teams and what most military and law enforcement units I train use. The biggest issue with the drop-leg holster is that it's worn too low on the leg. The holster was designed so you could clear your plate carrier and kit when you draw your pistol, so it doesn't need to be down to your knees. This is most common when shooters are issued a holster but don't realize that it can be or needs to be adjusted. If you run one, raise it up as high as possible where you can clear your kit when drawing.

4.1.1 – Holster raised up and top leg strap removed

You should be able to take off the upper leg strap and just use the lower one. This way, your pistol will shift much less when you're moving, and the distance the pistol needs to move from holster to target is shorter—that's a good thing.

Placement is another problem with every type of holster. Normally people will put the holster on the belt and then start practicing drawing their weapon. Sounds like a good formula, right? Well, it's backwards. The first thing you should do is start moving your hand naturally to where it wants to move if you need to draw a gun. Then just put your holster where your hand naturally moves. This way you don't have to retrain your body, and you've saved yourself countless hours of repetition.

For all weapons mounts, always remember to bring the sights to eyes. When you look at something, half the work is done; your eyes are lined up with the target, your gun is not. All you need to do is move your sights into the line of sight between your eye and the target. If you move your eye to the sights, you have to align the gun and your eyes when they are both moving, so you essentially made a moving target for yourself.

4.1.2 – Holster mounted too far back

4.1.3 – Holster mounted too far forward

Draw

Drawing your weapon from a holster is like any other skill—it's perishable. If you don't incorporate drawing your weapon into your training regimen, you're giving the tactical advantage to your adversary. Whether it's drawing your firearm against an active shooter or in competition, the fundamentals and end game should always be the same; your eyes, weapon, and sights quickly up and locked on a target, ready to engage. A lot of LE operators incorporate drawing from the holster only during their semiannual live-fire qualifications. You're only setting yourself up for failure, or worse, if you do this. The same goes for civilians who carry a concealed firearm. They will buy a holster, usually a cheap, poorly made one, and they never dry-fire or live-fire from the holster. You spend a lot of money on your firearm, and you should buy an equally acceptable holster. I'm not saying you have to buy the top-of-the-line (most expensive) holster out there, but the holster should be able to take a beating on a regular basis, be comfortable, and be operator friendly. And, yes, everyone should have a holster of some sort, even for a "pocket pistol." There are a few choice words I use for people who attempt to carry without a holster: gangsters, thugs, or simply idiots.

You can find websites or trainers who teach a varied number of steps, ranging from one to ten, on how to draw from the holster and get your pistol up and into the game. I teach a four-step process to draw your pistol, called the rubber band draw. I call it the rubber band draw because it's similar to the common four-step draw: Position 1 – 2 – 3 – 4. You will do it by the numbers!

4.1.4 – This holster says it's just right

Drawing your weapon from a holster is like any other skill—it's perishable.

4.1.5 – Position 1: Grip the pistol.

4.1.6 – Position 2: Draw the weapon and rotate the muzzle toward the target.

Traditional 4-Step Draw

Position 1: Grip the pistol.

Position 2: Draw the weapon and rotate the muzzle toward the target.

4.1.7 – Position 3: Grip the pistol with both hands high in the center of chest.

4.1.8 – Position 4: The pistol is pressed out, arms fully extended.

Position 3: Grip the pistol with both hands high in the center of chest.

Position 4: The pistol is pressed out, arms fully extended

This is a great way to start if you've never drawn a pistol before, but it's far from smooth, and that equals lost speed. Drawing to shoot is like sprinting and needing to come to a perfect stop on the edge of a cliff.

The Rubber Band Draw

The difference between the traditional four-step draw and the rubber band draw is that you need to imagine you have rubber bands attached to each of the positions and your muzzle as you drive your gun straight from the holster to a fully mounted position locked on a target. Doing this will smooth out the rough edges on your draw stroke and get you up on target much quicker. There are also a lot of smaller details that are often overlooked, so we'll look at them as we cover how to draw your pistol. I think learning this technique is easier too because the movement is like putting your hand in your pants pocket, pulling it out, and pointing at something—all things you have already practiced thousands of times.

4.1.9 – Rubber Band Draw. Flinch to the gun with half-moon arc

1. Flinch to the gun! How fast would your hand move if you were just shot at? That's how fast your hand needs to move to the holster. Move your hand in a half-moon arc so you grip your pistol from the back with your elbow driving straight back. By doing this you can establish a high grip and more easily break any weapon retention system on the holster (thumb break, hammer hood, and so on). Remember, "what you grab is what you get." During this flinch to the gun, you also need to drop into your fighting stance and your eyes need to lock onto the target like a laser. Once the gun starts moving from its holster, you want as few things moving as possible.

2. Remember that you have a rubber band attached to your muzzle and the farthest attachment point (the location of the most tension) right

4.1.10 – Drive the elbow down and press the front sight into the front of holster

4.1.11 – Drive gun up, hands meeting where you would clap

now is Position 4, or your target, so that as you begin to pull up on the pistol by driving the elbow down, the front sight is sliding up inside the holster. As soon as the muzzle clears the holster, the pistol will continue its pull toward the target, and the muzzle will be rotated to point at it.

3. Now that we've got a perfect grip, we're clear of the holster, and pointing at our target, the gun is driven like a freight train—no, a Japanese bullet train—up to the mounted position. Since you have a theoretical rubber band attached to that traditional Position 3, the gun will start moving

4.1.12 – Finish ready to shoot

to come into your field of view. As it does, you'll need to decide where your focus is going to be greater: the front sight or the target. Also, as you're punching out as fast as humanly possible, remember that you've still got that rubber band attached high up on the center of your chest, and that's a good thing. The closer you get to fully mounting the pistol, the more that rubber band is pulling you to a smooth stop at full presentation. What you don't want to do is stop abruptly and then have to take time for your sights to settle—all that speed wasted. Now is when you need to take your time and make an accurate shot.

upward and toward the centerline with the front sights angled slightly upward. Your hands will meet in the middle, and you'll establish the grip with your reaction hand.

4.   As you move between Positions 3 and 4, your front sight should start

Keys to success:

- Reverse engineering: To make sure that you're drawing with the proper grip, grip your pistol properly (see chapter 3 in Marksmanship) and, without changing your grip, holster the gun and check your grip. Now make sure that you're establishing that same grip every time you draw your pistol.

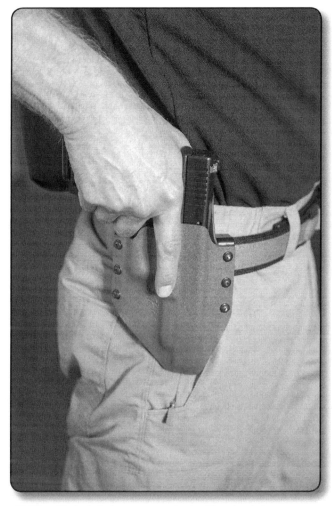

4.1.13 – Establish your grip in the holster

draw stroke time and trigger stroke time. You should draw your pistol like your life depends on how fast you can get this done. You then need to stroke that trigger like your life depends on

- Move your reaction hand up to the centerline of your body to be ready to meet the pistol. If you have time to rotate your hand so your fingers point down at about 45 degrees, even better.

- The only things that should move during your draw are your arms, hand, and gun.

- You should also establish a consistent head position prior to mounting, so your gun knows where to go.

- Drawing and shooting are two separate acts and can be broken into two times:

4.1.14 – Reaction hand ready

how smoothly you can get that job done, too. I see too many people on the range who, when I say slow-fire, do a slow draw, and then slap the trigger like it owes them money. They've got their priorities completely backwards. It should be: flinch to the gun — consistent grip — drive to the threat — smooth press to the rear.

- If you carry a gun for anything other than combat, 90 percent of your draws should be to "gunpoint," not drawing to shoot. Don't teach yourself bad habits.

- Your primary shooting grip must be effective on its own, in the event that the other hand never makes it to the party, because it's "reacting" to other stimuli.

High Ready

The high ready is an often-overlooked position, with both pistol and rifle. The main use of the high ready with the pistol is, after engaging a threat, you lower the weapon slightly so you can better see the battlefield.

To describe the different positions you'll be mounting your gun from, I normally start off from a good standing position and work backwards. When you first start practicing the positions, I recommend that you do the same thing: Start off from the fully mounted position and work backwards to get into the correct position. Once you know the position, this step is not necessary.

4.1.15 – The High Ready

Keys to the high ready:

1. After you engage a threat, don't be so quick to drop your guard. You need to ensure that threat is eliminated and that there are no other threats in front of you.

2. Finish your follow-through and be ready to shoot again if needed.

3. Lower your pistol just enough to see everything in front of you. Doing this is also important to open the tunnel vision brought on by your body alarm response. Take a deep breath, and assess what you need to do next.

4. To mount the gun from the high ready you just need to bring the sights up to your eyes. Engage, scan, or move as needed.

Inside Carry

The inside carry is a good position to use when your pistol is out of its holster but not pointed at a threat. It's also a good position to move around in with your pistol out since it's easier to keep your muzzle from pointing at anything you don't want to shoot. Some people teach a version of this position with a bent (weak) wrist, called Position Sul, but I do not recommend bending your wrist since it will be hard to hold onto your gun

4.1.17 – Position Sul (South)

if you're attacked. If you need to, move the pistol down to your strong side so you can keep it pointed straight down. Sul, which means "south" in Portuguese, can be used as a nonready position, on a range or around other people, where muzzle discipline is more important than being ready to quickly engage threats.

Keys to the inside carry position:

1. From the fully mounted position, the pistol is brought back to the center of the body with the muzzle directed toward the ground.

4.1.16 – Inside Carry

2. Wrist should be kept straight and strong.

3. You can release your reaction hand if needed.

4. To mount the gun from this position, simply put the rubber band in play, and drive it straight up.

High Port

In the high port position, you point the muzzle up rather than down, as with the inside carry position. The high port with the pistol is my preferred position if I'm static and scanning for threats with my gun out of the holster. If I'm moving it's a different story, and I normally like to have my muzzle down; for me it's safer and faster to move. The key to being an effective fighter is to be comfortable using any position, especially on ships and in urban areas, where the battlefield is truly multidimensional, and you never know where the next threat will present itself.

Keys to the high port:

1. Starting from the fully mounted position, bend your elbows and bring the muzzle straight back in line with your eyes: eyes – muzzle – target.

2. Keep the bend in your elbow outside of 90 degrees, which is a stronger position than if your elbows are bent inside 90 degrees.

4.1.18 – High Port

3. Keep the wrist of your strong hand straight.

4. To mount the gun from this position, drive it straight out, and remember to let the rubber bands bring you to a smooth stop on your target.

Retention

To retain something means to keep it, and that's the reason for using the retention position—keeping your pistol. Mostly I only see pistols in the retention position for law enforcement (LE) qualification courses of fire. Anyone who uses a pistol for personal defense really should practice it a lot more because as you move around you need to protect your firearm, which allows your free hand to complete other vital tasks.

Keys to the retention position:

1. Starting from a proper standing pistol position, let go with your reaction hand and bring your pistol straight back to your strong side by pushing your elbow straight back.

2. Always keep your reaction hand out of the line of fire.

3. Brace the pistol or your wrist/ arm (depending on your flexibility) against your side. This is a vital step to control the weapon if you need to fire from here.

4. You also need to cant the gun away from your body. If you need to fire from this position, the slide can hit you and cause a malfunction.

5. To mount the pistol from this position, drive the gun out as if you were starting from Position 2.

4.1.19 – Retention

6. To shoot from the retention position, use your body to adjust your shots while keeping the pistol pinned to your side. Do not aim by bending your wrist.

4.1.20 – Reaction Hand Draw – Step forward

4.1.21 – Pull holster closer if possible

Reaction Hand Draw

Drawing your pistol with your reaction hand is one of those skills that, of the very limited number of people who practice it, 99.9 percent of the time they will never need to use it. But if you're in that 0.1 percent, it could easily save your life. You don't need to practice it a lot, but you need to have some general idea of what you're going to do when your "good" hand is no longer "good." A lot of variations will occur due to the differences in holsters and holster placement, so I'll go over some common techniques that should help get your pistol from one side of your body to the other, so that you can stay in the fight.

4.1.22 – Release any retention devises

4.1.23 – Pinch between knees

Keys to drawing with your reaction hand:

1. Step forward with your strong-side leg if you have a drop-leg holster or, if your holster is on your waist, twist your body so your holster is closer to your reaction side.

2. If you can, grab your holster and pull it around your leg or waist, so it's even closer to your reaction side.

3. The final step to help make it easier to get your pistol out is to squat down slightly. You should of course do all three steps simultaneously, especially if someone is shooting at you!

4.1.24 – Re-grip gun

4.1.25 – Rotate gun toward target

4. Reach over and disengage any retention devices on the holster.

5. Draw the pistol (it will be backward) and place it between your knees. You will need to pinch the gun with your knees, so keep your feet slightly spread apart, making sure the muzzle

is pointing forward and is sticking out in front of your knees.

6. Let go with your hand and re-grip the gun properly. It's important that you establish a good grip now since you're not going to have time later.

4.1.26 – Press gun out

Training notes: _____

_____

_____

_____

_____

_____

_____

_____

_____

_____

_____

_____

_____

_____

_____

_____

_____

_____

7. Once you have a good grip, let go with your knees.

8. Rotate the gun up while keeping it pointed in a safe direction.

9. Press pistol straight up and switch your stance if it's more comfortable.

2

Carbine Mounts

You need to be able to mount your carbine from a variety of positions, and you'll need to modify each one, depending on the length of your carbine, sling type and length, your body type, and the situation you're dealing with. Two of the best things that will help you mount the gun right every time are to get comfortable holding your gun properly all the time, and to always put the buttstock into your shoulder.

What do I mean by holding the gun properly? Guys get lazy and sling their guns with their support hand way back by the magazine. They then stack up on a door or hear the threat command and, as the saying goes, what you grab is what you get. They mount their gun, and they're starting off at a disadvantage because their support hand is barely supporting their primary weapon system.

4.2.1 – Lazy support hand

Low Ready

In the low ready position, your barrel is angled down at about 45 degrees. It's commonly used in timed courses of fire and competitions, but it's also a very combat-effective ready position, depending on how wide a field of fire you need to cover.

Keys to the low ready:

1. Starting from your good, aggressive, standing carbine position, all you need to do is lower the barrel to a 45-degree angle.

4.2.1 – Lazy support hand

4.2.2 – One small adjustment and you're always ready to fight

The second problem you need to avoid is letting the gun decide where it's going to sit in your shoulder. Again, I think it is just laziness since everyone knows where they want the buttstock to sit—they just don't insist on being the boss. Remember, be the weapon's master, not its bitch.

4.2.3 – Low Ready

4.2.4 – Bring the sights up to your eyes

2. Keep the buttstock in your shoulder.

3. Keep your head up!

4. To mount the gun, bring it straight up, hinging on the buttstock.

High Ready

The high ready is much like the low ready, except that you're lowering the muzzle only enough that you're just looking over your sights. Apart from using the high ready to assess your threat after engaging a threat, it's also the position your gun needs to be

in when you're making a room entry during close quarters combat (CQB)—but that's a topic for another book.

Keys to the high ready:

1. Starting from your good, aggressive, standing carbine position, all you need to do is lower the muzzle just enough to see over your sights. You need to lower it enough so that you can see your threats, but the more you lower it, the longer it will take for you to come up and engage the threats you do find.

4.2.5 – High Ready

2. Keep the buttstock in your shoulder, and keep your head up. One of the biggest problems I see is a tendency for people to drop their head when they lower their muzzle.

3. To mount the gun, snap it straight up, hinging on the buttstock.

High Port

The high port is primarily used in CQB, but it's also good to know if you run with your muzzle up or any time your threat priority is above eye level. In the high port, the muzzle is pointed straight up, so make the crew chief happy next time you get on a helo and don't show off some other new position you just learned!

Keys to the high port:

1. Starting from the fully mounted position, punch the gun straight out and break it off your shoulder.

2. Now rotate the gun 90 degrees, so the buttstock is down and the muzzle is pointed straight up. The muzzle should be right in front of your eyes: eyes – muzzle – target.

3. Keep the gun close to you and keep your grips the same.

4. To mount the gun from this position, drive the muzzle straight out to your target, then pull the buttstock

4.2.6 – High Port – Eyes-muzzle-target

into your shoulder. When you first start learning this mount you should exaggerate the punch out until you learn how far the gun needs to

4.2.7 – Drive muzzle straight out

4.2.8 – Pull buttstock into shoulder

move to clear your gear or body. As you learn the mount, you can (and should) make this movement smaller and faster, but you should

always punch out so you can put the buttstock where you want it. If not, the buttstock will often run high off your shoulder.

4.2.9 – Inside Carry

Inside Carry

Boarding that helo, the inside carry is a good position. It's also good any time you've got a lot of people around and muzzle discipline is a high priority. Or if you've got two threats you need to cover, and they're 180 degrees apart, this is the best way to split the difference without a swim buddy.

Keys to the inside carry:

1. Starting from the fully mounted position, bring the muzzle down until it's pointing between your feet.

2. Rotate the gun about 90 degrees so that the magazine is pointing to your strong side.

3. Keep the buttstock in contact with your shoulder.

4. As with the other positions, keep your head and eyes up!

5. To mount the gun, snap it straight back up, hinging on the buttstock, and rotating it back 90 degrees.

Retention

Also called a high tuck, the retention position is used to mount the gun when your support hand is busy taking care of more important things like opening a door, or it can be used to fire from if that hand was injured.

Keys to the retention position:

1. Starting from an athletic fighting position, let go with your support hand and bring your gun straight back to your strong side by pushing your elbow straight back.

2. Always keep your reaction hand out of the line of fire.

3. Pinch the buttstock with your arm against your body. This is an important step to controlling the weapon if you need to fire from

4.2.10 – Retention

here, and it will also help you in manipulating the safety.

4. To mount the gun from this position, drive it straight out in the same way as with the high port. Your support hand should be moving up and forward in the same path as the gun, so as to not slow the movement down when you establish your grip with that hand. Remember to place the buttstock into your shoulder where you want it.

5. To shoot from the retention position, use your body to adjust your shots while keeping the gun pinned to your side. Do not try to aim by turning the muzzle with your hand.

Reaction Side

Being a Navy SEAL sniper, I thought that shooting off your reaction side was a no-brainer. If you could expose yourself less by switching shoulders, you did it. But as I've worked more with other units, I've learned that it's a lot more common among SEALs and even more so among SEAL snipers. Well, lucky you, to have me writing this book because you're going to learn how to do it right!

Most people think that shooting off the reaction side is only for tactical ninjas, but that's far from the truth. If you just think of it as mirroring everything you do, down to the smallest details, you'll find that it's pretty easy, especially with a little practice. In fact there are quite a few shooters who can naturally shoot a rifle off either shoulder. I'm not one of them, but maybe you are, and you'll never know it unless you give it a try.

Keys to shooting off your reaction side:

1. Probably the most important thing to keep in mind is that if you're not comfortable when you train this position, don't use it in competition or combat unless absolutely necessary.

4.2.11 – Your reaction side position should mirror the other side.

4.2.12 – Note the gun is mounted directly below each eye

4.2.13 – Using your thumb on selector

4.2.14 – Make sure your establish a good grip before shooting

2. If you use a red dot, keep both eyes open to shoot. If you're using iron sights, close your dominant eye to focus on the front sight.

3. When you mount the gun, place it directly below your eye (or as close as possible). This is the biggest problem I see when people say they cannot find the sights. The gun is too far out on the shoulder.

4. Remember to switch your feet. If you drop your strong leg back in your

4.2.15 – Using the trigger finger to come off fire

4.2.17 – Ready to get to work

4.2.16 – 2nd knuckle working fire control

using their thumb to come off safe, and then their trigger finger to put it back on safe. This is fine, but you need to remember to re-grip the gun properly, and this can take time. The other option (and the faster of the two) is using your second knuckle with a straight finger to do both. This technique will take more practice, but in the end you'll be a lot faster.

regular stance, you need either to step forward with that foot or back with the other. This should help make the position feel more comfortable.

5. If you don't have an ambidextrous safety, you have a few options. If you're a lefty, welcome to the world of the normal people—now you know what you've been missing all along. Use your thumb. If you're normal, I mean right-handed, you can either use your thumb or the knuckle of your (new) trigger finger. Starting off, most people will feel more comfortable

Most people think that shooting off the reaction side is only for tactical ninjas, but that's far from the truth.

4.2.18 – Transfer to Reaction Side, Single-point Sling

4.2.20 – Move your strong hand forward and reaction hand back

Transfer to Reaction Side, Single-point Sling

I normally run with a single-point sling, simply because I like to be able to move my weapon around quickly to different positions and I don't want a sling getting in the way. How you transfer the gun depends on which type of sling you have. Let's start with my favorite, the single-point.

4.2.19 – Start off on your strong side

4.2.21 – Move buttstock to other side   *4.2.22 – Move buttstock to other side*

To transfer:

1. Think about exactly how your body is positioned and where each of your hands is gripping the gun. The key is to mirror this position on the other side.

2. Move your strong hand forward to marry up with/mirror your reaction hand.

3. Move your reaction hand back to fire control (pistol grip).

4. Punch the gun out and move the buttstock to the other side of your chest. You will likely need to tilt the muzzle up or down to get the buttstock around your sling, and you might need to lift your chin slightly if you choose to go muzzle down.

4.2.23 – Switch your feet

4.2.24 – Switch your feet

Try out each, and see which works better for you.

5. When you start moving your hands, you should switch your feet at the same time. I normally step back with my reaction-side foot unless I'm moving.

6. Remember to place the buttstock into your shoulder where you want it.

7. Bring the sights up to your eyes. If you're craning your neck to find the sights, your position is wrong. Most likely the buttstock is too far out on your shoulder. Don't make a bad position worse—fix it!

8. To transfer the gun back to your strong side, just reverse the steps.

Transfer to Reaction-Side, Two-point Sling

If you do long patrols with a gun slung around your neck, or most of your shooting is done on a flat range and 90 percent of your mounts are from the low or high ready, a two-point sling will work fine for you. It can also be used effectively to support some of your shooting positions and will be more comfortable than a single-point. One of the trade-offs, though, is it's a little trickier to switch shoulders on the fly, but I developed my own technique for just such an occasion. It gets you up on your gun faster and also transfers the sling to the other side. The one major negative is that you will temporarily not have the weapon slung on any part of your body, so you will need to decide which is more important in each situation: speed or the ability to let go of your gun without dropping it.

To transfer fast:

1. Again, think about your position because you want to end up mirroring this on the other side.

2. Punch the gun out off your shoulder, and move it up and over your head.

3. As you bring the buttstock into your reaction-side shoulder, bring your reaction hand back, and move your strong hand forward. Damn, that was fast!

4.2.25 – Transfer to Reaction Side, Two-point Sling: Fast Method

4. Step back when you start the movement.

4.2.26 – Punch gun out and up

4.2.27 – Switch hands and shoulder

5. If you are going to run the gun on your reaction side for a while and want the sling switched, just slip your reaction arm out, and lift the sling in

front of the muzzle and over to the other side, ready to operate.

6. To transfer back to your strong side,

SECTION IV: **OPERATIONS**

2 • CARBINE MOUNTS

4.2.29 – Switch sling position if needed

You will need to decide which is more important in each situation: speed or the ability to let go of your gun without dropping it.

4.2.28 – Step back

reverse the steps. If you haven't moved the sling to the other side, just move the gun back over your head, and the sling will be set.

4.2.30 – Transfer to Reaction Side, Two-point Sling: Secure Method – Loosen sling

To transfer without possibly dropping:

1.   Keeping the muzzle up and covering any possible threats, reach back with the reaction hand and loosen the sling if possible.

2.   Pull your reaction arm back and down through the loop in the sling.

3.   Move your strong hand forward to marry up with/mirror your reaction hand.

4.   Move your reaction hand back to fire control (pistol grip).

4.2.31 – Pull reaction arm out

5.   Punch the gun out and move the buttstock to the other side of your chest.

6.   When you start moving your hands, you should switch your feet at the same time.

4.2.32 – Pull reaction arm out

4.2.33 – Switch to other side

7. Remember to place the buttstock into your shoulder where you want it.

8. Bring the sights up to your eyes.

9. To transfer the gun back to your strong side, just reverse the steps.

Training notes: _____

_____

_____

_____

_____

_____

_____

_____

_____

_____

_____

_____

_____

_____

_____

_____

_____

_____

Training notes: _____

_____

_____

_____

_____

_____

_____

_____

_____

_____

_____

_____

_____

_____

_____

_____

_____

_____

Remember as you work with your pistol to always keep your head and eyes up so you can see the battle space: Eyes, Muzzle, Target (EMT).

3

Pistol Manipulations

Remember as you work with your pistol to always keep your head and eyes up so you can see the battle space: eyes, muzzle, target (EMT). That means you should have your eyes, muzzle, and target all in line when you're working on your gun. There's nothing worse than spotting your enemy, looking down during a reload, and then looking up to see him gone. The way to accomplish this is to have a workbox up near your face (not in front of it). This box is where you use all the tools of your trade to get your gun up and running as fast as possible.

Loading

Every time you put a gun in your hand, it's an opportunity to train, and loading your gun is no exception. That's why it kills me to see so many people load their pistols like they're checking the time on a pocket watch.

4.3.1 – Always remember eyes-muzzle-target

4.3.2 – Move as little as possible

They treat it like it's unimportant, with their heads down and in a rush to get to the "real training." This is where your training begins, so let's do it right from the beginning.

To load:

4.3.3 – Loading – Draw

1. Draw your pistol according to previous instructions, that is, like your life depends on how fast you get those sights up on target.

4.3.4 – Dry fire

2. Practice a dry-fire repetition or two. (You should always know the condition of your weapon and make sure it is always pointed in a safe direction.)

4.3.5 – Bring straight back, lock the slide to the rear and grab a magazine

3. Bring the weapon straight back into your workspace, lock the slide to the rear and grab your primary pistol magazine.

4.3.6 – Make sure you "index" the magazine

4.3.7 – Insert magazine

4. Index the magazine (tip of the index finger near or touching tip of first bullet), and bring it straight to the magazine well.

5. Keep your eyes up on target. You can glance down to make sure the magazine is going to make it into the magazine well smoothly, but get your eyes right back up as soon as it finds the hole. To make sure you hit the magazine well smoothly, think, "aim small, miss small," just like in shooting. "Aim" with the top back of the magazine to the back of the magazine well. If you "miss," you'll be off by a little, but it will still go in.

4.3.8 – Glance down if needed to ensure the magazine will go in smoothly

4.3.9 – Ensure it's fully seated

6. Continue to guide the magazine into the well for about ½ inch to avoid the magazine locking sideways in the well. This tends to happen when people open their hand flat as soon as the top of the magazine reaches the well.

7. Once the magazine has begun its path, release the slide as you punch straight back out and get another opportunity to practice sight alignment and sight picture.

4.3.10 – Release the slide and mount the gun

8. If you decide not to shoot, practice a good scan and then holster.

9. If you want to do a press check, now is the right time.

Releasing the Slide

There are a few different methods you can use to release the slide, and each has advantages and disadvantages. Some people feel very strongly about one method over the others, but I actually practice them all because I sometimes find that my hand or the gun is in a slightly different position, and it's quicker for me to use a different technique than what I was planning on half a second previously. For the same reasons, I recommend you not only try them all out, but practice using them,

too. You should have one that you use most often and works best for you and your gun, but don't neglect the others.

Release Slide Stop

This is one of those places the "gross motor skill" naysayers will tell you that you can't release the slide stop in the heat of battle.

4.3.11 – Release slide stop with strong-hand

4.3.12 – Release slide stop with strong-hand

My guess is they've either never been in battle or have not trained enough! To release the slide, pull down on the slide stop with your strong-hand thumb (if your hands are big enough) or your reaction hand thumb as you establish your grip. This is my go-to slide release, since for me it works and it gets my hands back on the gun faster than any other method.

4.3.13 – Release slide stop with reaction-hand

4.3.14 – Release slide stop with reaction-hand

Slingshot

The slingshot method is probably the most used method out there but the one I use the least. To slingshot the slide, you pinch the rear serrations of the gun between your thumb and the inside of your index finger and pull back on the slide all the way and then let go. It's important not to ride the slide forward when using this technique, and to make sure you pull the slide back all the way. I find it's the hardest way to grip the slide, and it takes the longest to get my hands back on the gun. But if you like it, more power to you!

4.3.15 – Slingshot

4.3.16 – Slingshot

Power Stroke

This method is much like the slingshot, but instead of pinching with two fingers from the back, you come over the top and pinch the top rear serrations between all four fingers and the heel of your hand. This allows you to get a much better grip on the gun.

4.3.17 – Power Stroke

4.3.18 – Power Stroke

Magazine Mash

This is not so much a method as it is the result of seating your magazine with enough force to release the slide stop. I don't recommend training to use this method or relying on it under stress. It can by very unreliable, and with each iteration you're wearing down your gun. Not all guns will do it, but if you want to try it, make sure you have a full magazine (mass + velocity = force), and hit the bottom of the magazine at a 45-degree angle to the front.

4.3.19 – Magazine Mash

Press Check

Doing a press check (also called a status, brass, or chamber check) means checking the condition of your firearm by verifying there is a round in the chamber. I think the debate over doing press checks and the strong opinions people have on both sides is pretty interesting. One side says you should always know the condition of your gun, and doing a press check could lead to a self-induced malfunction. The other side says, "How can you be sure whether a gun is loaded without checking, especially if you're depending on this gun to save your life?" I actually agree with both sides. I should always know the condition of my firearm, and since I use mine to protect me and my family, if I ever have the slightest doubt about the condition of my gun I'm going to check it properly and ensure that it's ready when I need it. If you decide do to a press check, there are a few different techniques you can use; I'll show you my favorite two. Try them both to find the one you're more comfortable with, and use it anytime you need to verify the condition of your pistol.

Press Check Techniques

Practice your firearms safety rules at all times: Guns are always considered loaded, keep your finger off the trigger, don't point it at yourself, and practice in a safe area. You should practice doing both a visual and physical check for low-light conditions by seeing the brass and feeling for the brass with your finger. Of course I highly recommend practicing these techniques, and this is a great time to have a few dummy rounds on hand so you can practice safely.

Pull From Top

This is probably the easiest to learn and perform, and is one of the most common ways. Keep your regular strong-hand grip and pull back on the slide from the top using either the power stroke or slingshot grip. Pull back only far enough to be able to see if there is brass in the chamber and/or feel for brass with your trigger finger. You can grab in front of or behind the ejection port.

4.3.20 – Visual check while pulling

4.3.21 – Physical check while pulling

Push Under Front Serrations

This is probably my favorite method since I have more control of the gun and it's easier to physically check with my trigger finger. To do this, reach under the gun with your reaction hand and grab the front serrations. Push the slide to the rear to verify the condition of your gun. This one may be more difficult if you don't have front serrations, and of course you need to be careful not to point the gun at your hand when you reach forward.

4.3.22 – Visual check holding underneath

4.3.23 – Physically checking while holding underneath

Loaded Chamber Indicators (LCIs)

LCIs are becoming more and more common on modern handguns, so it's important that I cover them here. They are, as the name implies, small indicators on the gun that are supposed to tell you if there is a round in the chamber. It works by having a piece sticking up off the extractor, so if the piece is sticking up there is a round in the chamber, and if it's down, then the gun is empty . . . supposedly. Call me old-fashioned, but I don't even look at these, much less rely on what I see, if one does happen to invade my visual field. LCIs are of course manual and prone to malfunction, so I rely on my own indicators—my senses of sight and touch. If you do have one on your gun, I recommend you keep it (and the rest of your gun) clean to keep it running reliably.

Unloading

Since we're developing the habit of doing things the same way every time, we need to look at unloading our pistols in the same way. If you look at the history of accidental shootings, you'll find improper unloading high on list of causes. By learning the proper way and practicing it the same way every time, you will avoid being a statistic and live to fight another day.

To unload:

1. Get in one more repetition of drawing your pistol properly and lining up your sights.

4.3.24 – Unloading – Press magazine release and grab magazine

4.3.25 – Pull and lock slide back

2. Decide not to shoot!

3. Bring the weapon straight back into your workspace as your strong-hand thumb presses the magazine release and your reaction hand grabs the magazine.

4. Index the magazine and put it in your pocket or open magazine pouch.

5. Pull the slide back with your reaction hand and lock it to the rear by lifting up on the slide catch with the thumb of your strong hand.

6. Tilt the gun down to look forward into the chamber to make sure it's clear.

7. Tilt the gun back to make sure there is no magazine in the magazine well.

4.3.26 – Visually check the chamber

4.3.27 – Physically check the chamber

8. With your finger, feel the inside of the chamber to make sure there is no round.

9. With your finger, feel up inside the magazine well to make sure there is no magazine.

10. If someone else is there, ask them to do a "buddy check," verifying the same things.

11. Move the gun back up into your workspace, and release the slide as you punch out and acquire a target.

12. Practice one perfect dry-fire, and holster an empty weapon.

4.3.28 – Visually and physically check the magazine well

Reloads

Reloading your gun is a necessity outside the Hollywood world of bottomless magazines. Your main goal when reloading is to have the gun out of operation for as short a time as possible, while not losing situational awareness. One key to success is to know where your magazines are so you can grab them without looking for them or playing

"tactical patty-cake" as you pat yourself down. Knowing where they are should be easy since you put them there, but it's also important to move your magazines if and when you have time, to get them closer to the gun.

I have what I call my "sweet spot" for grabbing magazines if I'm in a hurry, and for me that's on my belt and it doesn't matter what I'm wearing for kit or body armor. So when I do my initial load, slide-lock, or speed reload, I will always grab from my sweet spot. The only time I don't do this is for a tactical load, discussed later. After I've finished loading and when I have time, I back-fill my sweet spot with a full magazine so it will be ready when I need it.

Before we get started, you need to consider where you put your magazine pouches. In the same way that I see people put their holsters wherever they find space and then learn how to draw from there, move your hands to where they naturally want to go, and then put your pouches there. Whenever I set up a new belt or chest rig, I continue moving and adjusting my gear until it's perfect. If you want to be a great shooter, you need to do the same.

Slide-lock Reload

The slide-lock reload needs to be your bread-and-butter reload. What's happened is that in the middle of your engagement process you've run out of ammunition, and you likely need more. It's a very lucky day if you just happen to eliminate all your threats or drop all your targets just as the last round is fired. It's more likely Mr. Murphy has come to pay a visit than Lady Luck, so we need to be ready for him.

To perform a slide-lock reload:

1.   Recognize you need to reload! You'd be surprised how often new shooters don't realize it's time to feed the beast.

2.   Use your thumb to release the magazine as soon as possible so you can use gravity and time to help it come out. If you can't press the magazine release button with your thumb, use your reaction-hand fingers to help roll the gun in your hand, don't "flip" it. (Figure 4.3.29).

3.   Keeping your eyes, muzzle, and target in line, bring the muzzle straight back into your workspace by bending your elbow and rolling the gun about 45 degrees so you can see into the magazine well.

4.   Use the side of your body or your kit as a reference for where to stop. You

4.3.29 – Using reaction hand to roll the gun

4.3.30 – Bring straight back

want the position of the gun to be as consistent and stable as possible so your hand with the magazine knows exactly where to go each time.

5. As soon as your reaction hand comes off the gun, it reaches for the magazine in your sweet spot.

6. Index the magazine and bring it straight to the magazine well.

7. Remember to keep your eyes up on target, except for a quick glance down to make sure the magazine finds its home.

8. Continue to guide the magazine into the well as you release the slide and punch straight back out and get back into the fight.

9. Eliminate all threats, and remember to keep moving ammo toward your gun when you get a chance.

Speed

A speed reload is done when you know you're getting low on ammunition in the gun and want to reload, but it's more important to have less downtime than to possibly lose a few rounds on the ground. It's not used that often but is good to know if you ever need it. When you get a chance, of course you should try to retrieve the magazine.

To perform a speed reload:

1. Once you decide to do it, commit and do it fast.

2. Keeping your gun up and ready

4.3.31 – Speed Reload

to engage, reach down with your reaction hand and index the magazine from your sweet spot.

3. Once you have the magazine, bring the muzzle straight back into your workspace, keeping your eyes, muzzle, and target in line and release the magazine with your strong-hand thumb.

4. Insert the fresh magazine and remount the gun.

4.3.32 – Tactical reload – Think before you act

4.3.33 – Hold magazine between index and middle fingers

Tactical

A tactical reload is more common than a speed reload, and the one I recommend using if you have time. They are used for the same reasons, but with a tactical reload you've determined that it's tactically safer

and/or more advantageous for you to retain the partially loaded magazine.

To perform a tactical reload:

1. Since you have the time to make an informed decision, think through the steps before you start.

4.3.34 – Release magazine and pinch between thumb and index finger

4.3.35 – Inset fresh magazine

2. Keeping your gun up and ready to engage, reach down with your reaction hand and index the magazine from where you keep your reserve ammunition. This is the one time you do not go for the sweet spot because you have time and you don't want

your primary mag pouch empty if everything goes to hell in the middle of your reload.

3. Once you have the magazine, bring the muzzle straight back into your workspace.

4.3.36 – Ensure it's fully seated

4.3.37 – Store magazine

4. Move the index finger of your reaction hand down the side of the magazine so the magazine is now between your index and middle fingers.

5. Release the old magazine with your strong-hand thumb and pinch it between your thumb and index finger.

6. Insert the fresh magazine and store the used magazine in the farthest spot from your gun.

Using Lights

Your firearms are without a doubt the most critical tools in your inventory, but we have many other items in our toolboxes that we use on a daily basis but are often neglected in training, particularly lights. As a Navy SEAL, I always had at least three separate lighting systems (helmet-mounted, handheld, and weapons-mounted) at my disposal during any operation. Part of properly employing these systems is testing them *every day* and having spare bulbs and batteries in your kit. Just because the briefing said the mission was only going to last one hour means nothing, and we know that things can change once the team is inserted and Mr. Murphy comes along for the ride.

Just because you bought or were issued that new tactical flashlight from Surefire or Streamlight doesn't mean that you should just throw it on your weapon and think you'll know how to use it. You need to train with it first. You should be dry-firing and going to the range and using your lighting systems in low-light and no-light conditions whenever possible. If you never shoot at night, you're just adding to the chain of events that leads to bad things happening. Break the chain now, and start training under realistic conditions.

Think tactically when using your lighting systems, and use them only when you need them. Lights on your weapons systems are used to ID threats and even temporarily incapacitate (blind) or cause a subject to

momentarily freeze, giving you a split-second advantage. Never move around with your light on the entire time, as this gives away your position. Sure, once bullets start flying the bad guys know you're there, but it's proved that they shoot at what they can see, so if an active shooter sees only your light coming down a passageway, that's what he's going to shoot. The human eye naturally focuses on the brightest object in dark environments.

One of the best uses of lights is to leave them off. If you have time, let your eyes adjust to the darkness, which takes approximately twenty to thirty minutes. You'll be surprised how easy it is to see your sights with a little ambient light. Just be certain of your target and use these techniques to shed some light on the situation.

Finally, if you're using a handheld light for any weapon system, even if it's all you're using, you need to think about where you're going to stash the light when it's not in use. It needs to be where you can quickly get it out and put it away. I'm not a fan of having a lanyard

4.3.38 – Just because it's dark, doesn't mean you need a light

around my wrist because I've seen it become a problem in dynamic situations, like prisoner handling. I have a chest-mounted pouch with a light if I'm in full kit, or if I'm carrying concealed, I carry the light in my reaction-side front pocket with the light facing up. In either case, I can quickly put it back in that pocket when it's not needed. The key is testing it and finding out what works for you.

Gun-mounted

A gun-mounted light is the easiest, but you still need to practice if you plan to use it during a violent encounter. If you've never practiced manipulating the switch during training, it's unlikely you're going to think about it with 100 gallons of adrenaline pumping through your veins. There are

various types of lights, and you'll need to see what works for you and your gun, but here's what I do with mine. Since I keep my light off more than on and I want to be always ready to shoot, I manipulate the light with my reaction-hand thumb rather than my trigger finger. I can do this pretty easily just by sliding my reaction hand forward slightly and still keep a solid grip on the gun.

The key with using a light in any tactical situation is to never stay in the same place once you turn a light off. So if I scan an area quickly, I turn the light off and physically move to a different spot.

Harries Technique

The Harries technique is used with a handheld light, and is easy, but costs some of your

4.3.39 – Gun-mounted   4.3.40 – Harries Technique

weapons control. To use the technique, grab the flashlight with a backhand grip (light pointing out bottom of hand) and cross your reaction-hand wrist under your strong hand. It's important that you go wrist-to-wrist for added support, and also keep your strong arm straight out. You've already taken one hand off the gun—don't make your position any weaker by bending your arm!

FBI Technique

The FBI technique, as the name implies, was developed for FBI for agents to use a handheld light but try to avoid getting shot by suspects shooting at the light. In the FBI technique, you hold the light the same as the Harries technique, but rather than crossing your wrists you extend the light up and away

from your head. This is a good technique if you are using a larger light. It can also be used effectively to cast shadows on objects that may be hard to see straight on.

Ayoob Technique

This is the newest technique in the group, but the one I've quickly learned to like the most. Developed by Massad Ayoob, it allows you to keep a better grip on your gun and to shoot and move more naturally. In this technique, you hold the light in the palm of your reaction hand, pointing out between your index and middle fingers. I find this works great with lights that have a pressure button on the bottom, as I pull the light into a knuckle on my strong hand to actuate the light.

4.3.41 – FBI Technique

4.3.42 – Ayoob Technique

Training notes: _____

_____

_____

_____

_____

_____

_____

_____

_____

_____

_____

_____

_____

_____

_____

Training notes: _____

_____

_____

_____

_____

_____

_____

_____

_____

_____

_____

_____

_____

_____

_____

_____

4

Carbine Manipulations

Just as with your pistol, "eyes, muzzle, target" should be your mantra with the carbine. I've heard some nonsense about keeping your gun pointed at the enemy while you're working on it, so he doesn't know your gun is down—this is the stupidest line of thinking I've ever heard! If they are close enough to see the angle of your gun, they can see what you're doing to it, and if you're relying on visual deception to cover for your bad technique, I recommend running as a better chance of keeping your lineage alive.

Now that we're moving the gun around, we must discuss sling length. The length of your sling depends on what your plans are with the gun—or it should. As with many pieces of kit, most people get a new sling in the mail and they think the length it's set at is how they should carry their gun. But you need to set the length so your sling

can be an asset and not a liability. What I use as a rule of thumb is my thumb. Make a fist with your thumb straight up, and put your thumb under your chin. The bottom of your fist should be resting on top of your buttstock with your gun hanging in front. It will vary between shooters, but this is good starting place and better than having a hot barrel banging you in the knees if you need to transition to your pistol on the move.

Loading

You'll see a lot of commonality between pistol and carbine manipulation. This is for consistency, which will save you a lot of training time and also save your ass when the shit hits the fan. Loading your carbine is an opportunity to train. Don't pass it up. Let's learn the right way.

One note on loading your carbine, for those who are "old school" or learned from an old-school instructor: It's okay to load your AR magazines with thirty rounds if you make sure you can seat your magazine with one in the chamber and that it doesn't cause malfunctions. I was taught as a tadpole that you never load thirty rounds in a magazine (always twenty-eight) because this will cause your gun to jam. And it did, back then. But now we have better guns and magazines, so test it out on the range, and if you can, always load thirty rounds because there's no reason to sell yourself two rounds short!

Before you get started, I see a lot of people on the range doing this backwards, so I want to set the record straight. Check your sling length, sights, and lights; tie your shoes; check your Twitter account—whatever you need to do *before* you load your gun. More often than not, people load up and then check all the things they should've checked first. Maybe nobody ever told them—you just lost your excuse!

Finally, as with your pistol loadout, set yourself up for success by putting your magazine pouches where your hands naturally want to go. Don't mess with years of evolution by forcing yourself to retrain your body in how it naturally wants to move. If you can, find that "sweet spot" for at least one magazine for your carbine, and put the others where you have room and time to find and load if needed.

4.4.1 – Always load your pistol first if using one

The primary load is how you should load your empty carbine when you're not under any stress. You're either getting ready to go on patrol, just stepping up to the firing line, or loading up to start a competition. The differences with this load and the others I cover are that you're going to check to ensure that your gun will go *bang* when you press the trigger and set up your magazines after you load. To load:

4.4.2 – Bring the gun back into your workspace

4.4.3 – Load from your sweet spot

1. Always load your secondary weapon first if you're using one. Why? Because it's on your first-line gear, the stuff you want when TSHTF.

2. As stated above, mess with all your gear and make sure everything is set now before you load. Start off with your bolt locked to the rear.

3. Bring your gun up like you just looked up and saw the Terminator drawing

down on you and your loved ones, standing behind you.

4. Practice a dry-fire repetition, put gun back on safe.

5. Bring the weapon straight back into your workspace by breaking it off your shoulder, bringing the buttstock back, and pinning it between your forearm and the side of your stomach.

4.4.4 – Remember E-M-T

4.4.5 – Glance down if needed

6. Grab the magazine from your sweet spot. Do not grab one from your pocket or one you have randomly tucked into your kit. When you grab your magazines, you have two choices: Index the magazine just like a pistol magazine, or use a "beer can" grip. How you grab the magazine depends on where you have it on your kit or belt. Much like other techniques, you should reverse-engineer this step: Start holding the magazine ready to insert it

into the magazine well, then put it back into its pouch. For me, my sweet spot is on my belt, where I run one mag of 5.56 and use a beer can grip. My other magazines are on the center of my chest where I index the magazines.

7. Keep your eyes up on target. Glance down to make sure the magazine is going to make it into the magazine well smoothly, but get your eyes right back up as soon as it finds the hole.

4.4.6 – Release the bolt with your thumb

8. Continue inserting the magazine in one continuous, firm motion until it locks into place, and quickly pull down to ensure it's set.

9. Roll your thumb up to the bolt release and press it. It's right there, why not use it?

10. Drive the gun straight out and use this golden opportunity to take one more step down the path of perfection.

4.4.7 – Mount the gun

11. Decide not to shoot, practice a good scan, and assess.

12. If you want to do a press check, now is when you should do it.

13. Move your magazines toward your sweet spot so you're ready to roll.

Press Check

4.4.8 – Index grip

4.4.9 – Beer can grip

I won't debate press checks again, but there is an easier way with the carbine that you can consider. When loading, check which side brass is on in the magazine (left or right), and remember it. After you load the gun, drop the magazine out and look to see what side the round is on. If it's on the other side, there is only one place it can be—in the chamber. Your gun is hot! At night or other low-light conditions, use your finger to feel which side the round is on. When you reinsert the magazine, pull on it to make sure it's seated.

If there is a magazine in and the bolt is forward, I use the same technique to do a press check. I release the magazine and then look and feel where the round is. Next I reinsert the magazine, making sure I push and then pull down on the magazine to make sure it's seated. Then I cycle the weapon by pulling all the way back on the charging handle and letting go, so the weapon goes fully into battery. I drop the magazine again, check where the round is, and reinsert again with a firm push-pull. If the round moved, she's hot! If there was a round in the chamber, yes, I'm down a round. But for me, this is a better outcome than causing a malfunction.

Note: The first round will always be on the right in a magazine with an even number of rounds, twenty-eight or thirty. What you do with this information is up to you.

4.4.10 – Easy press check – Look and feel which side the top round is on

4.4.11 – Load the weapon

4.4.12 – Release and feel again

4.4.13 – A traditional press check

The more traditional way to do a press check with a carbine is to rotate the gun so you can see inside the ejection port and then pull back on the charging handle with your reaction hand. I don't recommend this method because you can't feel for brass with your trigger finger in low-light operations, and the bolt often won't go into battery since you're riding the bolt home. If you do use this method, remember to pull back only far enough to identify the brass, and always hit the forward assist.

I can teach a monkey to pull a trigger, its all the other stuff that makes a great shooter.

4.4.14 – Unloading – Release the magazine

4.4.16 – Pull back on charging handle

4.4.15 – Unloading – Release the magazine

4.4.17 – Pull back on charging handle

Unloading

As with our pistols, we want to have as much carryover in training for everything we do, even unloading a carbine. Of course the best way to unload is via the muzzle, but sometimes that's impossible and we need to take the following steps.

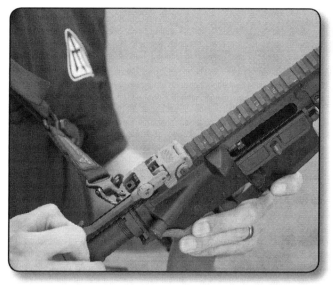

4.4.18 – Lock the bolt to the rear

To unload:

1. Drive into a solid fighting stance and bring your gun up on target.

2. Decide not to shoot.

3. Bring the weapon straight back into your workspace by breaking it off your shoulder and bringing the buttstock back and pinning it between your forearm and the side of your stomach.

4. Push the magazine release with your trigger finger and grab the magazine with your support hand. Put it away in a pouch as if you just did a tactical reload.

5. Grab the gun under the magazine well with your support hand with your thumb on the bottom of bolt release. Pull the charging handle back with

4.4.19 – Observe the chamber is empty

your strong hand and lock it to the rear by pressing down on the bottom of the bolt release with the thumb of your support hand. Lock the charging handle in the forward position.

4.4.20 – Physically inspect the chamber

4.4.21 – Physically inspect the magazine well

6. Tilt the gun down to look forward into the chamber to make sure it's clear.

7. Tilt the gun back to make sure there is no magazine in the magazine well.

8. With your finger, feel inside the chamber to make sure there is no round.

9. With your finger, feel up inside the magazine well to make sure there is no magazine.

10. Check to make sure the weapon's fire selector switch is in on safe.

11. If someone else is there, ask them to do a "buddy check," verifying the same things.

4.4.22 – The world is safe

4.4.23 – It's go time

Working the Fire Selector Switch (Safety)

Ever stop to think about why some people call it the "safety" switch? It's not like some magical switch that, when you have it switched off, the whole world is safe. It's possible that by not having the weapon on "fire" you could be harmed and thus unsafe. It's the same thing in traffic when some people call traffic lights "stop" lights when you could just as easily call them "go" lights.

Well, whatever you want to call the switch that controls when your gun goes bang, you need to know how to use it effectively. The key is dry-fire training. It's not just with your selector switch, but every detail of your shooting package. The great thing about dry-fire training is that you can get in a lot more repetitions and it's no less effective than live fire.

The key to being able to rotate the switch rapidly is to always hold your weapon properly. This means that you've got a solid grip with your strong hand, with your thumb on top of the selector switch. You also need to maintain a good grip with your support hand because driving the gun up helps with the process. So don't just bring the gun up, then move the selector; use your thumb coming down and the gun coming up against each other—you'll be ready to fire in half the time.

4.4.24 – Canting the weapon to see inside the chamber

Reloads

I'll cover two different reloads for the carbine: speed and tactical. These are slightly different from the pistol reloads, but the goals are the same: the least possible downtime with the highest possible success rate.

Speed

Like the slide-lock pistol reload, the carbine speed reload needs to become second nature. The reason is that whether you're in combat or competition, your brain needs to be thinking about other things while your body gets the job done. In combat you will often also have to make the tactical decision whether you're going to transition

4.4.25 – Use momentum to clear the empty magazine

or reload, so a lot of neurons are working, and the process must be as simple and smooth as possible.

To do a speed reload:

1. The first thing to learn is what your gun feels like when it's empty and needs refueling. At first you may need to cant the gun slightly so you can see into the ejection port, but in time you'll notice it feels a certain way when the gun fires and the bolt locks to the rear.

2. To start, bring the weapon straight back into your workspace by breaking

4.4.26 – Reach for new magazine

4.4.27 – Keep eyes up

it off your shoulder and bringing the buttstock back and pinning it between your forearm and the side of your stomach. As with all of your manipulations, remember: EMT (eyes, muzzle, threat) in line, all the time.

3. As you bring the weapon back, you must do two things at once: press the magazine release with your index finger as your reaction hand goes for the fresh magazine.

4. Grab the magazine from your sweet spot and twist your carbine quickly to use inertia to help propel the magazine out.

5. Keep your eyes up on target, glancing down only long enough to make sure the magazine will make it into the magazine well smoothly.

6. Continue inserting the magazine in one continuous, firm motion until it locks into place, and quickly pull down to ensure it's set.

7. Roll your thumb up to the bolt release and press it.

8. Drive the gun straight out as your reaction hand drives forward to secure its grip.

Tactical

The steps for a carbine tactical reload are the same as with your pistol. Since carbine magazines are bigger, the way you hold the magazines will be slightly different but will help ensure the procedure is quick and you don't lose a magazine in the process.

To do a tactical reload:

1. Since you have the time to make an informed decision, think through the steps before you start.

2. Keeping your gun up and ready to engage, reach down with your support hand and grab a magazine from where you keep your reserve ammunition. Do not go for the sweet spot because you have time and you don't want your primary mag pouch empty if everything goes to hell in the middle of your reload or before you have time to shift ammo. Hold the fresh mag by the bottom, with the front bottom edge of the magazine in the center of the palm, between the thumb and index finger.

3. Once you have the magazine, bring the gun straight back into your workspace.

4. Bring your support hand and magazine up to the magazine in the gun and lay it across, forming an "L,"

4.4.28 – Think before you start

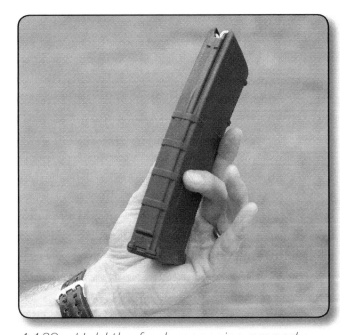

4.4.29 – Hold the fresh magazine properly

with the top of the magazine pointing forward. Hold onto both magazines.

5. Release the old magazine with your trigger finger and pull it out.

4.4.30 – Release the old magazine

4.4.32 – Rotate and insert the fresh magazine

4.4.31 – Form an "L" with the magazines

4.4.33 – Ensure magazine is fully seated

6. Insert the fresh magazine by rotating the fresh magazine up. Make sure the magazine is secure by pulling down on the magazine. (Make sure you're not pressing on the magazine release!)

7. Store the used magazine in the farthest spot from your gun.

Transitioning

Transitioning means moving from one weapon system to another. Since your hands are weapons, drawing your sidearm is technically a transition from empty-hand fighting to firearm fighting. Whatever weapon you're transitioning to, make sure you will gain a tactical advantage. What I mean is that just because your primary weapon malfunctions, don't automatically think that you have to or should transition to your sidearm, as many LE agencies teach. What if you're too far away to make effective shots with your pistol (this distance is different for everyone) or if you're behind effective cover? What if someone draws their pistol when you're interviewing them? Should you automatically draw your pistol and hope to win the fight? Statistically you're going to lose that fight if you do, yet most officers are trained to practice drawing from the interview stance so much that it's what they're going to do under stress.

So the most important part about any transition in training, combat, or competition is to predetermine under what circumstances you're going to transition so the decisions are well thought out in advance. Doing this will save your mental energy for all the other variables you need to be thinking about. That said, the specific transition that I'll cover is from your primary (carbine) to your secondary (pistol) weapon, and then how to transition back. As with anything else you're

learning, start super slow, making sure your movements are exact. As you practice more, speed will be a natural byproduct of training.

Note 1: There's something I need to clear up that is taught by well-meaning instructors, who may not know exactly how weapons work. You don't need to put your weapon on safe when transitioning due to a stoppage (a tactical transition is different). If your weapon doesn't fire when you pull the trigger, it's not going to fire when it's hanging in front of you. You are either out of ammo or there is a malfunction stopping the gun for firing, and neither will be fixed by letting go of your gun.

Note 2: Don't roll the gun to look at the ejection port before you transition, either. It

4.4.34 – Transitioning to your pistol – Bring carbine straight down with your hand on top

doesn't matter why it's not working. It's not working, and we've already predefined the circumstances where we're going to transition. You can look after you have a working weapon in your hands, or when the fight is over.

To transition from carbine to pistol due to stoppage:

1. As stated above, this is *not* the time to make decisions. Realize you have a stoppage and get to work!

2. Both your arms come down together: Your strong hand immediately lets go of the gun and makes a beeline for your pistol. The support hand lowers the carbine straight down. Rotate the carbine so when you let go, your hand

will be on top, not under the gun. If it is, your hand will have to move around the carbine to come up to the pistol. Also, do not waste time slinging your carbine off to the side. It takes longer and usually ends up coming back to land in front of you anyway.

3. Move your reaction hand up to the centerline of your body, and rotate your hand so your fingers point down at about 45 degrees, ready to meet the pistol.

4. Now, as usual, is one of the many times to stay consistent in your techniques and simply draw and mount your pistol using the rubber band draw covered earlier.

4.4.35 – Draw pistol as normal

4.4.36 – Fully transitioned

After transitioning and winning the fight, you should look for a tactically sound opportunity to get your long gun back up. Maybe this is after you've cleared a room and have effective security, or it may not be until the end of a competition. Every situation is different, but again, work out as many scenarios as possible ahead of time so you're not down a gun in the middle of a gunfight.

To transition back to a carbine from a pistol after a stoppage:

1. Bring your pistol back into the retention position.

2. Grab your carbine with your reaction hand and bring it up so you can see into the ejection port to identify the reason for the stoppage.

3. Here you will need to take one of two directions on your preplanned tactical road map: 1) Your carbine ran out of rounds and needs to be fed or has a malfunction that can be fixed quickly; continue to Step 4; or 2) Your carbine has a major malfunction. Keep your pistol out and look for cover or security for you to clear the malfunction.

4. Holster your pistol.

5. Bring the carbine up into your workspace and do a speed reload as described earlier.

4.4.37 – Transitioning back to your carbine Bring your pistol back to retention and check the chamber

4.4.38 – Holster

4.4.39 – Reload as normal

4.4.41 – Reload as normal

4.4.40 – Reload as normal

4.4.42 – Back in the fight

Using Lights

Using lights with your carbine depends on what you use it for and when it's employed. If you're part of a Special Operation or SWAT team, your ability to utilize your light properly could mean the difference between life and death for you. If you use a carbine for home defense and live with others, it could mean the difference between life and death for someone you love. But if on you use a carbine only in three-gun competitions, you'd be better served spending your time on other critical tasks. For the rest of you who could potentially end up using your carbine in low- or no-light situations, I'll try to shed some light on the subject. (Sorry, I'm a SEAL, not a comedian!)

I'm sure I'm starting to sound like a broken record, but to be effective, you need to train using your light. More than any other shooting accessory, it seems lights are the number one item for people to buy, put on a gun, and never train using properly. You should never rely on any accessory to make you a better shooter, but if you're not going to train with it, take it off your gun because it has a better chance of making your situation worse than of helping you. Switching your light on and off may seem simple, but if you haven't practiced, under stress it can feel like doing brain surgery with oven mitts on. We'll discuss using a weapon-mounted light, as well as a few handheld techniques I like to use as a backup if my weapon light stops working.

4.4.43 – Gun mounted

Gun-mounted

If you've had your ears open so far, you can predict the points I'm going to bring up for using a gun-mounted light on your carbine. First is deciding to use either the thumb switch or a pressure pad. A lot of people don't like pressure pads because in the past they were very unreliable, and I wouldn't use them them either. But nowadays there are quality pressure pads out there that have never failed me in the harshest environments. If you choose a thumb switch because that works better for your setup, that's great, but don't resort to that because you think a pad will fail. Buy quality when you're putting your life on the line.

Next up is placement of the light. Earlier I pointed out the importance of putting your accessories where your hands aren't. The most common place I see people mount their new light is right where they should

Forward Grip Hold

Although it's not the best place to mount a light, the forward grip hold does keep your grip the closest to how you naturally shoot and is the best way to support the gun. One big downside is the difficulty of turning the light off and on, so light discipline can be a problem. To use this method, simply pin the light between the forward rail of your gun and your hand.

4.4.44 – Cross-support

be establishing a proper grip with their support hand. This is one reason I really like a pressure pad since I can mount the light on the strong side of my gun and put the pressure pad on top, where my thumb naturally goes to control recoil.

Cross-support

The cross-support technique uses the handheld light much like the Harries technique with the pistol. To do this, grab the flashlight with a backhand grip (light pointing out bottom of hand) and cross your support arm under the front of your magazine. From here you can either support the gun with your wrist or around the middle of your forearm. I like it better on my forearm since this allows me to move the light around a little easier, but it's really shooter preference. This is the only technique I use, because it's the only technique that allows you to turn the light off and on quickly and easily.

4.4.45-46-47 – Forward grip hold

Positive Retention

Positive retention is the ability to let go of your carbine with both hands and secure it to your body so you can attend to other tasks. Think of it as a sort of "holster" for your carbine. Not everyone needs to secure their carbine, but it's one of those things that's often overlooked by those who do. If you ever have the need to go hands-on with someone or place someone in cuffs, that big, long piece of metal swinging around can hurt, and I've seen more than a few sights get broken when someone failed to secure their weapon properly.

Never just attach something to your kit and think you'll be able to use it effectively when the need arises.

There are a few different systems for putting a carbine into positive retention. One is the weapons catch, a U-shaped device with a Velcro closure that normally attaches to your belt. The other, becoming more popular, is the elastic band weapons catch, basically a piece of bungee cord attached to your plate carrier that you can wrap around the weapon and then back to your kit. Which system you should use depends on what positions you'll be in when your gun is in positive retention, as well as what type of kit you wear. Obviously if you don't wear a plate carrier, a bungee system will not work; likewise, if you need to fast-rope, a system that keeps the gun on your chest isn't the best choice. The good news is there are lots of variations out there; you just need to define your mission and then find or make one that works best for you.

Once again, never just attach something to your kit and think you'll be able to use it effectively when the need arises. You need to practice both putting your weapon into and taking it out of positive retention. As with every skill, you need to break down the movements to find the most efficient technique for you, your weapon, and your retention system. Speed is obviously important for taking your weapon out in the event you need to engage a threat, but speed can be just as important in securing the weapon. If your partner is covering a suspect and you need to put your gun away to go hands-on, you need to make it quick in case that's the time this guy decides he doesn't want to be cuffed and starts to run. Most likely your partner still can't shoot him, so you'll need to go hands-on quickly.

You also need to think about what is exposed or rubbing on your kit when your weapon is in retention. I've seen magazines get ejected, and selector switches rotated. If you can, mitigate the chances of these things happening by recognizing them and making adjustments. Of course, the only way you'll know if it's likely to happen is to practice, not only putting it into and taking it out of retention, but also doing whatever you're likely to do with the gun in retention. If it's fast-roping, find a rope and climb it. If it's cuffing someone, do some basic ground defense. Finally, make it a habit to check your gun every time you come out of retention. Check your selector switch and give your magazine a quick tug. A few simple steps could save your life—or at least not make you look dumb!

Left-Hand-dominant Shooters

Let's finish up with a few techniques for my friends who are very closely related to us genetically: left-handed shooters (just kidding)! Seriously, other than being a right-rear-door gunner or doing a right-hand buttonhook into a room, you guys have it pretty tough. I highly recommend that you either build or retrofit your gun with ambidextrous controls and avoid having to learn special techniques to work your weapon. If you're in the military or law enforcement, you may not have that option, so here are a few things I teach my southpaws on the range.

Loading

1. Load your secondary weapon first if you're using one.

2. Check all your kit, lights, and sights. Start off with your bolt locked to the rear.

3. Find a safe target and practice mounting the gun.

4. Practice a dry-fire repetition, then put gun back on safe.

5. Bring the weapon straight back into your workspace by breaking it off your shoulder and bringing the buttstock back and pinning it between your forearm and the side of your stomach.

6. Grab the magazine from your sweet spot. Do not grab one from your pocket or one you have randomly tucked into your kit unless this is where you keep them when your life is on the line. When you grab your magazines, you have two choices: index the magazine just like a pistol magazine or use a "beer-can" grip. How you grab the magazine depends on where you have it on your kit or belt, and you should reverse-engineer this step. Start holding the magazine ready to insert it into the magazine well, then put it back into its pouch.

7. Keep your eyes up on the target. Glance down to make sure the magazine is going to make it into the magazine well smoothly, but get your eyes right back up as soon as it finds the hole.

4.4.48 – Trigger finger releasing the bolt

8. Continue inserting the magazine in one continuous, firm motion until it locks into place, and quickly pull down to ensure it's set.

9. Use your trigger finger to press the bolt release. Here is one advantage for lefties: If you look in the ejection port, you can see the bolt picking up and chambering a round. (Figure 4.4.48)

10. Drive the gun straight out and use this golden opportunity to take one more step along the path of perfection.

11. Decide not to shoot, practice a good scan, and assess.

12. If you want to do a press check, now is when you should do it.

13. Move your magazines toward your sweet spot so you're ready to roll.

Unloading

1. Drive into a solid fighting stance and bring your gun up on a target.

2. Decide not to shoot!

3. Bring the weapon straight back into your workspace by breaking it off your shoulder and bringing the buttstock back and pinning it between your forearm and the side of your stomach.

4. Push the magazine release with your thumb as you grab the magazine with your support hand. Put it away in a pouch as if you just did a tactical reload. (Figure 4.4.49)

4.4.49 – Pushing magazine release with thumb

5. Pull the charging handle back with your support hand and lock it to the rear by pressing down on the bottom of the bolt release with your trigger finger. Lock the charging handle in the forward position.

6. Tilt the gun down to look forward into the chamber to make sure it's clear.

7. Tilt the gun back to make sure there is no magazine in the magazine well.

8. With your finger, feel the inside the chamber to make sure there is no round.

9. With your finger, feel up inside the magazine well to make sure there is no magazine.

10. Check to make sure the weapon's fire selector switch is on safe.

11. If someone else is there, ask them to do a "buddy check," verifying the same things.

Working the Fire Selector Switch (Safety)

Next up is something discussed previously for right-handed shooters when shooting reaction side and manipulating the fire selector switch. When they start, most people feel more comfortable using their thumb to put the weapon on fire, and using their trigger finger to put it back on safe.

4.4.50 – Using your thumb on selector

4.4.51 – Make sure your establish a good grip before shooting

4.4.52 – Using the trigger finger to come off fire

4.4.53 – 2nd knuckle working fire control

4.4.54 – Ready to get to work

This is fine, but you need to remember to re-grip the gun properly, and this can take time. If speed is high on your priority list, the other, faster option is using the second knuckle of a straight trigger finger to do both. This technique will take more practice, but in the end you'll be a lot faster.

Speed Reloads

1. The first thing you need to learn is what your gun feels like when it's on empty and needs refueling. Another advantage to being left-hand-dominant is that you can see the ejection port and should be able to see that you need to reload without canting the gun.

2. To start, bring the weapon straight back into your workspace by breaking it off your shoulder and bringing the buttstock back and pinning it between your forearm and the side of your stomach. Always remember: EMT (eyes, muzzle, threat) in line, all the time.

3. As soon as you start bringing the weapon back, you need to slide your support hand back and press the magazine release with your thumb. Pull the magazine straight out and release it as soon as it's clear of the magazine well.

4. Grab the magazine from your sweet spot.

5. Keeping your eyes up on the target, glance down only long enough to make sure the magazine is going to make it into the magazine well smoothly.

6. Continue inserting the magazine in one continuous, firm motion until it locks into place, and then quickly pull down to ensure it's set.

7. Press the bolt release with your trigger finger.

8. Drive the gun straight out as your reaction hand drives forward to secure its grip.

Tactical Reload

1. Since you have the time to make an informed decision, think through the steps before you start.

2. Keeping your gun up and ready to engage, reach down with your support hand and grab a magazine from where you keep your reserve ammunition. Do not go for the sweet spot because you have time and you don't want your primary mag pouch empty if everything goes to hell in the middle of your reload, or before

you have time to shift ammo. Hold the fresh mag with a beer can grip by the bottom half, with the front bottom edge of the magazine between the pinkie and ring finger.

3. Once you have the magazine, bring the gun straight back into your workspace.

4. Bring your reaction hand and magazine up to the magazine in the gun, and press the magazine release with your thumb. Hold onto both magazines.

5. Pull out the old magazine with your index finger between the two magazines.

6. Slide your pinkie under the bottom of the fresh magazine and insert it by moving both magazines over. Make sure the magazine is secure by pulling down on it.

7. Store the used magazine in the farthest spot from your gun.

Training notes: _____

_____

_____

_____

_____

All malfunctions get fixed in your workspace. Your head should be up where you can see the battlefield or your next target, or be able to move with the gun up, pointed in a safe direction so you can glance at it as needed to solve the problem quicker.

5

Malfunctions

I'm sure you've heard that the best offense is a good defense. Well, in gunfighting there are few places I find this to be true, other than defending against malfunctions. The reason is that the more you can keep your gun up and running, the more you can stay on the offense. This holds true in combat and competition. Malfunctions suck. First, try to avoid them, and then know how to fix them quickly.

First let's talk about how to avoid malfunctions. I use an acronym to remember the main causes of malfunctions: SCREAMED—something you likely did, with colorful language, when you got one, but surprisingly didn't help fix it.

S - Spring: If you've had the gun awhile, check this, because it has a service life. The spring can get compressed and not give you the recoil you need to properly cycle the weapon. Also under spring, I group the shooter who can cause malfunctions by not giving the spring anything to "spring" against. Make sure you're providing a solid platform for the gun to recoil off of if you're having failure-to-feed problems.

C – Clean: Is your gun dirty? Would you like to work properly if you were dirty? When your gun gets gummed up, it doesn't work properly, and you can have multiple problems including failure to go into battery. Read the manual that came with your gun and learn how to clean it. You should do some type of cleaning on your gun every time you use it. That doesn't mean you need to break it down each time, but learn what your gun needs and keep it clean.

R – Recoil guide rod: The guide rod can get dirty or dinged and, like the spring, will also slow down the proper function of your firearm.

E – Extractor: The extractor plays a vital role in getting ammo into and out of your gun on time. Very small defects in this little piece can cause major performance problems. Extractors can get worn out, no longer holding the casing in the proper position. The best thing to do to diagnose one of these problems is to know what it should look like and if you see something different, you'll know where the problem is.

Because magazines cause a large percentage of malfunctions, do not reload with the same magazine if at all possible.

A – Ammunition: You get what you pay for. After twenty years in the military, I learned that oftentimes the sale goes to the lowest bidder. We've had some really bad batches that, if it were a commercial purchase, I would've asked for my money back. SAAMI (Sporting Arms and Ammunition Manufacturers Institute) issues very exacting specification for each type of round, but there are allowable variances. This means that some ammo may not work with your gun, and some manufacturers many not have the best quality control, so what works one day at the range might not work the next.

M – Magazines: For those of us who keep our guns clean, magazines are the number one cause of malfunctions. There are several reasons, from being dirty to bad springs and followers, but the main cause I see is bent feed lips, and the reason is normally forcing rounds into the magazines with the edge of a loading bench. Toughen up your fingers and thumbs, and use those to put your ammo in the mag. If you've got a speed loader, use it, but don't slam it down and bend your feed ramps. If you're loading magazines and the rounds pop back out, this indicates that you have worn feed lips, which will cause malfunctions, normally double feeds. Sometimes they can be fixed, but not when you need them to work. Because magazines cause a large percentage of malfunctions, do not reload with the same magazine if at all possible. I recommend you mark all your magazines with your initials or some other identifying mark and number. This way you can keep track of magazines with problems. So if you keep getting double-feed malfunctions with number 3, consider that a bad magazine and fix it or get a new one.

E – Ejector: If you've got ejector problems, your spent casings will have a hard time finding their way out of your gun. Ejectors can become loose or cracked, causing ejection issues. As with your extractor, the best way to diagnose one of these problems is to know what they look like new, and if you see something different, you've diagnosed your problem.

D – Dry: Just as a dirty gun makes it run rough, not enough lube can do the same thing. Lubing your gun before you fire each day is a must, and if you're running a full-day course, you should do it at your lunch or dinner break. Failure to go into battery is a common problem with a dry gun.

I'm going to cover four malfunctions:

- Failure to feed

- Failure to go into battery

- Stovepipe

- Double feed

Note: These are not types of malfunctions by number as taught by many police and military units. I've found it easier just to give them names so everyone knows what I'm talking about.

For most of these, the answer could be a simple tap, rack, bang when you hear the "click." I know some sea lawyers are out there screaming, "You need to reassess your threat!" Well, no shit, Sherlock. You *always* reassess your threat, so I'm not sure why some people get so worked up about this only when it comes to malfunctions. If it makes you feel better (slows you down), ask your enemy in a gunfight if it's okay for you to keep going. Just don't be surprised when the last thing you hear is *bang*.

With all these treatments for your weapon, there are various ways to accomplish clearing, and I recommend you try them and see which you like best and also practice them because each has its time and place. One thought process is to diagnose the problem quickly before moving on to the treatment because this can save time in execution. The other thought process is to try the easy or most common fix, and if that doesn't work, move onto the next step (remedial action).

All malfunctions get fixed in your workspace. Your head should be up where you can see the battlefield or your next target, or be able to move with the gun up, pointed in a safe direction so you can glance at it as needed to solve the problem quicker.

Pistol

Failure to feed: The gun goes click or what we call "the sound of a dead man's gun." The magazine may not be seated: tap, rack, bang. Tap upward on the bottom of the magazine, rack the slide all the way back and release, and fire for effect. This is normally caused by weak-loading the magazine and not hearing the "confidence click." The other time we see a failure to feed is what I think should be called "should not breed," wherein the shooter loads an empty magazine into the gun. If this is where you're at in your gun handling skills, try not to get into a gunfight anytime soon.

4.5.1 – Gun goes click

4.5.2 – Tilt gun up if needed to diagnose

4.5.3 – Tap (hit really hard)

4.5.4 – Rack (Rip it and let go)

4.5.5 – Continue delivering customer service

If you want to diagnose the problem first, you can tilt the muzzle up slightly. If everything looks normal and the trigger went *click*, the mag is not seated — tap, rack, bang as above.

Note: As discussed in the pistol manipulations chapter, I like using the power stroke method as opposed to the slingshot for immediate action. If you use a slingshot, roll the pistol over toward your reaction hand to rack— it's faster.

Failure to go into battery: The trigger is mushy. The slide is not all the way forward — tap up on the bottom of the magazine, rack slide all the way back, release, and shoot.

If you want to diagnose the problem first, tilt the muzzle up slightly. You can see the slide is not fully forward, so assist it forward with fist or palm.

Note: You will lose a round doing the first method.

4.5.6 – Slide is not fully forward

4.5.7 – Heel strike back into battery

4.5.8 – Or hammer fist

4.5.9 – I can't see my front sight

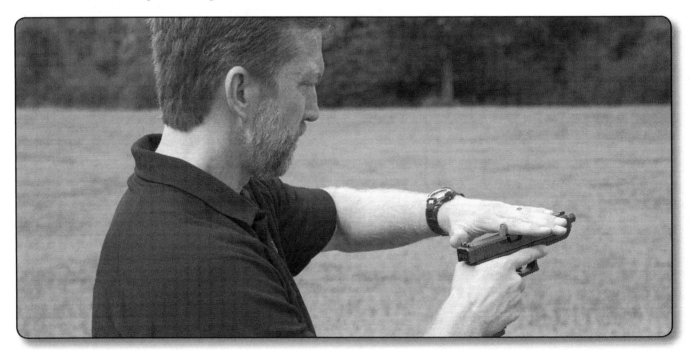

4.5.10 – Cut away with knife-hand

Stovepipe: The trigger is mushy. For this one, I teach only one method because if you don't see a piece of brass sticking out of the top of your gun, you're not looking at your sights and therefore shouldn't be shooting semiautomatic weapons. When you see this, power stroke over the top with a knife hand. You don't even need to cycle the weapon unless it's dry or dirty. If you notice it didn't go into battery, you many need to tap the back of the slide.

Note: Watch the path of your hand and fingers as you bring them over the top, so as not to put your hand in front of your muzzle.

Double feed: There is a lot going on with a double feed, and several options you could (and should) practice to see which you like and will work with your chosen bang-stick. With a double feed, you've got two rounds in chamber fighting for position. The traditional method would have you do your immediate action (tap, rack, bang), but there is no "bang" so you need to reassess, by looking into the chamber and seeing what I call the rat's nest. Lock the slide to the rear, strip the magazine, rack the slide three times, and reload.

If you want to try to diagnose the problem first, you can tilt the muzzle up slightly. You've got a mushy trigger and should be able to see that the slide is pretty far back and then see the bright chamber with all the shiny brass. Lock the slide to the rear, strip the magazine, rack the slide three times, and reload.

Bonus points: If you rack the slide once and see the brass ejected, that's all you need to do—it's clear. The reason you do it three times is for habit at night, when you can't see or in the event you miss it coming out.

Double bonus points: Push the magazine release while you rack the slide. This saves a step. If you can grab any part of the magazine, rip it and rack it. This may not work on all pistols, so try them out with dummy rounds or on the range.

Carbine

One of the keys to being successful if you run both a pistol and a carbine for your job, competition, personal security, or just for fun is to be able to keep things consistent across multiple shooting platforms. The more you can do this the better.

Failure to feed: Off safe — *click*. The magazine is not seated or is empty. Tap the bottom of the magazine, rack the charging handle, and bang away.

4.5.11 – Roll to asses if you want to waste some time

4.5.12 – Tap

4.5.13 – Rack

If you want to diagnose the problem first, you can roll the chamber up slightly. If everything looks normal and the trigger went *click*, the mag is not seated. Tap, rack, bang as above.

4.5.14 – Bang

Failure to go into battery: The trigger is mushy. The slide is not all the way forward. Tap the bottom of the magazine, rack the charging handle, and bang away.

If you want to diagnose the problem first, you can roll the chamber up slightly. You can see the bolt is not fully forward, so forward assist with your thumb.

4.5.15 – With a mushy trigger, it's worth it to look

4.5.16 – Forward assist with thumb

4.5.17 – Forward assist with thumb

4.5.18 – Forward assist with palm

4.5.19 – Assess the situation

4.5.20 – Sweep away in one quick motion

4.5.21 – Sweep away in one quick motion

4.5.22 – You may need to hit the forward assist

Stovepipe: This is not as common with the carbine as with the pistol, but we do see it when shooting with the ejection port close to a wall or tilted over to the ground. You've got brass sticking out. You'll likely not notice it at first and do immediate action, which may or may not work. If it works, get back into the fight. If it doesn't, assess your weapon and see what you've got and sweep the brass so you can get back to delivering excellent customer service.

If you want to diagnose the problem first, roll the chamber up slightly. You'll see there is the proverbial rat's nest, and you can just sweep it away and get back to business.

4.5.23 – Tapping will not help this

4.5.24 – Lock the bolt back

4.5.25 – Rip the magazine out

4.5.26 – Rack as needed to clear

Double feed: You've got two rounds in chamber fighting for position. Traditional doctrine has you perform an immediate action (tap, rack, bang) and find it doesn't work (in this case it may even make it worse). You'll then reassess the situation, see the shit-show, strip the magazine if possible, pull the bolt to the rear with the side of the magazine on the charging handle if needed, and push rounds loose with your fingers inside the magazine well. Load and go. If you're not able to strip the magazine, take tension off the magazine by locking the slide to the rear, then go through the other steps.

NAVY SEAL SHOOTING   CHRIS SAJNOG

If you want to diagnose the problem first, you can roll the chamber up slightly and look to see what you have. You notice the problem and roll the other way; hold with your support hand; rack and lock back the bolt; push the charging handle forward with your strong hand; strip the magazine (three racks if it's nighttime or you're not sure it's clear); reinsert and power-stroke (note: same hand position as pistol); and fire. If the chamber is not clear, do what you can to clear it.

There are many other less common malfunctions, but I've got to save something for my next book! Work on firing-hand-only techniques: tap with knee, drop weapon straight between legs, and rack. Watch legs and feet, and be careful with trigger! Always practice dry first!

A final note on malfunctions: No matter what type they are, I see the majority of shooters clear out a malfunction and just move on with their day as if nothing happened. Most likely they are just happy to have it cleared, but they are missing out on one of the most important aspects of proper training, and that's learning. What caused your malfunction? You always need to ask this question, and write it down in your training notebook. This way you can go back and check your gun, magazines, and past malfunctions for trends, so you can help avoid them in the future.

Training notes: _____

_____

_____

_____

_____

_____

_____

_____

318   NavySEALshooting.com

Training notes: _____

_____

_____

_____

_____

_____

_____

_____

_____

_____

_____

_____

_____

_____

_____

_____

Failing to train is training to fail.

6

Movement

When they say the shit hits the fan, the assumption is that it's moving. So unless you're doing bull's-eye shooting, you need to know how to shoot while moving. We all know that saying, "Train how you fight, and you'll fight how you train." This is part of the warrior or fighter mentality and will ultimately play a vital role in your survival as a law enforcement officer (LEO), soldier, sailor, or civilian who carries a concealed weapon. The effort that you put forth in training will directly impact whether you succeed or fail in your objective; and in the U.S. military and law enforcement, we know failure is not an option.

As a Navy SEAL CPO and training department head, I never wanted an operator who disliked training. Think back to your own experiences, and without a doubt you can remember those who complained, didn't

put forth the effort, or simply had a "medical appointment" or some "personal issue" that always came up during training. Remember those guys, and remember that when things went bad during an operation, that person was a huge reason why the failure occurred.

When they say the shit hits the fan, the assumption is that it's moving.

Undoubtedly, or at least I hope, most military and LE operators' favorite training day is going to the range for live-fire exercises. I'm no exception! My favorite live-fire exercises are shooting while moving and shooting from unstable platforms. Sure, static shooting has its place in any good training regimen, but this should be just your foundation to build marksmanship skills and confidence.

You should spend the better part of your time at the range moving on your feet while shooting your weapons, because your survival and your teammates' survival depends on it. Start slow and seek instruction from a seasoned shooter and operator.

Remember that whatever you put into training is what you're going to get out of it. Your teammates' or loved ones' lives rely on your training regimen, and your life depends on theirs. Training should be harder than the actual operation—this way you know your team and you are ready when you accept the mission.

Walking

This is always one of the hardest things for me to teach to people who have been shooting for a long time. The reason is that when I first learned to shoot on the move as a young Navy SEAL, I was taught with nothing in my hands—we just walked properly. Once we could do it consistently correctly, we moved up to holding our guns, and finally, only after everything was perfect were we allowed any ammunition. It's difficult for some high-speed operators who never learned the basics of shooting on the move and went straight to shooting to take a step back to move forward. So whether you're new at this or a salty old dog, start off with the basics to build a solid foundation for movement.

4.6.1 – Walking heel to toe

4.6.2 – Walking heel to toe

4.6.3 – Walking heel to toe

Start without a gun and just walk, keeping a low center of gravity by bending your knees and using them as shock absorbers. If you can, learn to disassociate your upper and lower body when moving. Think of your lower body as the tank treads (mobile shooting platform) and your upper body as the tank turret (gun). Walk heel to toe and keep your head height the same. You never want to be flat-footed when you're shooting, and this is especially true when you're moving. Stay relaxed and think about gliding rather than walking. A great dry-fire drill you can do to practice this is holding a glass of water (or hot coffee if you feel like living on the edge) filled to the rim and walking without spilling the water. When you can walk on the surface you plan to shoot on without spilling any, you're ready to bring some ammo to the party.

Forward

Shooting and moving forward should be the first movement you learn, as it will set the foundation for your other movements. You can practice some subtle techniques to refine your movement, which will make you a more proficient and confident shooter. These include taking smaller steps and as you step, let your heel strike first and let your foot roll forward on the outside of the foot to your toes. You can also tighten your abs, which will help stabilize your shooting platform and keep the path of your feet narrow. This can help reduce side-to-side

4.6.4 – Low center of gravity

4.6.5 – Use knees as shock absorbers

4.6.6 – Keep your feet on a straight line to keep your sights straight

motion as you shift weight to each foot. If you over exaggerate these motions in training, you'll do it properly when it's time to do God's work.

Keys to success:

- Start without a gun.

- Dry-fire before live-fire.

- Lower your center of gravity (bend your knees).

- Tighten abs.

- Take smaller steps.

- Walk a straight line.

- Walk heel to toe.

- Roll on outside of foot.

Lateral

After you've mastered moving forward, it's time to move sideways across your targets. My golden rule is to avoid crossing your feet when moving. It's terrible for balance, and you can easily be caught off guard. Walk as described above and when it's time engage a threat, lock on with your eyes and bring the sights up to your eyes. Keep aware of your foreground and background as you move, because they will be constantly changing. If you have a clear shot, try to stay ahead of your targets by engaging them at a 45-degree angle. The closer you wait until

4.6.7 – Always be aware of your changing foreground and background

4.6.8 – Keep your targets in front of you

4.6.9 – Don't cross your feet

4.6.10 – Keep your hips open when shooting toward your strong side

90 degrees, the harder it will be to shoot across your body, and you will be moving the fastest relative to your target due to the sharper angle.

With both pistol and carbine, it will always be easier to shoot toward your reaction side. So if you're a right-handed shooter and you're moving left to right, you're shooting toward your reaction side. The difficulty with lateral movement is when you need to shoot toward your strong side—this is when we need to do the Groucho. Open up your hips by widening your stance and then point your strong side toe outward, toward the threat. This allows your upper body to rotate more

4.6.11 – It's harder to twist your body with a narrow gait

4.6.12 – Crossing your feet leads to bad things

so you can engage threats as they get closer to a 90-degree angle. In shooting toward your strong side, it's even more important to stay ahead of your targets by engaging at around 45 degrees.

The other thing you can do with your carbine if you're comfortable with it is shooting from your reaction side, but make sure you spend time training shooting off your strong side, as you will likely not have time to switch shoulders in combat or competition. But it is a good tool for the toolbox. Another tool for the carbine is to shift hips and walk backwards once a target/threat is past your 90, plus shooting while walking backwards

(on a smooth surface) is easier than moving forward. One option for shooting a pistol to your strong side is shooting one-handed.

If the distances are close and you feel confident shooting one-handed, you should at least try it out at the range to find your limits. This is a drill I do a lot when I run law enforcement courses, and it leads students to support their buddies and shoot on the move. A final note on lateral movement is that if you're not engaging a target, you're just walking with a gun in your hand. You don't need to Groucho across the battlefield or competition course. Save it for when your gun is making noise.

4.6.13 – The "Groucho"

4.6.14 – Diagonal movement

Diagonal

Obviously moving at a diagonal to your targets is somewhere between moving forward and moving laterally, and the techniques you need to put effective rounds on target are also somewhere in the middle, depending on the angle you're moving in relation to your threat.

Sidestepping

Sidestepping is an important movement that is often overlooked. It's used in the CQC environment if you're moving down your wall to clear an area and is the basis for learning off-line-of-attack movements. Sidestepping also allows you to keep your plates and natural point of aim toward your enemy and opens up your field of view in that direction.

You should learn to do the movement first just as I suggested you learn to walk—with nothing in your hands. When sidestepping, squat down and put your hands up like you're a lineman in football. Bring one foot to the other, and then put it down and push off, widening your stance. Like most movement drills, if done properly your legs should get a good workout and you should look like you're warming up for a football game.

4.6.15 – Sidestepping

4.6.16 – Maintain a solid shooting platform

Off-line-of-attack/ Get off the X

In any situation where someone just started shooting at you, it isn't advisable to stand in a static position. In the SEAL Teams, we're always taught to "get off the X," the "X" being the target area your enemy just designated and can equal death or serious physical injury. Actively engaging your targets while moving to cover is paramount.

Off-line-of-attack movements are any dynamic movements in any direction, and they should be used not just for attacks but also during reloads or clearing malfunctions. The key theory at work with getting off the line of attack, or getting off the X, is that action is quicker than reaction. So when someone is aimed at you and shooting, once you move that person now has to react off of your movement before he can accurately engage you again, and hopefully this will give you time to draw your weapon and neutralize the threat before that happens. When making your dynamic movement, remember these points:

- Make one movement, no matter how far you go. If you keep moving you've just made yourself a moving target. Harder to hit, but you no longer have the action-reaction advantage.

- If you're going for your pistol in its holster, there are two things you need to

do: Get off the X and draw your pistol. If you enjoy life, do them in that order.

- Don't raise your weapon up onto the target until after you've made the movement. If you do, your momentum will make it hard for you to stop on the threat (overtravel) and you'll likely miss the threat in the direction of your movement. At best it will take you longer to acquire the target and engage.

- Moving toward the threat at a 45-degree angle changes the angle of attack more than moving 90 degrees straight to the side. This great angle can make it harder for your adversary to lock in and engage.

Backwards

Shooting while walking backwards on a smooth, flat surface is actually easier than shooting while moving forward. The problem comes in that there are very few places, even flat ranges, where the surface is completely obstacle-free, so being able to shoot while walking backwards is of limited use. This is because even a small rock or bump can throw you off balance very quickly. We'll discuss a few methods to shoot backwards, but before you choose to employ this skill, ask yourself why you're doing it, and if it's really necessary. Could you run back, turn, and shoot faster and more accurately? Could you cover more distance, be less of a target to any threats, and reduce the possibility

4.6.17 – Always look before you walk backwards

4.6.18 – Then walk back toe to heel

4.6.19 – The right leg is pushing back to check for obstacles

4.6.20 – Then bring the feet together

of ending up on your ass? There are times you might want to move backwards while shooting. I've just seen students learn to shoot moving backwards and then think it's the key to solving every tactical dilemma.

The first technique is simply to walk in the same manner as when moving forward, only now walk toe to heel as opposed to heel to toe. It's important to look behind you first to check the path you plan to move. If you've decided that the threat is so bad that you must move backwards while engaging, remember that falling would dramatically compound your problems.

The other method for moving backwards while shooting—and the one I recommend— is the push step. I like the push step because it allows you to keep your eyes (and sights) up on your threat, maintains a solid shooting platform, and nearly eliminates the chance of busting your ass. This is the technique we used in the SEALs onboard vessels, because of all the things you can trip on or fall in while rocking back and forth. If you need to shoot while moving backwards, this is your best bet.

The push step is much like the sidestep, only you're moving backwards. Maintaining your aggressive shooting stance, push your strong leg backwards and use it as a feeler, searching for any obstacles. When you've stretched out a comfortable length, simply move your reaction foot back to your shooting stance. Try not to bring your feet

too close together because you will be off balance when you do, and of course this is when the ship takes a roll or a teammate bumps into you.

Turning

Turning is really pretty easy, but for some reason people tend to lose their heads when you put a gun in their hands. Don't let that happen to you. Just like anything else you want to learn to do with a gun, learn to do it first without one. We turn left, right, and change directions every day without a gun in our hands, and your movement when you're shooting should be the same.

One common rule for turning any direction is always looking before you turn. Just as when shooting multiple targets, you need to look at the next target with laserlike focus. So if I were to be turning left and then shooting, the first thing I need to do is snap my head and eyes to the left and lock in on a target. If you can't do that, why would you be shooting anyway? When you practice, it might help to imagine what you would do if you heard gunfire coming from that direction. Your reaction would likely be to crouch and turn as your left hand flinches up to protect your face. Once you locate a threat, your body swings around to come online with your eyes.

Next it's important to remember that it doesn't matter what you do with your feet. What's important is turning as quickly and

4.6.21 – Always look before you turn

as smoothly as possible. Everyone is built differently and moves differently, so use what God gave you to turn to address your threat. You should try to turn in place rather than do what I call a barn-door turn, where you hinge on one foot and bring your body around just like a barn door. Oftentimes the terrain or situation will dictate what your feet need to do to turn anyway, so don't think about your feet, just turn.

Also, no matter how you actually move, the most important thing in turning to shoot is that there must be no lateral movement. Whether you're coming from a holster or bringing up your carbine, your gun needs to come straight up to the target. Don't raise your gun up when you're turning to a target. Not only is it slower to turn, but it's not safe and it's harder to stop on your target due to the momentum created and the overtravel that can occur.

> "I fear not the man who has practiced 10,000 kicks once, but I fear the man who has practiced one kick 10,000 times"
> **– Bruce Lee**

4.6.22 – Right turn

4.6.23 – Look first

4.6.24 – Then drive the gun straight up

90-degree Turns

The biggest problem I see with students turning 90 degrees is that they often take much bigger steps than needed. Try this: With your feet shoulder width apart and facing to the right, see if you can just rotate 90 degrees to the left on the balls of your feet. Don't move your feet, just put the weight on your toes and rotate. Can you get close to a shooting position? Could you get your gun up on target quicker? You may not be in a perfect shooting position, but it should show you that your movements

4.6.25 – Left turn

4.6.26 – Look

can be much less than you might think, and this equals speed. And if that position is not perfect, you can always improve your fighting position. Your feet aren't stuck in cement, so get off that first shot quickly and then continue moving your feet into a better fighting position. I'm not saying this is the way to turn either, so pick up and move your feet as much as you need to. How you move your feet and hips turning to the left will be different than how you do it to the right, so practice both.

4.6.27 – Drive the gun to the threat

4.6.28 – Turning 180 degrees

4.6.29 – Break the hips to be able to see the threat

180-degree Turns

With a little practice, turning to engage a target behind you is just as easy as turning 90 degrees. For this one, the problem usually comes with not turning far enough to actually see your threat. This leads to poor turns and slow shot times since you're not locked onto your threat and need to acquire it while you're turning. To avoid this and be able to see all the way behind you, the key is breaking your hips. This means bending your knees and turning your hips, not just your head. If done correctly, you should be able to easily see up to 270 degrees in either direction.

4.6.30 – Don't worry about your feet, drive the gun straight up

To make the turn, think about pivoting in place rather than swinging around to avoid the barn door. If you are bringing a carbine to the fight, it should be pointed straight down, so imagine you're spinning around on the muzzle. Remember not to bring it up until it's in line with your target. If you're coming from the holster, you should establish your grip with your strong hand and defeat any retention systems (bails, breaks, and so on) but do not draw out of the holster until your hips are facing the threat. Again, doing this will only slow down the time it takes to get your first shot off effectively.

Use the same techniques I discussed for turning 90 degrees to see how much you actually need to move your feet to get your hips pointed downrange where you can safely and effectively engage threats. Once you've got those first rounds on target, advance your fighting position by moving your feet to better support your shooting platform and dial in your natural point of aim.

Scanning/Search and Assess

In any real-life shooting scenario, you need to make sure there are no other threats that require customer service. To do this, you need to maintain your awareness not only 360 degrees, but also for any possible threats from above or below. This can be especially challenging in urban and maritime environments. Another important reason for doing a post-shooting scan is to lower your

body alarm response (BAR). No matter how cool and collected you think you'll be, the first time (or anytime) you're in a gunfight you're likely to have tunnel vision, audio exclusion, increased breathing and heart rate, and loss of fine motor control, among other responses. By breaking that target fixation, looking around, and breathing, you're going to come back to reality more quickly and be ready to deal with any additional threats or help out your team or family.

Of course, you need to practice scanning for threats and checking on your teammates, family, or bystanders every time you shoot to make it a habit. If you don't practice on the range, you won't do it in a gunfight, and this could cost you your life.

To properly scan, do the following:

1. Do a good follow-through and be prepared to take another shot if needed. If you've determined that target is no longer a threat, move on to Step 2.

2. After you engage a threat, don't be quick to drop your guard. You need to ensure that threat is eliminated and that there are no other threats in front of you.

3. Finish your follow-through and be ready to shoot again if needed.

4. Lower your pistol just enough to see everything in front of you (high ready position).

5.   Take your finger off the trigger and bring it to a safe, tactical ready position.

6.   Do a 360-degree scan for additional threats. This does not mean just shaking your head from left to right, but really seeing and assessing what's around you. If there are people around you, look at their hands. Get off the X! Quickly assess your environment for any available cover, and move to it if it makes tactical sense. Often this is not possible on a range, but practice thinking about where you could go. Again, don't just look—see and assess!

To do this:

1.   Turn your head to either the left or the right. If you know in which direction there is a higher probability of threats, you should turn that way first. It's important to see all the way behind you, and to accomplish this, tilt your head down slightly. You will thereby open your field of view by as much as 60 degrees. (During the scan, make sure you are also looking for any threats that might be either above or below the level you're on.) Also, don't be afraid to move your feet to scan 360.

2.   Now look back at your original threat and make sure it's still down. Did he have on body armor, and now he's getting back up? He may be asking for seconds.

4.6.31 – Always do a scan appropriate for your environment

3.   Turn the opposite direction you originally checked, again making sure you look behind, above, and below you.

4.   Finally, look back again at your original threat to make sure it's still down.

5.   Even after you holster, do another scan.

How widely you'll need to scan and assess depends on your environment and situation.

4.6.32 – You should always be able to shoot if you see something

4.6.33 – Think 360

If your back is against a wall, you don't need to look back at it.

Your scan may not need to include looking high and low, but think about your environment, and always ask yourself what you're missing.

Always expect more threats: If there was one threat, be prepared for two; if there are two threats, be prepared for three, and so on.

After your scan, make sure you know the condition of your weapon, and plus-up as needed.

If you're kneeling or prone, always search and assess before you get up and yell "standing." Search and assess at each level, because your view of the battle space changes with elevation change.

4.6.35 – How much would you expose if you knew someone was shooting at you?

Barricades

Barricades are anything you can shoot over, around, or under. They can be cover—things that can stop you from being injured—or concealment, things that prevent you from being seen. They can be cars, trees, walls, or windows. The key to shooting around any barricade is that you have as much of your body behind the barricade as possible and still be able to take effective shots. Staying behind the barricade could save your life in combat and save your score in competition. If you choose to stick yourself and/or your weapon around or in front of the barricade, that's fine—let's just not call it a barricade. If you're resting your weapon on it, you can call it weapons support and if you're not

4.6.36 – Don't get too close to barricades

really standing behind it, it's just an obstacle you're moving around.

One of the best ways to practice working barricades is through dry-fire practice with a partner. I like to use blue training guns for this because there's no weapons manipulation needed, and blue guns ensure safety. For any barricade position, just have your partner watch from the other side and notice the first thing they see come around the barricade. The best thing would be if they see the muzzle of the gun and your eye or sights together. If they see your foot, leg, or elbow first, those are the things you can expect to get shot off or at least signal to the bad guy you're coming.

4.6.37 – Standing pistol

4.6.38 – Kneeling pistol

As a general rule, stay as far back from the barricade as possible. I normally try to stay at least an arm's length away from any barricade I'm shooting around. I also don't like to rest my weapon directly on a barricade when shooting. It may feel more stable, but your recoil will be directed differently with each shot so it likely won't be as accurate. If you do need to rest your gun on something, use your hand between the gun and surface of the barricade as padding.

Also, if you are going to use a barricade for support, or extend your muzzle past the end of a barricade, make sure you know what's on the other side. If you're in a close-quarters

4.6.39 – Prone pistol

4.6.40 – Standing carbine

4.6.41 – Kneeling carbine

gunbattle, be aware that someone could grab your gun if you don't know they're there. On the other side of the spectrum, make sure you know the difference between where your sights are and where your muzzle is. You need to be always aware of the mechanical offset you're going to need to compensate for so you don't end up looking at a target and hitting a barricade. Depending on the size of a hole you may need to shoot though, this might be a good reason to stick your barrel into the hole to ensure a clear shot.

When shooting around barricades, you want to keep your natural shooting positions

4.6.42 – Prone carbine

as much as possible. Don't try coming up with new ways to shoot just because you're behind something. Just make an effort to stay small and keep all arms and legs tucked in. Normally I'll see elbows or feet come out first, so it's always important to lean out first and clear the area with your eyes and gun, then slide your feet out behind them. It will help to lower your center of balance more than normal the farther you lean out.

Always have your gun up ready to fight *before* you come peeking around a barricade. When I teach room clearing, I always say there are two things you need to do to clear a room and live: Get your gun up and enter the room. If you do them in that order, you'll be fine. So remember, get your gun up, then come around the barricade.

When engaging targets around barricades, you always want to try to engage them from outside to inside. This is because the targets on the outside are the ones you'll see first. And if you can see them, they can see you, too! Of course things can always change and targets can pop up or come around another corner, but all things being equal, remember: outside to inside.

I've heard some people talk about standing a certain way behind barricades so if they get shot they will fall behind the barricade and their partners can rescue them. I'm calling the BS flag on this one. First off, never go into a gunfight with getting shot as part of your tactics. Second, how in the world do you know what way you're going to fall when you're shot? Fight your fight and plan on winning. You'll have a better chance with a good shooting position and lots of practice.

Unstable Platforms

Especially for maritime operators, shooting from unstable platforms is a certainty. But even if you're not a Navy SEAL, improving your balance while shooting is a great way to improve your shooting overall. Some of us are lucky enough to be able to practice shooting from vessels while at sea, but many of you may not have this luxury. You don't want your first time shooting from an unstable platform to be during an actual operation. You need to train from unstable platforms so you know how your shooting is going to be affected and the countermeasures you must take to overcome those environmental factors and stressors. Even without going out to sea, you still improve your unstable-platform shooting—you just need to use a little ingenuity.

You can come up with and build your own unstable platform for minimal costs and time. A simple sheet of plywood mounted on any type of partially inflated bladder system works well, or you can suspend the platform at each corner with ropes or chains attached to some 4x4 railings. The quickest and cheapest way to get some unstable live-fire training is to bring that crazy-looking half-ball from the gym, the BOSU Ball. It's a half sphere with an attached platform. You can stand on either side of it and get some great training and improve your skill set. The closer you move your feet to the center, the more unstable it's going to be. Remember to consciously think about weapons discipline and control during this training because you could fall down. So don't mount that trigger until the decision to shoot has been made. If you do fall, just keep your weapon downrange and if you so choose, continue your engagement from the ground as you move back to your feet, just as you should during an engagement.

Another tool I use on the range is a bongo board. This is like a skateboard with one big roller on the bottom. If your range surface is grass, gravel, or dirt, you'll need to bring a piece of plywood to put the bongo board on so it will roll smoothly.

Of course, before you start doing these high-speed moves on the live-fire range, you're practicing them at home dry-fire.

Your progression should be something like this:

1.   Practice on the board at home. No weapon in hand until you're very comfortable.

2.   Practice on the board at home. Dry-fire until you're very comfortable.

3.   Practice on the board at the range. Dry-fire until you're very comfortable.

4.   Live fire at the range. (Make sure you get approval from range master as appropriate.)

Not only will working on these drills with and without weapons help you should you ever need to shoot from an unstable platform, but they will significantly improve your shooting stance and your accuracy when shooting on the move. A solid stance and shooting on the move require solid core strength and balance, both of which you'll get from training on balance boards.

Training notes: _____

_____

_____

_____

_____

The more you train, the more experience points you have to draw from and the greater your chance of success.

7

Mastery

"Fast is fine, but accuracy is final."
—**Wyatt Earp**

When it comes to mastering your art, it is important to realize that everything is useful some of the time, but nothing is useful all of the time. This chapter will attempt to cover some of the intangible techniques required to excel at shooting. Many of the lessons covered here are purely cerebral and will require a change in your thinking, as opposed to the physical techniques covered up to this point.

Multiple Targets

One of the first skills you'll need to learn to move past the "basics" and to the next level is how to quickly and accurately engage two or more threats. The techniques can be used in competition to improve your score, in hunting to put more food on the table, or in a combat or self-defense shooting with more than one threat.

Most instructors teach to continue shooting a threat all the way to the ground until it's no longer a threat. This is great advice if you only have one threat, but history has taught us that rarely is there a single threat. If you have one threat, expect two; if you have two, expect three. The point is to always assume there are other threats out there in a dynamic shooting environment, so let's break the tunnel vision and keep our heads on a swivel.

Let's assume you have two threats directly in front of you. They are ten yards away, one yard apart, and both pointing automatic weapons at you. Your gun is also up and pointed at them. There is no cover. Which one are you going to keep shooting all the way to the ground? Are you going to put two rounds in the first and then two in the second? It's not as easy as it looks on TV,

4.7.1 – Multiple targets

4.7.2 – Eyes first

but you need to know these answers before test time!

The first thing you'll need to learn is shooting tempo or rhythm. This means making your gun sound like music as you shoot and not discombobulated like Steve Martin in *The Jerk*. So if my plan was to shoot bad guy number one with two rounds and then move to bad guy number two and shoot him with

---

If you're shooting bad guy number one all the way to the ground while number two is shooting you, who wins?

---

two rounds, it should sound like four evenly spaced shots, not two shots, long delay, two shots. This is critical because by forcing tempo upon ourselves, we force ourselves to compress the time between targets (which is longer) and not the time between shots on each target (which is shorter). It's the same way I teach a team room entry. It's more important that everyone comes in together (compressing the time between people) than it is for each guy to come in fast (individual time). Normally what people will focus on to shoot faster is the time it takes to shoot each target, but that's not going to help you if both guys are shooting at you.

The key to mastering this skill is to force yourself to start off slow with your targets close together. If you're hitting each target

4.7.3 – Then drive the muzzle to your eyes

with two rounds each, it can really be hard to slow down on each shot, but it will force you do drive the gun between targets. As you get comfortable with the tempo and your shots are where they need to be, you can speed up, or better yet, just let speed happen. You can also start spreading your targets and changing the number of rounds with each engagement.

I mentioned earlier remembering "eyes, muzzle, target," and here is another place you'll need to use it to effectively engage multiple threats. What you want to do is always move your eyes, then move your muzzle to the target. While I'm following through on the last shot of a target, I move my eyes to the next target and pick out the smallest thing center mass I can see: Aim

small, miss small. Then, rather than settling my sights back on the first target, I let the recoil help me move the sights to line up with my eyes on the new target. By doing this, you will not only increase your speed, but you'll be far less likely to throw a round on the second target by moving your gun and eyes together.

Another consideration when you're presented with multiple threats is deciding how many rounds you're going to deliver to the first threat before moving on to the next. In basic law enforcement, you traditionally shoot two rounds and then reassess the threat. This is known as the "standard response" and is starting to lose favor due to its shortfalls in effectiveness. More departments are learning a "nonstandard response," which is basically anything other than two rounds. This is a great improvement on traditional training and with a single threat is the way to go, but again, if you're shooting bad guy number one all the way to the ground while number two is shooting you, who wins?

One technique to think about is what I've heard called "boarding house rules," which means everyone gets a serving before anyone gets seconds. In theory, you shoot everyone once, knock them down long enough to engage all your known threats, and then go back to see who is asking for a second helping. I'm not suggesting this is how you should deal with every multi-threat encounter you have, but it is something you should practice and might be the best option in certain circumstances. As a general rule (if there is such a thing in a gunfight) for how many rounds to shoot before scanning: Shoot until you see a positive effect on your target. This could be a positive ballistic effect (head goes boom), a positive physical effect (person drops weapon) or a positive psychological effect (person runs away). Every situation, even in training, will be different, and your response should adjust accordingly. Just don't get caught in the rut of "shoot two rounds then see if they are still shooting at you." Almost anything is better than that. The more you train, the more experience points you have to draw from and the greater your chance of success.

Now that you've got your timing and round count figured out, you can do a few things with your body to shoot multiple targets

Shoot until you see a positive effect on your target.

that are spread apart quickly and effectively. First, you must have a bend in your knees. I'll assume your knees are already bent. You don't want to rotate at the hips; you need to move your entire lower body so your upper body position stays the same. If you rotate only at the hips, your upper body position

will break its form. By shifting your whole lower body, you'll be able to maintain the same upper body shooting position.

The final thing to consider has to do with how high your ready position should be in different circumstances. It's helpful for timed evolutions on a range or if you're covering multiple threats. As a rule of thumb, the closer your threats, the higher your muzzle needs to be if you need to recognize a threat and engage. For instance, if I'm covering a hallway and a threat could come from either direction, my muzzle would be down all the way, so I could best react to a threat from either direction. On the other hand, if I had two threats I was covering that were close to each other, my muzzle would be much higher. Just realize that rapid movement of your muzzle on a horizontal plane will cause delays in locking onto a target and should be minimized as much as possible. The shorter the horizontal movement, the less momentum is created and the easier it will be to stop and acquire the proper sight alignment and sight picture.

Moving Targets

Sometimes you'll be lucky enough to have a bad guy sit in one place long enough for you to shoot him, but I wouldn't count on it. More often than not, once the shooting starts, everyone is moving and your ability to acquire and track the enemy will improve your survivability. Hitting movers is a basic skill that just requires lots of practice.

The techniques are not hard to learn, but normally even dedicated shooters have a hard time finding places to train shooting movers. If you're a hunter you will likely have a few more opportunities to practice on live targets, but you need to make sure you'll be successful by learning on paper or steel.

If you can avoid shooting a moving target and instead shoot a stationary target, you should.

There are two main techniques for shooting moving targets: ambush and tracking. As the name implies, in the ambush method you wait for the target to come to you, whereas you track the target in the tracking method. Both have their strengths and weaknesses.

Before we get started on the various methods, let's cover some basic elements about shooting movers that apply to any method. First, if you can avoid shooting a moving target and instead shoot a stationary target, you should. This sounds obvious, but how you can make that a choice may not be. What I mean is that, for instance, if you're shooting a target that is moving directly toward or away from you, you are shooting a stationary target. Also, if you can time your shot when the target is turning (picture a guard on patrol walking back and forth), that too is a stationary target.

4.7.4 – Aim in front of your target, wait for your target to move into your sights to fire .

4.7.5 – Aim at your target and swing your aim to match target speed. Fire when ready.

For targets that are moving laterally to you, you may need to lead the target, depending on the target's speed, distance, velocity of your round, and angle of attack. Leading the target means aiming in front of your target or aiming where your target is going be when the round gets there, not its current location. The best comparison is in football when the quarterback throws a ball downrange to a receiver. The speed the receiver is running, the distance down the field, and what pattern he is running all determine how far in front of the receiver the quarterback will throw the ball. If he were to throw the ball where the receiver was when he let go, he's more likely to get an interception than a catch.

Leading the target means aiming in front of your target or aiming where your target is going be when the round gets there.

It would be counterproductive to list the exact lead conversion formulas comparing miles per hour (MPH) of your target, feet per second (FPS) of your projectile, and then an angular multiplier to come up with your final lead in feet for each target. Just writing that sentence bored me, and won't help you hit the broad side of a barn. It's important to understand the football analogy and get out on the range and practice. But as a rule

of thumb, for a pistol inside twenty-five yards, don't lead unless it's a car or plane. If a human is moving faster than that, they are not a threat to you and should be out of your hair soon. With a carbine, I use seventy-five yards as the outside range where I normally don't lead the target.

The first method I'm going to cover is the easiest one, the ambush method. The reason it's easiest is that you are not moving your gun and shooting at the same time. You pick a spot to set up on that the target is going to (or you hope it's going to) move across. When the target gets to your pre-determined lead or in your sights, you fire. Because you're not moving, timing your shot is the critical component of being successful with the ambush method. It's much easier on a target moving at a constant pace, and you need to think about the timing of your shot sequence. This means the time it takes you internally to pull the trigger, and then the internal working of the gun from sear release to bullet leaving muzzle. It may seem like it all happens too fast to matter, but with the ambush method, bad timing is the biggest reason for misses. This is a good choice for a target at a constant pace or one that stops or turns at set points. This is not the best method to use when you're being engaged by the enemy, meaning that if someone is shooting at you, it's not a good decision to point somewhere in front of him and wait.

Next up is the tracking method. This is a bit harder to master, but can be used in any situation. With the tracking method, your muzzle's movement and speed will match those of your target. There are several variations on the technique itself, but just understanding and mastering the basics will allow you to hit moving targets within your weapon's maximum point-blank range.

If part of your strategy to survive a gunfight is hoping the other guy is a worse shot than you, I recommend you stay away from guns!

One important safety note when using the tracking method is to know what's in front of and behind your target for the full field of fire. It can be difficult to track a target and scan the environment in front of the target, so it's best to scan the area first and note a cutoff point where it's no longer safe to fire. One technique that will help is shooting with both eyes open. This will allow you to better track the movement and the surroundings while also maintaining your sight alignment and any lead you may be using. A great dry-fire drill for this is tracking a horizontal line, whether it be a fenceline or the line where your wall meets the ceiling. As you're swinging the sights across the line, practice dry-firing and continuing your movement. Stopping to shoot is the most common

error with the tracking method because we normally practice a follow-through that is straight up and back down to the same place. Remember, your target is moving so you want to follow through by bringing your sights back down to where your target is, not where it was. If you do this drill every time you train, you'll be surprised at how well you'll hit movers the next time you get the chance.

Accuracy

One of the great debates when it comes to firearms training is speed vs. accuracy. I don't engage in such nonsensical discussions since that's like asking which wheels on a car are more important, the front or the back. They are both equally important, and if you want the car to work properly, you just need to make sure they're balanced. I should be clear on what I mean by accuracy. For me, this means putting effective rounds on target. It doesn't mean keyholing shots unless that is the size of your target. I teach students to quickly find the biggest target available at that moment, set their sights on the center of it, and fire for effect. But with that we also need to constantly remind our shooters: "You can't miss fast enough." That means, for instance, that if you decide you're going to slap the trigger like it owes you money because it's faster, you're going to throw your rounds all around the guy shooting at you, hoping that he doesn't have the discipline to slowly press back on his trigger with you in his sights. If part of your strategy to survive a gunfight is hoping the other guy is a worse shot than you, I recommend you stay away from guns!

Top Five Reasons Accuracy is King

1. Especially when I'm training LEOs, I remind students that every round that leaves their weapon has a very small lawyer attached to it, just to see where it hits. Like miniature ambulance chasers along for the ride, these guys are waiting to end a career, or worse.

2. If going to jail for killing the wrong person doesn't bother you, think about it in financial terms. With the economy in its current state, we need to save every penny we can! One shot, one kill could have very easily first been uttered from a smart shooter looking to save some money on ammo so he could head to the local gun shop on his way home to buy another bang-stick. Even when I was in a SEAL platoon at the range, we made sure that every round downrange was effective and accurate. Did we think about how much the ammo cost? Hell, no! We just wanted to shoot better than the guy next to us so we could make fun of him later, and of course shoot better than the enemy.

3. I'm not a statistician, but I'd be willing to bet that statistically the longer you're in a gunfight your chance of eating a lead sandwich increases accordingly. Just get it over with, and hit the target(s) on the first shot. This way you get to fight another day and deliver effective customer service to more bad guys.

Every round that leaves their weapon has a very small lawyer attached to it.

---

4. Raise your hand if you like to clean your weapon. Okay, there are a few bullet heads out there who actually enjoy cleaning guns, but the rest of us would rather punch the bore with hollowpoint rounds than a bore brush. Every gun I've ever shot works the same way: The more you shoot, the more you need to clean it. For SEALs, this might be the biggest reason not to miss. We SEALs are well known for our laziness (if my fellow frogmen are offended, please change *laziness* to *masters of efficiency*). I'm not saying don't shoot your gun or even shoot less, I'm just saying if I'm going to foul that bore, I better have a long list of confirmed kills to justify it.

5. Every round you waste is one less tool in your toolbag (magazine) to deal with any tactical situation you are trying to sort out. When I was running SEAL sniper school, I would have my students load single rounds into their M4s while shooting the Navy Rifle Qualification Test. Just knowing you have only one round to put downrange helped shooters score higher. I would discourage this technique in a combat situation, but keep in mind that you might need those extra rounds to deal with the next threat that comes knocking at your door.

Wyatt Earp said it best: *"Fast is fine, but accuracy is final."* You can shoot as fast as you want, but if you're not hitting the target you're just wasting time, money, or worse. The good news is that becoming accurate is simple: train more! By training as much as you can on and off the range, you'll learn what your limits are for accuracy *and* speed. Just like everything else in life, it's all about balance.

I remember listening to a radio show one day on "military snipers." At the end of the show, they were talking about how fast sound travels compared to the speed of bullets. The guy they interviewed said, "Past 800 yards, I can shoot at someone all day long, and they will never know I'm there." Obviously he's not a SEAL sniper. If we shoot at you, you'll know we were there; in fact, that will be the last thing you know!

Speed

After this talk about accuracy, don't get the idea that speed does not matter. Speed can be the deciding factor in gunfights and timed competitions, just as easily as a missed shot can affect your score or mission success. The biggest problems I see with speed are that most people don't understand what steps they should speed up to shoot faster, or they just force themselves to shoot faster. Don't force yourself to go fast. Speed happens as a natural byproduct of good training. When you try to force speed, you start fumbling and making mistakes. If you just let speed happen and concentrate on good training, you'll be surprised at how fast you're shooting without even trying. Ray Chapman once said: *"Smoothness is five-sixths of speed."* Go for smoothness, and speed will take care of itself. Go for speed and you're likely to mess up fast.

Speed happens as a natural byproduct of good training.

Now let's talk about when to go fast. For new shooters, I recommend that they go slowly for everything, from draw to trigger squeeze. You need to perfectly engrain the movements into your neural pathways, but as you progress you need to let that speed happen. Let's say you're practicing a course of slow aimed fire with your pistol: ten rounds in ten minutes at twenty-five yards. Plenty of time for you to take accurate shots, but I'm always amazed by how many people do a slow, robotlike draw and then rush the shot from the time they see the sights until they slap the trigger. This is backwards and sums up my point: Flinch to the gun (super-fast), drive the gun to the target (really fast), and then take a slow, aimed shot. This is how you get fast. You make up time on your draw and presentation and then use all that time to pay homage to the king: accuracy.

4.7.6 – Shooting with both eyes open

Shooting with Both Eyes Open

Shooting with both eyes open is one of the most important skills to learn for any dynamic situation. On a static range it's not a big deal if you want to close off half your vision to line up the sights, but when the situation becomes dynamic, you'll want to take in as much visual information as possible. You

If rapid target acquisition and accurate shooting are on your nice-to-have list, keep both eyes open.

need two eyes to locate threats quickly, and it's impossible to close one eye without affecting the other at least slightly. I read one study that said vision is degraded in the opposite eye by as much as 20 percent, and that the pupil will compensate for the closed eye by dilating. Normally this is a good thing as it lets in more light, but the amount of dilatation is not consistent with the lighting and this further deteriorates vision. So if rapid target acquisition and accurate shooting are on your nice-to-have list, keep both eyes open. This becomes even more important if you are on a two-way range and you plan on moving at some point (highly recommended). I don't need a study to tell me it's easier to walk (or run) with both eyes open.

One of the questions I get asked most when new shooters are learning to shoot with both eyes open is how to get rid of the second image so they can only see one sight picture. The truth is you don't want to. Everyone will see two sight pictures—we have binocular vision and this is why we want to keep both eyes open. Learning to shoot with both eyes open is just teaching your brain to ignore

4.7.7 – To shoot and move, you need both eyes open

the visual input from your nondominant eye when you're shooting. Your eye will still be sending the same information to your brain,

---

Learning to shoot with both eyes open is just teaching your brain to ignore the visual input from your nondominant eye when you're shooting.

---

but you're training your eye to use only the input from your dominant eye.

4.7.8 – I'm right eye dominant. This is what my right eye sees.

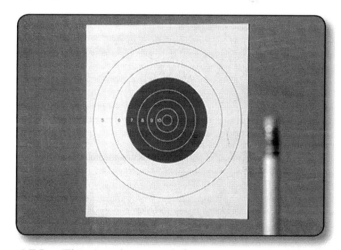

4.7.9 – This is what my left eye sees.

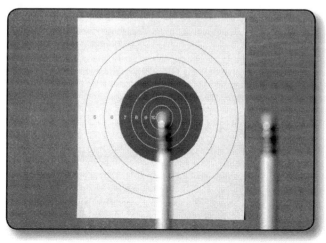

4.7.10 – This is what I see with both eyes open.

Before you try shooting with both eyes open, it's important to learn to shoot with just one eye open. Basically, you need to walk before you run. If I were to ask you to juggle three balls while riding a unicycle, you would do a lot better by learning to juggle first, then learning to ride a unicycle before putting them together. It's the same thing with shooting with both eyes open. Learn to shoot first with one eye closed until your dominant eye has that image engrained in it, and then learn to keep the other eye open. Until you can shoot effectively with one eye open, you'll be spinning your wheels going straight to two.

Before you try shooting with both eyes open, it's important to learn to shoot with just one eye open.

Now that you understand the importance of shooting with both eyes open, stop thinking it's a magical technique that only Joint Special Operations Command (JSOC) Jedi operators can use. Yes, for some it does come a little easier, but almost everyone can learn it and start sending effective fire downrange within a week. There are a few people with vision issues that do not allow them to focus with both eyes open, but don't put yourself in that group too fast. It's going to be hard for anyone who's never done it before to learn, but the benefits are well worth the effort. You'll start out seeing

4.7.11 – Practice this before you use it at the range

4.7.12 – Teach your mind what image to use

4.7.13 – Most people can learn quickly with a little practice

double and it will probably be blurry, but there are some easy drills you can do to speed up the process of teaching your mind which picture (eye) to focus on.

Grab a pen or pencil (or an unloaded weapon, observing all safety rules) and hold it at arm's length with the thinnest part (front sight post width is good) pointing up. Now close your nondominant eye and aim the tip of your writing instrument at an object at least three feet away. Without moving anything, open your nondominant eye. This will train your brain what it should look like to have both eyes open when you shoot. Practice this for a few minutes, then move on to step two.

Next, do the same thing, but this time in reverse. Start off with both eyes open and try to aim at the object. Once you're sighted in, close your nondominant eye and check to see if you're pointed directly at the object. If you are, great! If you're not, move the tip to point where you want it, and open both eyes again to teach your brain what visual data to pay attention to when both eyes are open. Do this for a few more minutes and then move on to step three.

This drill is not only good for training your eyes and brain to shoot with both eyes open, but also for working on front sight focus and working the muscles in the eye that adjust focus. Start off with both eyes open and the tip of your pen or pencil three or four inches in front of your dominant eye. The tip should be lined up with your target, and you should be focusing on your target. Now slowly extend your arm out all the way while keeping the tip aimed at your target. As you extend past halfway out, your focus should start to shift to your aiming tip. Focus, press, and repeat.

If you are closing an eye when you shoot, make sure you close that eye when you draw or start to raise your firearm.

The next thing you can do is to put a piece of Scotch tape or smear some Vaseline on your shooting glasses over the nondominant side. It only needs to be big enough to cover the part of your vision where the front sight post would be. Then shoot with both eyes open, and this will help train your mind to associate the correct eye to the sight. I guess now is good time to mention dry-fire training, since all this can be trained without going to the range.

If you practice these three drills for ten to fifteen minutes a day for one week, you'll be able to shoot with both eyes open on the range. You can (and should) do all the same drills dry-fire with whatever weapons you use. Then plus-up some magazines and test it out on the range, I'm sure you'll do fine if you've done your homework.

Once you've perfected this skill, keep that pencil handy and move on to multiple targets, shooting while moving (can't sit in that desk all day), and moving "targets" (coworkers). And although your fellow workers may think you're a bit strange, they can't call the cops for brandishing a #2 pencil. What could be better than training for combat from the comfort of your desk or couch?

If after all this you still can't hit the broad side of a barn with both eyes open, then shut that other eye tight and fire away! Better to make accurate shots than to miss and potentially hit an innocent bystander. If you are closing an eye when you shoot, make sure you close that eye when you draw or start to raise your firearm. The sooner you do this, the quicker you'll be able to lock in and engage the target. This should become part of your training so you naturally close that other eye as part of the mounting process.

Finishing the Fight

Sometimes being faster and more accurate than your enemy is not enough to win a gunfight. Knowing your weapon's stopping power and terminal ballistics, and a bit of human anatomy, can go a long way in helping you finish the fight as quickly and painlessly (for you) as possible. I don't want to get into so much of this stuff that you mistake this book for a college anatomy and physiology textbook, but I want you to understand why you statistically have an 85 percent chance of surviving being shot, which is good for

you, but not so good when you realize this applies to your enemies too.

So let's talk about shot placement and human anatomy. A little insight can change the outcome of a major event. The short answer is center mass—that's where you want to shoot 99 percent of the time. For one, you'll do it a lot faster because there's no thinking. One thing I hate seeing in training is someone spot a threat target with

Practice shooting center mass, and then adjust fire if your threat does not go down.

body armor on, adjust the sights up to the head, and then shoot. They think they saved time because they skipped shooting them in the chest and went for the head. In reality they were getting shot while looking at the body armor and would likely not be able to take the head shot. Practice shooting center mass, and then adjust fire if your threat does not go down. So where is center mass? It's the center of the biggest thing you see at that moment. If you're facing someone and you see their whole body, center mass is the center of the chest. If someone is poking their head around the corner and all you see is their head (and gun), the center of their head is now center mass. Center Mass Groups is not just a great idea; it's a great name for a company!

Another consideration should be the location of vital organs like the brain, heart, and cervical spinal cord. Hitting these will provide instant cessation of hostilities, like turning off a light switch. Even getting close to these and hitting their main blood supply can incapacitate quickly, since during a gunfight their bodies (and yours) shunt blood toward the vital organs. Another good location, if available, is the pelvic area or the hips. A shot in the middle of the pelvis can drop someone very quickly, taking away their mobility. Don't be surprised if you shoot someone multiple times and they're not going down. Remember these points and find a way to finish the fight.

Your weapon's stopping power is another thing you need to consider on a two-way range. Stopping power is the ability of your firearm and ammunition to quickly incapacitate your enemy (or dinner if you're hunting). It takes several factors into account, such as bullet dynamics, energy

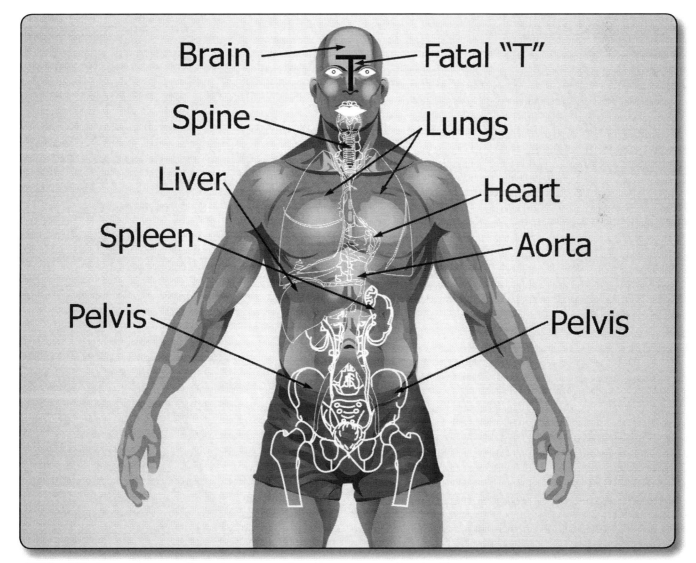

4.7.14 – Vital organs are all center mass. Another reason to aim there.

> ## *You've got plenty of choices, and decisions need to be made yesterday.*

transfer, and terminal ballistics. Due to the wide range of firearms and ammunition available, stopping power is difficult to study, and manufacturers tend to overstate the results they do get to increase sales. The key is for you to think about the stopping power of your weapon and ammunition before you buy, so you will have some idea of what to expect when you need to use it. Stopping power should not be your only consideration. Bigger is not always better except in elephant hunting. Know what your gun and ammo can do and then adjust your training and loadout to fit your system.

How many times do you need to engage a threat target? You've got plenty of choices, and decisions need to be made yesterday. As I covered earlier, you've got the "standard response" of two rounds and then assess your threat that every LEO has had drilled into their minds. Then you've got the "nonstandard response," which is anything other than two rounds. This is often taught along with continuing to shoot until the threat is gone, both great improvements on what has been taught for years. I've come up with my own variation on this trend of "more is

better" and call it STD or "shoot 'til dead." In any event, if your life is in danger and you've chosen to use deadly force, you shouldn't stop engaging a threat if it's still standing. Just be conscious of the fact that there may be other threats that need your attention. The number of rounds you need to engage each threat will vary with every situation. You might get lucky and hit one in the spinal cord and he drops immediately, while bad guy number two takes ten rounds to the chest but is still coming at you. Just make sure you're practicing shooting a different number of rounds, and use as much force as is necessary to stop any threats you face.

> ## *If your life is in danger and you've chosen to use deadly force, you shouldn't stop engaging a threat if it's still standing.*

So what's the answer? Unfortunately, the answer is going to be different for every one of you, and different for each deadly force confrontation you find yourself in. Sometimes you'll need to use speed, sometimes accuracy, and others you'll need to use some of this newfound intelligence to outwit your opponent. The more knowledge you have, the better chance you'll have of finishing the fight.

Low-light Shooting

Earlier I discussed different ways to hold your lights, but now we need to master the night. Statistically during any twenty-four-hour period, you've got a 50 percent chance that it's going to be dark when you need to engage a target. Do you do 50 percent of your training with low or no light? That's crazy talk! Nobody does that! Okay, but do you train at all? There are hundreds of techniques out there for shooting in low light, but they are all worthless if you don't practice them.

One consideration to think about in a low-light situation is that any light you use may be shining on or silhouetting you or someone on your team. The best way to learn how different lighting techniques work is to go into different rooms with others and shine lights on each other (no guns needed) and take turns seeing what the bad guy would see. Shine lights on the floor, ceiling, or directly into the face of your "enemy." This is also a good time to see if you can

Sometimes you'll need to use speed, sometimes accuracy, and others you'll need to use some of this newfound intelligence to outwit your opponent.

locate others on your team if you're not fighting alone. Oftentimes we think about not wanting to be seen by the enemy, but just as often you want to know where the rest of your team is for safety and control.

Do you do 50 percent of your training with low or no light?

Our eyes consist of rods (night vision/black and white) and cones (daytime/color vision) and understanding the basics of how they work can improve your nocturnal prowess. Your rods are super sensitive to light, which helps us see in extremely low light. The problem is they are so sensitive that if they get overexposed (flashlight to the eyeball), your night vision will be washed out and it can take you up to thirty minutes to completely return to normal. Knowing this, you might consider keeping one eye shut if you think you're about to be exposed to a bright light, saving your night vision in at least one eye. Another important fact about your rods is that they are located along the outside walls of your eyes. This means that if you are looking directly at something at night, you're using your cones, which are very poor at night. But if you look away from the object at about 45 degrees, you will be able to see it much better.

One thing that will make the actual shooting part of low-light shooting easier is the proper

4.7.15 – First decide if you even need a light

equipment. If you ever plan to shoot at night, get tritium sights. At a minimum get a dot on your front sight. If you plan to line up your sights, I recommend you get them on both the front and rear, since you need to see them to line them up. As for handheld lights, I recommend you spend some money to

---

Just as you can temporarily blind yourself from your light's backsplash, you can do the same when you fire the first round.

---

invest in a Surefire. They've got many models out there to fit your needs—just make sure to get one around 80 lumens. Some people will try to convince you to get a brighter model, but you can actually ruin your own night vision from light backsplash inside or near reflective surfaces. Surefire does make models now with high and low settings, so you might consider that option. Lasers are

4.7.16 – Light can both help and hurt you

another option you should consider. Just keep in mind that although they're great for hitting your target, they are all but useless for finding it, so you will almost always need to

4.7.17 – A light pointed down covers a very small area

4.7.18 – Pointing your light at the ceiling can illuminate the whole room

use them in tandem with a light. The final part of your loadout is often overlooked, and that's the type of ammunition you use. Different loads will produce different muzzle flashes, and some are much worse than others. Just as you can temporarily blind yourself from your light's backsplash, you can do the same when you fire the first round. Some ammunition is specially made to reduce the flash, but it's best to test your ammo at night and see what you see—or don't see.

The biggest problem with using lights is that bad guys see you as well or better than you

see them. For this reason, always do as much as you can without a white light. I remember the first night shoot I ever did in the SEALs. We weren't allowed to use any light, and I thought it was going to be impossible to hit our targets, but I was surprised at how much I could see with just the ambient light. When

The biggest problem with using lights is that bad guys see you as well or better than you see them.

you do need to use your light, practice the way we did during land warfare assaults: I'm up, they see me, I'm down. Applying this to lights means: I'm lit up, they see me, I moved. Use your light in short (half-second) bursts as you're moving to locate any threats. Use your light in longer (one-second) flashes to identify the threat. Engage the threat with light if needed, but if possible (and it's more possible than you might think) keep your light off. If you are trying to use a handheld light during an engagement, don't worry about shining the light directly at the threat. It's more important to line up your sights, and you just need enough light on your target to see your sights and the threat.

In addition to knowing and practicing how to shoot in low light, you should also know how to operate in low light. This means the things you will be doing in low light 99.9 percent of the time—the things that could keep you from even ending up in a shootout. So many people concentrate on shooting techniques, but what are you more likely to do as a law enforcement officer entering a dark building:

1. Move around and use your radio?

2. Shoot someone in the face?

Obviously 99.9 percent of the time, it's moving around and using your radio, but when it comes to low-light training, how many LEOs practice anything but shooting? Don't get me wrong, that 0.1 percent is vital and needs to be trained more than 0.1 percent of

the time. Just don't neglect other functions that, if done well, can often keep you out of trouble. Spend time with the different lighting techniques identifying threats. The more you practice, the easier it will get, and may just avoid a lawsuit. If you use a gun for home defense, this should include simply walking through your home at night with all the lights off. What can you see? What light sources are available? Where are the shadows? Mirrors? Reflections? Just moving comfortably in your home at night should give you a huge advantage over an intruder, since you know the layout and he doesn't.

Just moving comfortably in your home at night should give you a huge advantage over an intruder, since you know the layout and he doesn't.

It's very important that you practice everything in daylight first. Until you're good enough to do it there, don't do it in the dark! I see this all the time: Units I train will show up to a night range with a new piece of gear, lights, or night vision and they haven't tried using it during the day. Think of daylight training before low-light operations the same as doing dry-fire training before live fire. They will both save you a lot of time and effort.

Training notes: _____

_____

_____

_____

_____

_____

_____

_____

_____

_____

_____

_____

_____

_____

_____

_____

_____

*If you're hammering the basics
and really working to be the weapon,
this journey in self-mastery
will not soon end.*

Now What?

"You never know when danger is going to show up at your doorstep and you'll only get one chance to do the right thing. Are you ready?"

Whenever people ask me how they can shoot like a Navy SEAL, I always say the same thing: Train your ass off! That's the short answer. I never mention any particular technique or even the fundamentals of marksmanship I cover in this book. Nope, what you need to do is train. Sure, there are plenty of other great little tricks out there, and I'm always trying to acquire new tools for my toolbox, but no matter what skill or technique I'm working on I'm, well, working. By reading this book you now have the knowledge to be an accurate shooter. You just need to apply yourself, or this knowledge will go to waste. Everyone is looking for the one trick to make them a better shooter, but one thing that's never changed is what it takes to be a great gunfighter: hands-on training.

But as we push on into the information age, the way many people view what is considered "training" is changing. I've noticed a disturbing trend lately when I talk to people about firearms training. I'm finding many people are no longer willing to put in the hard work needed to learn the art of

Skin that smoke wagon and do a little ballet with that boom-stick.

warfare, since it would be so much easier to just buy the latest training book or training video. Then all they have to do is kick back on the couch with a few cool ones and "train." Don't get me wrong: I've got no beef with getting more information or learning how to do something through a shooting book or video. There are some great ones, including this one, of course! But the caveat is that once you've got the information, you need to use it. Don't just sit there like a wallflower. Skin that smoke wagon and do a little ballet with that boom-stick.

So what does this mean for you? Well, if your skill level is already as good as you want it to be, you don't need to do anything. But if you want to improve your skills you can't just sit around waiting for the next "Dyno-Reflexive Combat-Carbine" video to come out so you can improve those mad ninja skills. It means you should take the information you already have or just got from this book to the range and see where your skill level is. Milk the knowledge you've already got for all it's worth and if you get to a point where your training is stagnating, hop back online and order away! But if you're hammering the basics and really working to be the weapon, this journey in self-mastery will not soon end. Even when you get to the point that you think you've mastered the basics, remember that advanced shooting is just the basics done smoother and faster.

Go to **http://chrissajnog.com** for my latest free firearms training.

Two things are involved in firearms training. One is a weapon and one is a tool. Which are you going to be?

Training notes: _____

_____

_____

_____

_____

_____

_____

_____

_____

_____

_____

_____

_____

_____

_____

_____

_____

You need to assess not only the target and what the shooter's doing, but also what they are thinking and seeing before, during, and after the round leaves the muzzle.

Appendix A:
Shot Corrections:
Analyzing Errors of the Bullet Fairy

Fixing your shooting problems is not as hard as you may think. Many people these days figure that to make any change in your life you'll need years of psychotherapy. But what happened to you as a child does not matter in shooting. In fact, what you did last time at the range has nothing to do with making immediate and major improvements to your shooting. With proper diagnosis, small changes to your technique can yield huge results.

The difficulty comes in analyzing targets and figuring out what you're doing wrong. When I say difficult, what I really mean is *impossible*. In fact, anyone who looks at your target and tells you what you're doing wrong is guessing at best and, at worst, has no idea what they're doing.

Diagnosing a shooting problem from a target is like diagnosing a stomach problem when someone is throwing up. You have a list of common things it could be, but you'll never know until you examine the patient. The same is true for shooting. No matter where the rounds hit a target, there are multiple potential reasons, and you'll never know without watching and talking to the shooter.

Anyone who looks at your target and tells you what you're doing wrong is guessing at best and, at worst, has no idea what they're doing.

One popular target for diagnosing shooting problems is the downloadable "shot correction" target, which looks like a pie chart and purports to show what you're doing wrong depending on what slice of the pie you're hitting. The problem with these is they show only some of the possible causes of error, and they don't account for the fact that oftentimes the shooter is making more than one mistake.

If you're trying to diagnose from a target like this, keep in mind that they were designed for shooting with one hand and don't take into account support-hand errors. They also do not allow for many possible errors with shooting position, natural point of aim, grip, sight alignment, sight picture, focus, or mindset. Other than that, they are very effective—smell that?

I've used these targets, and they can help give you a starting point for what to look for, but as in medicine: Treat the patient, not the test result. You still need to look at what the shooter is actually doing to produce that result. As a firearms instructor, I've found this is one of the hardest jobs—if you need help, make sure you find someone qualified. You need to assess not only the target and what the shooter's doing, but also what they are thinking and seeing before, during, and after the round leaves the muzzle.

In trying to diagnose your own errors, make sure you have a plan. Don't just go to the range and shoot up a target and then look

5.1.1 – In my improved shot correction target, you can see how many possible problems overlap.

at it. Use video if you don't have anyone to watch you. Always go slowly so you can see in the video what you're doing. Play it back, and if you see an error, fix it and film it again. Did it get better? If so, keep doing it! If not, look for something else. Keep doing this until you find and fix all your shooting problems.

If you don't have the ability to video or just need a list of possible reasons for your shooting woes, here you go.

Top Twenty Most Common Shooting Problems

1. **Bad mindset:** If you're shooting with a negative mindset, you'll never get good results. This can also lead to anxiety and stress during matches, or "buck fever." Training your mind is the first step to becoming a better shooter, and the first place to look for errors.

2. **Not having a training plan:** If you don't have a plan or are not executing your plan, how can you expect to shoot well? After a bad mindset, not having a well-defined plan is the surest way to achieve poor results. If you're not where you want to be, come up with a plan to get there.

3. **Not training:** This will be surprising to some and upsetting to others. Lack of training is a very common reason for shooting problems. Have you read this whole book and you're still not shooting better? Have you practiced? There is no substitute for training. If you don't do it, you will not get better. Not hitting the target? Are you practicing?

Your training method is far more important than your shooting method.

4. **Bad learning skills:** Before we even get into the first errors in physical techniques to check, you could be following a training plan religiously, but the way you're trying to learn may be flawed. One of the most common I see is lack of slow, deliberate dry weapons training. If you're trying to learn or fix a shooting problem, the last place to work on it is the live-fire range. Well, literally the last place would be in combat, competition, or on the streets, but the range should come only after lots of dedicated dry-fire practice, engraining the new skill into your muscle memory. If you go to the range first, it will take much longer to learn or fix errors—yet this is the course most shooters take. Make sure you're learning the right way.

5. **Bad body mechanics:** Often when diagnosing shooting problems, people work backwards, from the gun to the

finger to the grip. As far as mechanics go, we usually stop there, but we shouldn't. Just as the power of a well-thrown punch comes from legs, a good shot starts with good body mechanics. Are you using muscle or bone support? Are your arms bent? Are you off balance? Weight forward? Look at the whole shooter, not just the part holding the gun.

6. **Natural point of aim (NPA) is off:** This is a simple check before you get started and is especially important with iron sights. If your NPA is off to the right when you line up on your target, when you go to focus on the front sight post and relax, your body will naturally go toward its NPA. Check before moving on.

7. **Wrong grip:** Are you high enough up on the gun? Is as much of your hand as possible touching the gun? This is your connection to the gun. If it's not right, your shots won't go where you want. Assess your grip before worrying about what's happening downrange.

8. **Weak grip:** Stronger grip strength will cure 98.7 percent of all shooting problems. (Is that the same huge made-up statistic I used earlier?) Okay, it's not the cure-all, but it is the "cure-many." If your plan revolves around balancing a gun that is lighter than your trigger weight, you'll drop

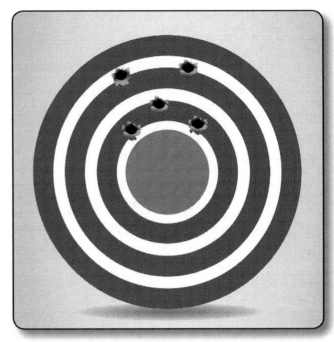

5.1.2 – A weak grip can cause rounds to go high

a lot of rounds. Put your gun in a vise (your hands) and you'll be amazed at what you do without disturbing the sights. Check that your grip strength is above average. If it's not, work on it!

9. **Inconsistent grip:** If you gripped a football differently every time you threw one, you wouldn't be accurate. Make sure that every time you grab your gun, you do it the same way. Consistent grip equals consistent groups.

10. **Milking the gun:** This means squeezing the whole hand while pressing the trigger. Your rounds can be either to the left or right depending on how you're gripping the gun. There are two ways to fix this. One is to try to balance the gun in your hands as you manipulate the

5.1.3 & 4 – Milking the gun can cause your groups to be either left or right depending on your grip and dominant hand.

trigger straight to the rear. The other is to squeeze the gun hard enough that when you move the trigger, your hand can't squeeze any more. If you've read this book, you know the right choice.

11. **Looking at the target:** This is a natural tendency and something you need to self-correct. If you haven't had that "aha!" moment yet, give it a try. Generally, if you're looking at the target your groups will be spread out all over the target—if this is the only thing you're doing wrong.

12. **Not focusing on front sight:** You may be looking at the front sight, but not focusing on it. This could be you if your groups are small, but you can never seem to keyhole shots.

Focusing takes practice, and if your eyes dart off the front sight post for even a tenth of a second before you shoot, it's the same as not focusing

5.1.5 – If you're looking over your sights as you shoot, you could have a low group.

5.1.6 – If there is no group, you're likely not focusing.

5.1.7 – Most people would say this is a breathing problem, but unless you're shooting long range it's much more likely to be something else.

at all. Calling your shots will help you maintain focus throughout each shot.

13. **Pushing and snatching:** I put these two together because both can be cured the same way, with a proper grip and knuckle alignment. Pushing and snatching refer to not having enough finger on the trigger (pushing) or having too much finger on the trigger (snatching the muzzle over). If you're doing either, start off with a proper grip. Put your finger where it naturally goes. Keep your second knuckle pointed at your target—you cannot push or pull with your trigger finger.

14. **Jerking:** This is an attempt to make the gun fire at an exact time by applying sudden pressure on the

trigger, thus disturbing the alignment, or as I like to say, "slapping the trigger like it owes you money." It's hard to self-diagnose this without video. If you can video or have someone watch you, look at the hammer of your gun. It should move at the same pace all the way back before snapping quickly forward. If it moves back slowly, then very quickly before snapping forward, that's a jerk. Dry-fire is the cure to what's ailing you.

15. **Heeling:** This is when you're putting too much force on the back of the gun with the heel of your hand as the gun is going off. If your group on target is above 12 o'clock, make sure you're not doing this. If you're focusing on the front sight you'll be able to tell.

5.1.8 – "Center Mass Group" (one of my students)

5.1.9 – If you're right handed and you have a group low and left, it could be jerking, anticipation or flinching. Lefties would be low and right.

16. **Anticipation:** This is pretty common with newer shooters and hard to diagnose, as it's usually blended in with the gun's recoil. If your rounds are going low to your reaction side, this could be a culprit. The best way to diagnose this is putting a few dummy rounds in your magazine and shooting slow fire. You'll naturally anticipate the dummy round and look like you're having a convulsion. The best fix is: dry weapons training! Teach your body not to move before the trigger falls, and it will remember this when you're on the range.

17. **Flinching:** Flinching is like the ugly cousin to anticipation, and you could put them in the same group, but they are a little different. Flinching is involuntary muscular tension in anticipation of recoil. This could be moving your head, closing your eyes, tensing your arms or hands, moving your shoulder, or any combination thereof. The best fix I've found is dry weapons training or shooting with your eyes closed. If you choose the latter, make sure you're doing it with an experienced firearms instructor to make sure it's done safely.

18. **Bucking:** This means moving the shoulders forward as the gun (normally a rifle) recoils. Others can observe this pretty easily, and you can fix it with a better shooting position.

19. **Rhythm:** If your shooting rhythm resembles Steve Martin in *The Jerk*, you're not going to shoot well. If you need to shoot just one shot at a time this may not be a concern, but if you can shoot slow-fire well but go down the tube shooting fast, work on a constant rhythm. If need be, get a metronome or listen to music as you dry-fire. It sounds crazy, but it works. Once you get your rhythm down, it's really just a matter of turning up the speed to shoot faster.

20. **No follow-through:** How quickly do you bring the gun down after you fire? If it's right away, you're not following through. If you're not getting a second sight picture and are not ready to shoot another round, you're not following through. If this is all you're doing wrong, your rapid fire will not be as good as your slow fire, and your group is likely low. Make sure you're following through by always getting a second sight picture.

Training notes: _____

_____

_____

_____

_____

_____

_____

_____

_____

_____

Training notes: _____

_____

_____

_____

_____

_____

_____

_____

_____

_____

_____

_____

_____

_____

_____

_____

_____

_____

"Mediocrity is like a virus. Once you're infected, it's spread to those around you and it's very hard to cure."
– Snowman

Appendix B:
Comparison of Bullet Impacts when Sighting in at Different Distances

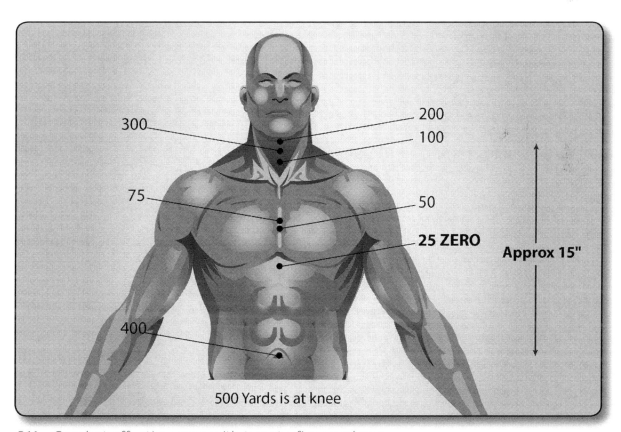

6.1.1 – Combat effective zone with twenty-five-yard zero

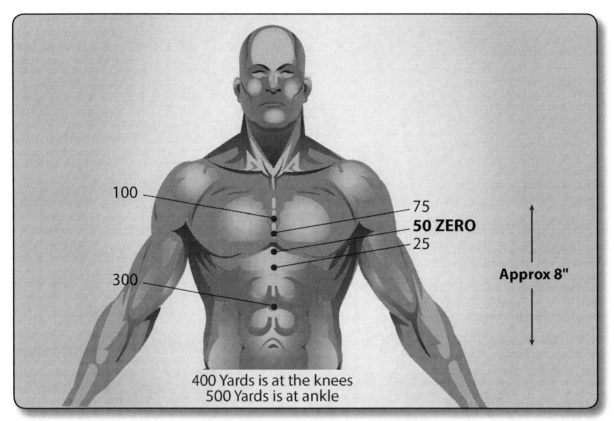

6.1.2 – Combat effective zone with fifty-yard zero

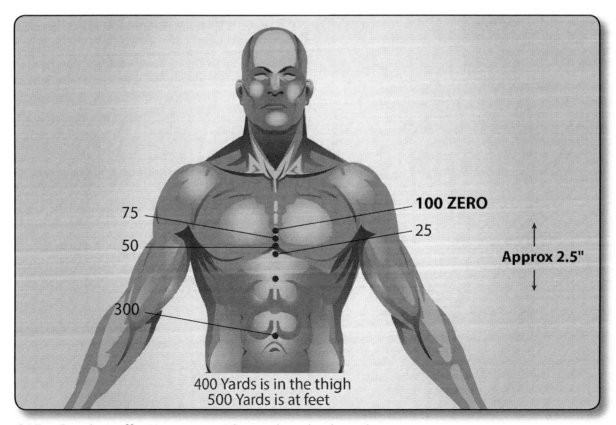

6.1.3 – Combat effective zone with one-hundred-yard zero

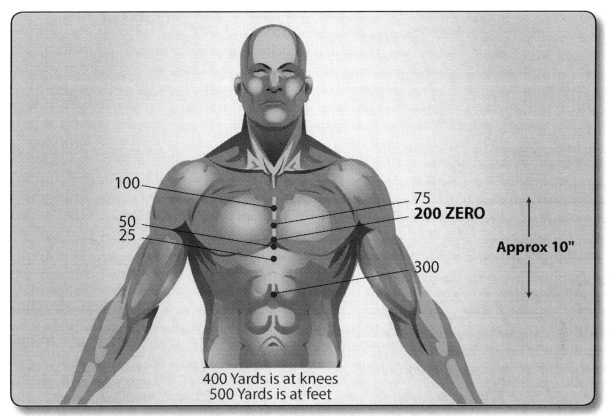

6.1.2 – Combat effective zone with 200-yard zero

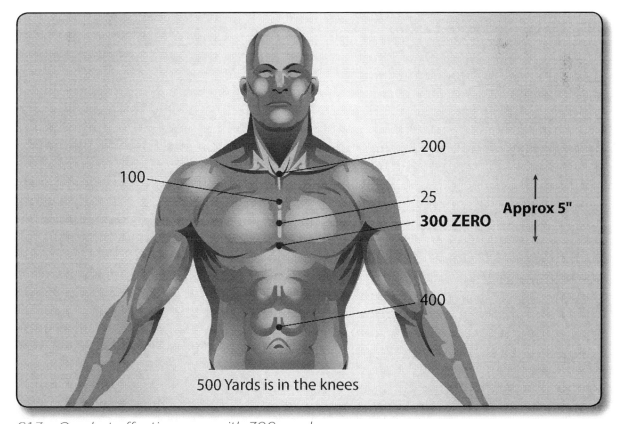

6.1.3 – Combat effective zone with 300-yard zero

About the Author

Chris Sajnog is a retired Navy SEAL Master Firearms Instructor, Neural-Pathway Training (NPT) Expert, speaker and Disabled Veteran Small Business Owner. He is one of the most experienced and respected firearms trainers in the world, being hand-selected to develop the training for the US Navy SEAL Sniper program. As a Navy SEAL he was the senior sniper instructor, a certified Master Training Specialist (MTS), BUD/S and advanced training marksmanship instructor.

After retiring from the SEAL Teams in 2009 to spend time with his family, Chris began training civilians and law enforcement officers. He is the founder of the New Rules of Marksmanship, a revolutionary approach to firearms training and has a passion for finding innovative ways to teach elite-level shooting skills online as rapidly as possible to his students.

He is a federal and state certified firearms instructor and has trained DOD, DHS, FBI, CIA, Law Enforcement, and multiple foreign allies in all aspects of combat weapons handling, marksmanship, and tactics.

He lives in San Diego, CA with his wife, Laura, and two boys, Caden and Owen.

Chris is the author of the following books:

> *How to Shoot Like a Navy SEAL*
>
> *Fundamentals of Freestyle Goju-Ryu*

Other Training products:

> *The New Rules of Marksmanship*
>
> *Navy SEAL Firearms Instructor Manual*
>
> *Mental Marksmanship*
>
> *Navy SEAL Mind and Body*
>
> *Vision Exercises for Shooting*
>
> *Online memberships*

Go to **chrissajnog.com** to continue learning.

Made in the USA
San Bernardino, CA
31 August 2015